Travelers

Phrase Book

◆

English-Italian

◆

Rand McNally & Company

Chicago • New York • San Francisco

Preface

Webster's Travelers Phrase Book is designed to offer quick, efficient assistance to the traveler who does not speak Italian—businessman, student, tourist. The book's unique four-part arrangement makes it easy to find the information needed in any situation.

I   Guide to pronunciation
Assistance in pronouncing the language is provided in a compact guide that uses the regular alphabet.

II   Essential phrases
All phrases are grouped under more than 700 key finding words, which are arranged alphabetically. If you are in a restaurant, for example, and want the check, or if you are in need of cash and want to cash a check, there is no need to figure out whether the phrase you need is under *Eating*, *Restaurant*, *Money*, or *Bank*. You go directly to the key word **Check**. Moreover, under many key words, additional related phrases are provided. Under **Automobile**, for example, you will find the phrases needed to 'fill it up,' rent a car, deal with a flat tire, and ask about the next gas station.

III   Signs and Notices
More than 60 vital signs and notices are translated.

IV   Basic vocabulary
More than 3,000 individual words are listed alphabetically for quick reference.

Guide to Pronunciation

After quickly finding the necessary phrase, you will need to pronounce it easily with a minimum of hesitation. Here again, this new guide offers rapid assistance by showing pronunciation in symbols that are familiar. The pronunciation of all sentences in this book is indicated by use of the English alphabet. Capital letters are used to indicate the stressed syllables. When you become accustomed to hearing Italian spoken, you will find it easier to imitate and your pronunciation will improve rapidly so that you will seldom need to refer to the pronunciation guide.

Vowels

Symbol	Approximate Sound	Italian Example	
ah	f*a*ther	c*a*rta	KAHR-*tah*
e	m*e*t	b*e*llo	BELL-*loh*
eh	l*a*te	c*e*na	CHEH-*nah*
ee	mach*i*ne	*i*l	EEL
oh	h*o*me	*o*gni	OH-*nyee*
oo	m*oo*n	l*u*na	LOO-*nah*

Consonants

Symbol	Approximate Sound	Italian Example	
p	*p*it	permesso	*pehr-*MESS*-soh*
b	*b*ed	borsa	BOHR*-sah*
t	*t*ill	tratta	TRAHT*-tah*
d	*d*o	dentro	DENN*-troh*
k	*k*ing	calore	*kah-*LOH*-reh*
g	*g*et	gusto	GOO*-stoh*
f	*f*or	fiamma	FYAHM*-mah*
v	*v*ase	vecchio	VEKK*-kyoh*
s	*s*end	segno	SEH*-nyoh*
z	*z*oo	sbagliato	*zbah-*LYAH*-toh*
sh	*sh*all	scienza	SHYENN*-tsah*
ch	*ch*eck	centrale	*chenn-*TRAH*-leh*
j	*j*ust	giro	JEE*-roh*
m	*m*eet	marrone	*mahr-*ROH*-neh*
n	*n*ot	noce	NOH*-cheh*
l	*l*eave	largo	LAHR*-goh*
r	rolled or trilled	rasoio	*rah-*ZOH*-yoh*
w	*w*it	uomo	WOH*-moh*
y	*y*es	ieri	YEH*-ree*

Aboard

When can we go aboard?

Quando potremo salire a bordo?

KWAHN-doh poh-TREH-moh sah-LEE-reh ah BOHR-*doh?*

Accept

Do you accept U.S. currency (travelers checks, credit cards)?

Accetta valuta americana (assegni per viaggiatori, le carte credito)?

*aht-*CHETT-*tah vah-*LOO-*tah ah-meh-ree-*KAH-*nah (*LYEE *ahss-*SEH-*nyee pehr vyahd-jah-*TOH-*ree, leh* KAHR-*teh* KREH-*dee-toh)?*

Accident

There has been an accident.

C'è stato un incidente.

CHEH STAH-*toh oon een-chee-*DENN-*teh.*

Get a doctor!

Chiamate un medico!

*kyah-*MAH-*teh oon* MEH-*dee-koh!*

Call the police!

Chiamate la polizia!

*kyah-*MAH *teh lah poh-lee-*TSEE-*ah!*

Send for an ambulance!

Chiamate l'ambulanza!

*kyah-*MAH-*teh lahm-boo-*LAHN-*tsah!*

Take me (take him, take her) to the hospital.

Portatemi (portatelo, portatela) all' ospedale.

*pohr-*TAH-*teh-mee (pohr-*TAH-*teh-loh, pohr-*TAH-*teh lah) ahl loh-speh-*DAH-*leh.*

He (she) is injured.

È ferito (ferita).

*eh feh-*REE-*toh (feh-*REE-*tah).*

Don't move him (move her).

Non muovetelo (muovetela).

*nohn-mwoh-*VEH-*teh-loh (mwoh-*VEH-*teh-lah).*

He (she) has fainted.
È svenuto (svenuta).
*eh zveh-*NOO*-tah (zveh-*NOO*-tah).*

Help me carry him (carry her).
Aiutatemi a portarlo (portarla).
*ah-yoo-*TAH*-teh-mee ah pohr-*TAHR*-loh (pohr-*TAHR*-lah).*

I feel dizzy.
Mi gira la testa.
mee JEE-*rah lah* TEH-*stah.*

He (she) has a fracture (bruise, cut, burn).
Ha una frattura (una contusione, un taglio,
   un'ustione).
ah OON-*ah fraht-*TOO*-rah (*OON*-ah kohn-too-*ZYOH*-neh)
   oon* TAH-*lyoh, oon-oos-tee-*OH*-neh).*

He (she) is bleeding.
Sanguina.
SAHNG-*gwee-nah.*

Are you all right?
Come si sente?
KOH-*meh see* SENN-*teh?*

Where does it hurt?
Dove le fa male?
DOH-*veh leh fah* MAH-*leh?*

It hurts here.
Mi fa male qui.
mee fah MAH-*leh kwee.*

I cannot move my _____.
Non posso muovere _____.
nohn POHSS-*soh* MWOH-*veh-reh* _____.

Pease notify my husband (my wife).
La prego di informare mio marito (mia moglie).
lah PREH-*goh dee een-fohr-*MAH*-reh* MEE-*oh mah-*REE-
   *toh (*MEE-*ah* MOH-*lyeh).*

Accommodate

Can you accommodate me (can you accommodate two, three, four)?

Può alloggiarmi (può alloggiare due, tre, quattro persone)?

pwoh ahl-lohd-JAHR-mee (pwoh ahl-lohd-JAH-reh DOO-eh, TREH, KWAHT-troh pehr-SOH-neh)?

Does the train to _____ have sleeping accommodations?

Il treno per _____ ha le carrozze letto?

eel TREH-noh pehr _____ ah leh kahr-ROHT-tseh LETT-toh?

Accompany

May I accompany you?

Posso accompagnarla?

POHSS-soh ahk-kohm-pah-NYAHR-lah?

Account (Bank)

I would like to (where do I) open a checking account.

Desidero (dove posso) aprire un conto corrente.

deh-SEE-deh-roh (DOH-veh POHSS-soh) ah-PREE-reh oon KOHN-toh kohr-RENN-teh?

Account (Calculation)

May I see an account of the bill?

Desidero vedere il conto.

deh-SEE-deh-roh veh-DEH-reh eel KOHN-toh.

Ache – see Hurt

Acquaintance – See Also Meet

I am happy to meet you (make your acquaintance).

Piacere (di fare la sua conoscenza).

pyah-CHEH-reh (dee FAH-reh lah SOO-ah koh-noh-SHENN-tsah)

Address

Please forward all mail to this address.

La prego d'inoltrare la posta a questo indirizzo.

lah PREH-goh dee-nohl-TRAH-reh lah POH-stah ah KWEH-stoh een-dee-REET-tsoh.

Here is my address
Ecco il mio indirizzo.
EHK-*koh eel* MEE-*oh een-dee*-REET-*tsoh.*

What is your address (and telephone number)?
Qual'è il suo indirizzo (e numero di telefono)?
kwah-LEH *eel* SOO-*oh een-dee*-REET-*tsoh (eh* NOO-*meh-roh dee teh*-LEH-*foh-noh)?*

Admission
What is the price of admission?
Qual'è il prezzo d'ingresso?
kwah-LEH *eel* PRETT-*tsoh deen*-GRESS-*soh?*

Advertise
I would like to advertise for a _____.
Vorrei mettere un'inserzione per _____.
vohr-RAY METT-*teh-reh oon een-sehr*-TSYOH-*neh pehr*

_____.

Advertisement
I am answering your advertisement.
Rispondo alla sua inserzione.
ree-SPOHN-*doh* AHL-*lah* SOO-*ah een-sehr*-TSYOH-*neh.*

I would like to run an advertisement.
Vorrei fare un'inserzione.
vohr-RAY FAH-*reh oon een-sehr*-TSYOH-*neh.*

Afford
I cannot afford that.
Costa troppo.
KOH-*stah* TROHP-*poh.*

Afternoon
Good afternoon.
Buon giorno.
bwohn JOHR-*noh.*

I would like to arrange it for the afternoon.
Vorrei fissare l'appuntamento per il pomeriggio.
vohr-RAY *fees*-SAH-*reh lahp-poon-tah*-MENN-*toh pehr eel poh-meh*-REED-*joh.*

Again
I hope to see you again soon.
Spero di rivederla presto.
SPEH-*roh dee ree-veh*-DEHR-*lah* PREH-*stoh.*

Please say it again.
Ripeta, per favore.
*ree-*PEH-*tah, pehr fah-*VOH-*reh.*

Age
What is your age?
La sua età, per favore.
lah SOO-*ah eh-*TAH, *pehr fah-*VOH-*reh.*

Aid – see Help

Air
My tire needs (my tires need) air.
La gomma ha (le gomme hanno) bisogno di aria.
lah GOHM-*mah ah (leh* GOHM-*meh* AHN-*noh) bee-*ZOH-
nyoh dee AH-*ryah.*

Air Conditioning
Does it have air conditioning?
C'è l'aria condizionata?
CHEH LAH-*ryah kohn-dee-tsyoh-*NAH-*tah?*

I want a room with air conditioning, please.
Desidero una camera con l'aria condizionata, per
favore.
*deh-*SEE-*deh-roh* OON-*ah* KAH-*meh-ruh kohn* LAH-*ryah
kohn-dee-tsyoh-*NAH-*tah, pehr fah-*VOH-*reh.*

Air Main – see Mail

Airplane – see Flight

Airport
The airport, please.
L'aeroporto, per favore.
*lah-eh-roh-*POHR-*toh, pehr fah-*VOH-*reh.*

Airsick
I feel sick.
Ho nausea.
oh NOW-*seh-ah.*

A la Carte
Please show me the a la carte menu.
Per favore, mi faccia vedere la lista alla carta.
*pehr fah-*VOH-*reh, mee* FAHT-*chah veh-*DEH-*reh lah* LEE-*stah* AHL-*lah* KAHR-*tah.*

All
This is all I have (I need, I want).
Questo è tutto quello che ho (che mi occorre, che desidero).
KWEH-*stoh eh* TOOT-*oh* KWELL-*loh keh oh (keh mee ohk-*KOHR-*reh, keh deh-*SEE-*deh-roh).*

Allergic
I am allergic to this.
Sono allergico a questo.
SOH-*noh ahl-*LEHR-*jee-koh ah* KWEH-*stoh.*

All Right
It is all right.
Va bene.
vah BEH-*neh.*

Alone
Please leave me alone.
Non mi dia fastidio, per favore.
nohn mee DEE-*ah fah-*STEE-*djoh, pehr fah-*VOH-*reh.*

Are you alone?
È solo (sola)?
EH SOH-*loh (*SOH-*lah)?*

I am (I am not) alone.
Sono (non sono) solo (sola).
SOH-*noh (nohn* SOHN-*noh)* SOH-*loh (*SOH-*lah).*

Ambulance
Call me an ambulance.
Chiami l'ambulanza.
KYAH-*mee lahm-boo-*LAHN-*tsah.*

American
I am an American.
Sono americano.
SOH-*noh ah-meh-ree-*KAH-*noh.*

Do you accept American money?
Accetta valuta americana?
aht-CHETT-tah vah-LOO-tah ah-meh-ree-KAH-nah?

American Embassy

Please direct me (take me) to the American Embassy.
Per favore, mi dica come andare (mi porti) all'
Ambasciata Americana.
*pehr fah-VOH-reh, mee DEE-kah KOH-meh ahn-DAH-reh
(mee POHR-tee) ahl lahm-bah-SHAH-tah ah-meh-ree-
KAH-nah.*

American Express

Please direct me (take me) to the American Express
office.
Per favore, mi dica come andare (mi porti) all' American
Express.
*pehr fah-VOH-reh, mee DEE-kah KOH-meh ahn-DAH-reh
(mee POHR-tee) ahl lah-MEH-ree-kahn ek-SPRESS.*

Do you accept the American Express credit card?
Accetta la carta credito dell'American Express?
*aht-CHETT-tah lah KAHR-tah KREH-dee toh dell
lah-MEH-ree-kahn ek-SPRESS?*

Amount

What is the total amount?
Quanto è?
KWAHN-toh EH?

Another

Let's have another drink.
Prendiamone un altro (un' altra).
prenn-DYAH-moh-neh oon AHL-troh (oon AHL-trah).

Please get me another drink.
Me ne porti un altro (un' altra).
meh neh POHR-tee oon AHL-troh (oon AHL-trah).

Answer

They do not answer; please try again.
Non rispondono; provi ancora, per favore.
*nohn ree-SPOHN-doh-noh; PROH-vee ahng-KOH-rah, pehr
fah-VOH-reh.*

Antiques

Please direct me (take me) to an antique shop.

Per favore, mi indichi un antiquario (mi porti da un antiquario).

pehr fah-VOH-reh, mee EEN-dee-kee oon ahn-tee-KWAHR-yoh (mee POHR-tee dah oon ahn-tee-KWAHR-yoh).

I am interested in antiques.

M'interesso di oggetti antichi.

meen-teh-RESS-soh dee ohd-JETT-tee ahn-TEE-kee.

Do you sell antiques?

Vendete oggetti antichi?

venn-DEH-teh ohd-JETT-tee ahn-TEE-kee?

Apologize

I apologize.

Chiedo scusa.

KYEH-doh SKOO-zah.

Appointment

I would like to make an appointment for _____.

Vorrei fissare un appuntamento per _____.

vohr-RAY feess-SAH-reh oon ahp-poon-tah-MENN-toh pehr _____.

Arrive

When does the plane (the bus, the boat, the train) arrive?

Quando arriva l'aereo (l'autobus, la nave, il treno)?

KWAHN-doh ahr-REE-vah lah-EH-reh-oh (low-toh-BOOSS, lah NAH-veh, eel TREH-noh)?

When do we arrive at _____?

Quando arriveremo a _____?

KWAHN-do ahr-ree-veh-REH-moh ah _____?

Article – see Things

Asleep

My husband (my wife) is asleep.

Mio marito (mia moglie) dorme.

MEE-oh mah-REE-toh (MEE-ah MOH-lyeh) DOHR-meh.

Assistance – see Help

Authority

I will report this to the authorities.

Riferirò questo alle autorità.

ree-feh-reer-OH KWEH-*stoh* AHL-*leh ow-toh-ree*-TAH.

Automobile

I want to rent an automobile, please.

Desidero noleggiare un'automobile.

deh-SEE-*deh-roh noh-ledd*-JAHR-*reh* oon *ow-toh*-MOH-*bee-leh.*

Where is the nearest gas station (garage)?

Dov'è la stazione di rifornimento (l'autorimessa) più vicina?

doh-VEH *lah stah*-TSYOH-*neh dee ree-fohr-nee* MENN-*toh (low-toh-ree*-MESS-*sah) pyoo vee*-CHEE-*nah?*

My car has broken down.

La mia macchina ha un guasto.

lah MEE-*ah* MAHK-*kee-nah ah oon* GWAH-*stoh.*

I am out of gas.

Non ho benzina.

nohn oh benn-DZEE-*nah.*

I have a flat tire.

Ho una gomma a terra

oh OON-*ah* GOHM *mah ah* TEHR-*rah.*

Can you help me?

Mi può aiutare?

mee PWOH *ah-yoo*-TAH-*reh?*

Can you tow (push) me to a garage?

Mi può rimorchiare (spingere) fino a un'autorimessa?

mee PWOH *ree-mohr*-KYAH-*reh (*SPEEN-*jeh-reh)* FEE-*noh ah oon ow-toh-ree*-MESS-*sah?*

I have (I do not have) an international license.

Ho (non ho) la patente internazionale.

oh (nohn oh) lah pah-TENN-*teh een-tehr-nah-tsyoh*-NAH-*leh.*

Here is my license.
Ecco la mia patente.
EHK-*koh lah* MEE-*ah pah*-TENN-*teh.*

Can you recommend a good mechanic?
Mi saprebbe indicare un buon meccanico?
mee sah-PREB-*beh een-dee*-KAH-*reh oon bwohn mekk-*
KAH-*nee-koh?*

Fill it up, please.
Faccia il pieno, per favore.
FAHT-*chah eel* PYEH-*noh, pehr fah*-VOH-*reh.*

Give me _____ liters, please.
Mi dia _____ litri, per favore.
mee DEE-*ah* _____ LEE-*tree, pehr fah*-VOH-*reh.*

The _____ does not work.
Il/la/l'/lo _____ non funziona.
eel/lah/l-/loh _____ *nohn foon*-TSYOH-*nah.*

Please check the _____.
Controlli per favore il/la/l'/lo _____.
kohn-TROHL-*lee pehr fah*-VOH-*reh eel/lah/l-/loh* _____.

Can you repair it while I wait? When?
Può fare la riparazione mentre aspetto? Quando?
PWOH FAH-*reh lah ree-pah-rah*-TSYOH-*neh* MENN-*treh*
ah-SPETT-*toh?* KWAHN-*doh?*

What is wrong?
Cosa è guasto?
KOH-*sah eh* GWAH-*stoh?*

Can you wash it (now)?
La può lavare (ora)?
lah PWOH *lah*-VAH-*reh* (OH-*rah)?*

There is a rattle (squeak).
Qualchecosa sbatte (fa rumore).
kwahl-keh KOH-*sa* ZBAHT-*teh (fah roo*-MOH-*reh).*

Something is leaking here.
C'è una perdita qui.
CHEH OON-*ah* PEHR-*dee-tah kwee.*

Will you accept this credit card (travelers checks, a
  personal check)?
Accetta questa carta credito (assegni per viaggiatori,
  un assegno personale)?
ahl-CHETT-*tah* KWEH-*stah* KAHR-*tah* KREH-*dee-toh*
  *(ahss-SEH-nyee pehr vyahd-jah-*TOH-*ree, oon ahss-*SEH-
  *nyoh pehr-soh-*NAII-*leh)?*

I am staying at _____.
Sono alloggiato all' _____.
SOH-*noh ahl-lohd-*JAH-*toh ahl* _____.

I am a member of the Automobile Club.
Sono socio dell'Automobile Club.
SOH-*noh* SOH-*choh dell-low-toh-*MOH-*bee-leh* KLOOB.

Available
Are there any rooms (seats) available?
Ci sono camere (posti) disponibili?
chee SOH-*noh* KAH-*meh-reh (*POH-*stee) dee-spoh-*NEE-
  bee-lee?

Awaken – see Call

Away
Go away!
Vada via!
VAH-*dah* VEE-*ah!*

Please take it away.
Lo porti via, per favore.
loh POHR-*tee* VEE-*ah, pehr fah-*VOH-*reh.*

Baby Sitter
Can you recommend a baby sitter (who speaks
  English)?
Mi potrebbe raccomandare una signorina per i bambini
  (che parla inglese)?
*mee poh-*TREBB-*beh rahk-koh-mahn-*DAH-*reh oon-ah see-
  nyoh-*REE-*nah pehr ee bahm-*BEE-*nee (keh* PAHR-*lah
  een-*GLEH-*seh)?*

Bachelor
I am a bachelor.
Sono scapolo.
SOH-*noh* SKAH-*poh-loh.*

Is he a bachelor?

È scapolo?

eh SKAH-*poh-loh?*

Back

How do I get back to _____?

Qual'è la strada per tornare a _____?

kwahl-EH *lah* STRAH-*dah pehr tohr*-NAH-*reh ah* _____?

Please come back later.

Torni più tardi, per favore.

TOHR-*nee pyoo* TAHR-*dee, pehr fah*-VOH-*reh.*

I want (I do not want) to sit in the back.

Vorrei (non vorrei) sedermi dietro.

vohr-RAY *(nohn vohr*-RAY) *seh*-DEHR-*mee* DYEH-*troh.*

When are we due back?

A che ora dovremmo essere di ritorno?

ah keh OH-*ra doh*-VREHM-*moh* ESS-*seh-reh dee ree*-TOHR-*noh?*

Please take me back to the _____.

Per favore mi riporti a _____.

pehr fah-VOH-*reh mee ree*-POHR-*tee ah* _____.

Bad

This is bad. (Please take it away).

Non è buono. (Lo porti via, per favore).

nohn eh BWOH-*noh. (loh* POHR-*tee* VEE-*ah, pehr fah*-VOH-*reh).*

Bags, Baggage

May I leave my bag (my bags) here?

Posso lasciar qui la mia valigia (le mie valigie)?

POHSS-*soh lah*-SHAHR *kwee lah* MEE-*ah vah*-LEE-*jah (leh* MEE-*eh vah*-LEE-*jeh)?*

Please help me with my bags.

Per favore, mi aiuti con le valigie.

pehr fah-VOH-*reh, mee ah*-YOO-*tee kohn leh vah*-LEE-*jeh.*

Please take my bags to _____.

Per favore, mi porti le valigie a _____.

pehr fah-VOH-*reh, mee* POHR-*tee leh vah*-LEE-*jeh ah*

_____.

Where is the baggage room?
Dov'è il deposito bagagli?
*doh-*VEH *eel deh-*POH*-zee-toh bah-*GAH*-lyee?*

How much baggage am I allowed?
Che peso è permesso per il bagaglio?
keh PEH*-so eh pehr-*MESS*-soh pehr eel bah-*GAH*-lyoh?*

Where is my baggage?
Dov'è il mio bagaglio?
*doh-*VEH *eel* MEE*-oh bah-*GAH*-lyoh?*

I cannot find my bags.
Non trovo le mie valigie.
nohn TROH*-voh leh* MEE*-eh vah-*LEE*-jeh.*

I need a porter.
Mi occorre un facchino.
*mee ohk-*KOHR*-reh oon fahk-*KEE*-noh.*

Bank

Where is the nearest bank?
Dov'è la banca piu vicina?
*doh-*VEH *lah* BAHN*-kah pyoo vee-*CHEE*-nah?*

At what time does the bank open (close)?
A che ora si apre (si chiude) la banca?
uh keh OH*-ra see* AH*-preh (see-*KYOO*-deh) lah* BAHN*-kah?*

Where can I cash this?
Dove posso riscuotere questo?
DOH*-veh* POHSS*-soh ree-*SKWOH*-teh-reh* KWEH*-stoh?*

Will you cash a personal check?
Potete incassare un assegno personale?
*poh-*TEH*-teh een-kahss-*SAH*-reh oon ahss-*SEH*-nyoh
pehr-soh-*NAH*-leh?*

Can I cash a money order here?
Posso riscuotere un vaglia qui?
POHSS*-soh ree-*SKWOH*-teh-reh oon* VAH*-lyah kwee?*

Where is the window for cashing travelers' checks?
Dov'è lo sportello per riscuotere gli assegni per
viaggiatori?
*doh-*VEH *loh spohr-*TEHL*-loh pehr ree-*SKWOH*-teh-reh
lyee ahss-*SEH*-nyee pehr vyahd-jah-*TOH*-ree?*

Please give me (don't give me) large bills.
Per favore, mi dia (non mi dia) biglietti di grande
  taglio.
*pehr fah-VOH-reh, mee DEE-ah (nohn mee DEE-ah) bee-
  LYETT-tee dee GRAHN-deh TAHL-yoh.*

Can you change this for me, please?
Mi può cambiare questo, per favore?
*mee PWOH kahm-BYAH-reh KWEH-stoh, pehr fah-VOH-
  reh?*

I would like to change some American dollars into
  _____.
Vorrei cambiare dei dollari americani in _____.
*vohr-RAY kahm-BYAH-reh day DOHL-lah-ree ah-meh-ree-
  KAH-nee een _____.*

What is the rate of exchange?
Qual'è il tasso di cambio?
kwahl-EH eel TAHSS-soh dee KAHM-byoh?

Bar
Where is the bar? Is there a bar open?
Dove'è il bar? È aperto il bar?
doh-VEH eel BAHR? EH ah-PEHR-toh eel BAHR?

When do the bars close (open)?
A che ora si chiudono (si aprono) i bar?
*ah keh OH-ra see KYOO-doh-noh (see AH-proh-noh) ee
  BAHR?*

Barber
Can you recommend a good barber?
Mi saprebbe indicare un buon parrucchiere?
*mee sah-PREB-beh een-dee-KAH-reh oon bwohn pahr-
  rook-KYEH-reh?*

I want a haircut (and shave), please.
Vorrei capelli (e barba), per favore.
*vohr-RAY kah-PELL-lee (eh BAHR-bah), pehr fah-VOH-
  reh.*

Not too short, please.
Non tagli i capelli troppo corti, per favore.
*nohn TAH-lyee ee kah-PELL-lee TROHP-poh KOHR-tee,
  pehr fah-VOH-reh.*

Don't cut any off the top.
Non mi tagli i capelli in alto.
nohn mee TAH-*lyee ee kah*-PELL-*lee een* AHL-*toh.*

I part my hair on the right (the left) side.
Porto la riga a destra (a sinistra).
POHR-*toh lah* REE-*gah ah* DEH-*strah (ah see*-NEE-*strah).*

No hair oil, thank you.
No, grazie, niente brillantina.
NOH, GRAH-*tsyeh,* NYENN-*teh breel-lahn*-TEE-*nah.*

Bath

A room with bath, please; a private bath is not
   necessary.
Una camera con bagno, per favore; un bagno
   privato non è necessario.
OON-*ah* KAH-*meh-ra kohn* BAH-*nyoh, pehr fah*-VOH-*reh;
   oon* BAH-*nyoh pree*-VAH-*toh nohn* EH *neh-chess*-SAH-
   ryoh.

Bathing

Is bathing permitted here?
È permesso fare i bagni qui?
eh pehr-MESS-*soh* FAH-*reh ee* BAH-*nyee kwee?*

Where can I rent (buy) a bathing suit?
Dove posso affittare (comprare) un costume da bagno?
DOH-*veh* POHSS-*soh ahf-feet*-TAH-*reh (kohm*-PRAH-*reh)
   oon koh-STOO-*meh dah* BAH-*nyoh?*

Bathroom

Where is the bathroom?
Dov'è la stanza da bagno?
doh-VEH *lah* STAHN-*tsah dah* BAH-*nyoh?*

Bathtub

I prefer a bathtub (to a shower).
Preferisco la vasca da bagno (alla doccia).
preh-feh-REES-*koh lah* VAH-*skah da* BAH-*nyoh (*AHL-*lah
   *DOHT-*chah).*

Battery

Do you sell flashlight (radio, transistor, electric razor) batteries?

Vendete pile per lampadine (radio, transistor, rasoio elettrico)?

venn-DEH-teh PEE-leh pehr lahm-pah-DEE-neh (RAH-dyoh, trahn-SEES-tohr, rah-ZOH-yoh eh-LETT-tree-koh)?

Beach

Is there a beach nearby?

Ce'è una spiaggia per nuotare qui vicino?

CHEH OON-*ah* SPYAHD-*jah pehr nwoh-*TAH-*reh kwee vee-CHEE-*noh?*

Beauty Parlor

Can you recommend a good beauty parlor?

Mi seprebbe indicare un buon parrucchiere da signora?

mee sah-PREB-beh een-dee-KAH-reh oon bwohn pah-rook-KYEH-reh dah see-NYOH-rah?

Can I make an appointment for _____?

Posso fissare un appuntamento per _____?

POHSS-*soh feess-*SAH-*reh oon ahp-poon-tah-*MENN-*toh pehr* _____

I have (don't have) an appointment (with _____).

Ho (non ho) un appuntamento (con _____).

*oh (nohn oh) oon ahp-poon-tah-*MENN-*toh (kohn* _____).

I want a shampoo, cut, and set, please.

Vorrei shampoo, taglio e messa in piega, per favore.

*vohr-*RAY *shahm-*POO, TAH-*lyoh eh* MESS-*sah een* PYEH-*gah, pehr fah-*VOH-*reh.*

Just trim it, please.

Spunti soltanto i capelli, per favore.

SPOON-*tee sohl-*TAHN-*toh ee kah-*PELL-*lee, pehr fah-*VOH-*reh.*

Not too short.

Non troppo corti, per favore.

nohn TROHP-*poh* KOHR-*tee, pehr fah-*VOH-*reh.*

I want a permanent (a rinse), please.
Vorrei una permanente (un cachet) per favore.
*vohr-*RAY OON-*ah pehr-mah-*NENN-*teh (oon kah-*SHAY)
*pehr fah-*VOH-*reh.*

I want a facial (a manicure, a massage), please.
Vorrei un trattamento al viso (una manicure, un
massaggio), per favore.
*vohr-*RAY oon traht-tah-*MENN-*toh ahl VEE-*zoh (oon-ah
mah-nee-*KOO-*reh, oon mahss-*SAH-*joh, pehr fah-*VOH-
reh.

I part my hair on the right (on the left, in the middle).
Porto la riga a destra (a sinistra, in mezzo).
POHR-*toh lah* REE-*gah ah* DEH-*strah (ah see-*NEE-*strah
een* MEDD-*dzoh).*

I wear bangs.
Porto la frangia.
POHR-*toh lah* FRAHN-*jah.*

I want a French twist (chignon), please.
Per favore, mi facci il chignon.
*pehr fah-*VOH-*reh, mee* FAHT-*chah eel shee-*NOHN.

Can you wash and set (and cut) my wig (my fall)?
Mi può lavare e mettere in piega (e tagliare) la
parrucca (il toupet)?
mee PWOH *lah-*VAH-*reh eh* METT-*teh-reh een* PYEH-*gah
(eh tah-*LYAH-*reh) lah pahr-*ROOK-*kah (eel too-*PAY)?

Please (don't) tease it.
Per favore, (niente) cotonatura.
*pehr fah-*VOH-*reh,* NYENN-*teh koh-toh-nah-*TOO-*rah.*

The water is too hot (cold).
L'acqua è troppo calda (fredda).
LAHK-*kwah eh* TROHP-*poh* KAHL-*dah (*FREDD-*dah).*

The dryer is too hot (cold).
Il casco è troppo caldo (freddo).
eel KAH-*skoh eh* TROHP-*poh* KAHL-*doh (fredd-doh).*

Becoming

I'm sorry, it is not becoming.
Mi dispiace, ma non mi sta bene.
mee dee-SPYAH-cheh, mah nohn mee stah BEH-neh.

It is becoming.
Mi va.
mee VAH.

Bed

A room with double bed (with twin beds), please.
Una camera con letto matrimoniale (a due letti), per
  favore.
OON-*ah* KAH-*meh-rah kohn* LETT-*toh mah-tree-moh-*
  NYAH-*leh (ah* DOO-*eh* LETT-*tee), pehr fah-*VOH-*reh.*

Please make up (don't make up) the bed (the beds) now.
Per favore, rifaccia (non rifaccia) il letto (i letti) ora.
*pehr fah-*VOH-*reh, ree-*FAHT-*chah (nohn ree-*FAHT-*chah)
  eel* LETT-*toh (ee* LETT-*tee)* OH-*rah.*

Bedroom

We would like two separate bedrooms.
Vorremmo due camere da letto separate.
*vohr-*RAYM-*moh* DOO-*eh* KAH-*meh-reh dah* LETT-*toh seh-*
  *pah-*RAH-*teh.*

Bellboy

Please send the bellboy to me.
Per favore, mi chiami il fattorino.
*pehr fah-*VOH-*reh, mee* KYAH-*mee eel faht-toh-*REE-*noh.*

Berth

I want an upper (lower) berth.
Vorrei una cuccetta superiore (inferiore).
*vohr-*RAY OON-*ah koot-*CHETT-*tah soo-peh-*RYOH-*reh
  (een-feh-*RYOH-*reh).*

Better

I like this one better (best).
Preferisco questo (questa).
*preh-feh-*REES-*koh* KWEH-*stoh (*KWEH-*stah).*

Have you anything better?

Ha qualchecosa di meglio?

ah kwahl-keh-KOH-sah dee MEH-lyoh?

Bicycle

Have you a bicycle repair outfit?

Ha una borsetta con il necessario per riparare la
  bicicletta?

*ah oon-ah bohr-SETT-tah kohn eel neh-chess-SAH-ryoh
  pehr ree-pah-RAH-reh lah bee-chee-KLETT-tah?*

Where can I rent (buy) a bicycle?

Dove posso noleggiare (comprare) una bicicletta?

*DOH-veh POHSS-soh noh-ledd-JAH-reh (kohm-PRAH-reh)
  oon-ah bee-chee-KLETT-tah?*

Where can my bicycle be repaired?

Dove posso far riparate la mia bicicletta?

*DOH-veh POHSS-soh fahr ree-pah-RAH-reh lah MEE-ah
  bee-chee-KLETT-tah?*

Big

This is too big.

Questo (questa) è troppo grande.

KWEH-stoh (KWEH-stah) eh TROHP-poh GRAHN-deh.

This is not big enough.

Questo (questa) non è abbastanza grande.

*KWEH-stoh (KWEH-stah) nohn eh ahb-bah-STAHN-tsah
  GRAHN-deh.*

I want something bigger.

Vorrei qualchecosa di più grande.

vohr-RAY kwahl-keh-KOH-sah dee pyoo GRAHN-deh.

Bill (currency)

Can you change this bill?

Mi può cambiare questo biglietto?

mee PWOH kahm-BYAH-reh KWEH-stoh bee-LYETT-toh?

Bill (invoice)

The bill, please.

Il conto, per favore.

eel KOHN-toh, pehr fah-VOH-reh.

Blanket

May I have another blanket, please?

Potrei avere un'altra coperta, per favore?

*poh-TRAY-ee ah-VEH-reh oon AHL-trah koh-PEHR-tah,
pehr fah-VOH-reh?*

Bleed — see Accident

Board

When can we board?

Quando potremo imbarcarci?

KWAHN-doh poh-TRAY-moh eem-bahr-KAHR-chee?

Are meals served on board?

I pasti sono serviti a bordo?

ee PAH-stee soh-noh sehr-VEE-tee ah BOHR-doh?

Boardinghouse (Pension)

Can you recommend a boardinghouse?

Mi potrebbe raccomandare una pensione?

*mee poh-TREHB-beh rahk-koh-mahn-DAH-reh oon-ah
penn-SYOH-neh?*

Boat

Where can I rent a boat? I wish to rent a boat.

Dove posso noleggiare una barca? Vorrei noleggiare
una barca.

*DOH-veh POHSS-soh noh-ledd-JAH-reh OON-ah BAHR-
kah? vohr-RAY noh-ledd-JAH-reh OON-ah BAHR-kah.*

When does the boat leave for _____?

Quando parte la nave per _____?

KWAHN-doh PAHR-teh lah NAH-veh pehr _____?

Book

I would like a book of tickets.

Vorrei un libretto di biglietti.

vohr-RAY oon lee-BRETT-toh dee bee-LYETT-tee.

Do you have a book about _____?

Avete un libro che tratta di _____?

ah-VEH-teh oon LEE-broh keh TRAHT-tah dee _____?

I would like to book passage to _____.

Vorrei prenotare un posto per _____.

vohr-RAY *preh-noh*-TAH-*reh oon* POH-*stoh per* _____.

Bookstore

Where is a bookstore?

Cerco una libreria.

CHEHR-*koh ah* OON-*ah lee-breh*-REE-*ah.*

Border

How many kilometers is it to the border?

Quanti chilometri ci sono dalla frontiera?

KWAHN-*tee kee*-LOH-*meh-tree chee* SOHN-*noh dahl-lah frohn*-TYEH-*rah?*

When do we arrive at the border?

Quando arriveremo alla frontiera?

KWAHN-*doh ahr-ree-veh*-RAY-*moh* AHL-*lah frohn*-TYEH-*rah?*

Borrow

May I borrow _____?

Posso farmi prestare _____?

POHSS-*soh* FAHR-*mee preh*-STAH-*reh* _____?

Boss

Where is the boss?

Dov'è il padrone?

doh-VEH *eel pah*-DROH-*neh?*

Both

I want both.

Li (le) vorrei tutti e due (tutte e due).

lee (leh) vohr-RAY TOOT-*tee eh* DOO-*eh* (TOOT-*teh eh* DOO-*eh).*

Bother

Stop bothering me.

Smetta di darmi fastidio.

ZMETT-*tah dee* DAHR-*mee fah*-STEE-*dyoh.*

They are (he is) bothering me.

Mi stanno (mi sta) dando fastidio.

mee STAHN-*noh (mee stah)* DAHN-*doh fah*-STEE-*dyoh.*

Bottle — see Wine

Brand
Is this a good brand? What is the best brand?
È una buona marca? Qual'è la marca migliore?
eh OON-*ah* BWOH-*nah* MAHR-*kah? kwah*-LEH *lah* MAHR-*kah mee*-LYOH-*reh?*

Break
The _____ is broken. (Please have it fixed).
Il (la) _____ è rotto (rotta). (Lo (la) faccia riparare, per favore).
eel (lah) _____ *eh* ROHTT-*toh* (ROHTT-*tah*). *(loh (lah)* FAHT-*chah ree-pah*-RAH-*reh, pehr fah*-VOH-*reh).*

Breakfast
When is breakfast (lunch, supper) served?
A che ora è servita la prima colazione (la colazione, la cena)?
ah keh OH-*rah eh sehr*-VEE-*tah lah* PREE-*mah koh-lah-*TSYOH-*neh (lah koh-lah*-TSYOH-*neh, lah* CHEH-*nah)?*

I want breakfast (lunch, dinner) in my room.
Vorrei la prima colazione (la colazione, il pranzo) in camera.
vohr-RAY *lah* PREE-*mah koh-lah* TSYOH-*neh (lah koh-lah*-TSYOH-*neh, eel* PRAHN-*dzoh) een* KAH-*meh-rah.*

Is breakfast included?
E compresa la prima colazione?
EH *kohm*-PRAY-*sah lah* PREE-*mah koh-lah*-TSYOH-*neh?*

Bring
Please bring a _____.
Mi porti un (un', una, uno) _____.
mee POHR-*tee oon (oon,* OON-*ah,* OON-*oh)* _____.

I did not bring a _____.
Non mi son portato (portata) un (una, un', uno) _____.
nohn mee sohn pohr-TAH-*toh (pohr*-TAH-*tah) oon (*OON-*ah, oon,* OON-*oh)* _____.

Building
What is that building?
Cos'è quell'edificio?
koh-SEH *kwell-leh-dee*-FEE-*choh?*

Bus

When does the bus leave for _____?
Quando parte l'autobus per _____?
KWAHN-*doh* PAHR-*teh low-toh*-BOOSS *pehr* _____?

How much is the bus fare?
Quanto costa il biglietto dell'autobus?
KWAHN-*toh* KOH-*stah eel bee*-LYETT-*toh dell low-toh*-BOOSS?

Where is the bus stop (station)?
Dov'è la fermata (il capolinea) dell'autobus?
doh-VEH *lah fehr*-MAH-*tah (eel kah-poh*-LEE-*neh-ah) dell-low-toh*-BOOSS?

Which bus goes to _____?
Quale autobus va a _____?
KWAH-*leh ow-toh*-BOOSS *vah ah* _____?

Business

I am here on business.
Sono qui per affari.
SOH-*noh kwee pehr ahf*-FAH-*ree*.

Busy

I am busy.
Sono occupato (occupata).
SOH-*noh ohk-koo*-PAH-*toh (ohk-koo*-PAH-*tah)*.

Are you busy?
È occupato (occupata) lei?
EH *ohk-koo*-PAH-*toh (ohk-koo*-PAH-*tah) lay?*

The line is busy.
La linea e occupata.
lah LEE-*neh-ah eh ohk-koo*-PAH-*tah*.

Buy

Where can I buy _____?
Dove posso comprare _____?
DOH-*veh* POHSS-*soh kohm*-PRAH-*reh* _____?

I wish to buy _____.
Vorrei comprare.
vohr-RAY *kohm*-PRAH-*reh* _____.

Cab – see Taxi

Cabin

Where is cabin number _____?
Dov'è la cabina numero _____?
doh-VEH *lah kah*-BEE-*nah* NOO-*meh-roh* _____?

Cablegram – see Telegram

Call

I want to put a call through to _____.
Vorrei fare una telefonata a _____.
vohr-RAY FAH-*reh* OON-*ah teh-leh-foh*-NAH-*tah ah* _____.

Please call me at _____.
Mi chiami per favore al numero _____.
mee KYAH-*mee pehr fah*-VOH-*reh ahl* NOO-*meh-roh*

_____.

How much is a call to _____?
Quanto costa una telefonata a _____?
KWAHN-*toh* KOH-*stah* OON-*ah teh-leh-foh*-NAH-*tah ah*
_____?

What is this (that) called?
Come si chiama questo/questa (quello/quella)?
KOH-*meh see* KYAH-*mah* KWEH-*stoh*/KWEH-*stah (*KWELL-
loh/KWELL-*lah)*?

Camera

Do you rent cameras?
Date macchine fotografiche a nolo?
DAH-*teh* MAHK-*kee-neh foh-toh*-GRAH-*fee-keh ah* NOH-
loh?

I need film for this camera.
Mi occore una pellicola per questa macchina.
mee ohk-KOHR-*reh oon-ah pell*-LEE-*koh-lah pehr* KWEH-
stah MAHK-*kee-nah.*

Something is the matter with this camera.
Questa macchina è guasta.
KWEH-*stah* MAHK-*kee-nah eh* GWAH-*stah.*

Can you fix it?
La può riparare?
lah PWOH *ree-pah*-RAH-*reh*?

Please direct me to a camera shop.
Mi indichi per favore un negozio di articoli fotografici.
mee EEN-*dee-kee pehr fah-*VOH-*reh oon neh-*GOH-*tsyoh*
  *dee ahr-*TEE-*koh-lee foh-toh-*GRAH-*fee-chee.*

Camp

May we camp in your field?
Possiamo campeggiare nel vostro campo?
*pohss-see-*AH-*moh kahm-pehdd-*JAH-*reh nehl* VOH-*stroh*
  KAHM-*poh?*

Is there a campsite nearby?
C'è un campeggio vicino?
*cheh oon kahm-*PEHDD-*joh vee-*CHEE-*noh?*

Can

Can you help me?
Mi può aiutare?
mee PWOH *ah-yoo-*TAH-*reh?*

Cancel

Please cancel my reservation.
Cancelli la mia prenotazione, per favore.
*kahn-*CHELL-*lee lah* MEE-*ah preh-noh-tah-*TSYOH-*neh,*
  *pehr fah-*VOH-*reh.*

Is the flight cancelled?
È cancellato il volo?
*eh kahn-chell-*LAH-*toh eel* VOH-*loh?*

Candle

Do you have any candles?
Ha delle candele?
ah DELL-*leh kahn-*DEH-*leh?*

Car – see Automobile

Card, Calling

May I have your calling card?
Potrei avere il suo biglietto da visita?
*poh-*TRAY *ah-*VEH-*reh eel* SOO-*oh bee-*LYETT-*toh dah*
  VEE-*zee-tah?*

Card, Post

I wish to buy some postcards (postal cards).

Vorrei comprare delle cartoline illustrate (cartoline postali).

vohr-RAY kohm-PRAH-reh DELL-*leh kahr-toh-*LEE-*neh eel-loo-*STRAH-*teh (kahr-toh-*LEE-*neh poh-*STAH-*lee).*

Careful

Please be careful.

Faccia attenzione, per favore.

FAHT-*chah aht-tenn-*TSYOH-*neh, pehr fah-*VOH-*reh.*

Please drive more carefully.

Faccia più attenzione quando guida.

FAHT-*chah pyoo aht-tenn-*TSYOH-*neh* KWAHN-*doh-*GWEE-*dah.*

Please handle this with care.

Per favore, tratti questo con cura.

*pehr fah-*VOH-*reh,* TRAHT-*tee* KWEH-*stoh kohn* KOO-*rah.*

Carry

Please carry this (my bags).

Mi porti questo (le mie valigie), per favore.

mee POHR-*tee* KWEH-*stoh (leh* MEE-*eh vah-*LEE-*jeh), pehr fah-*VOH-*reh.*

Cash

Can you cash this check?

Mi può incassare questo assegno?

mee PWOH *een-kahss-*SAH-*reh* KWEH-*stoh ahss-*SEH-*nyoh?*

Cashier

Where is the cashier?

Dov'è il cassiere?

*doh-*VEH *eel kahss-*SYEH-*reh?*

Castle

Are there tours of the castle?

Si può visitare il castello?

see PWOH *vee-zee-*TAH-*reh eel kah-*STELL-*loh?*

Catalog

May I have one of your catalogs?

Potrei avere uno dei vostri cataloghi?

poh-TRAY *ah*-VEH-*reh* OON-*oh day* VOH-*stree kah*-TAH-
loh-ghee?

Catch

I have to catch a train.

Devo prendere un treno.

DEH-*voh* PRENN-*deh-reh oon* TREH-*noh.*

Cathedral

Please direct me to the cathedral.

Per favore, mi indichi la strada per la cattedrale.

pehr fah-VOH-*reh,* mee EEN-*dee-kee lah* STRAH-*dah
pehr lah kaht-teh*-DRAH-*leh.*

Please direct me to the cathedral.

Mi indichi la strada per la cattedrale.

mee EEN-*dee-kee lah* STRAH-*dah pehr lah kaht-teh*-DRAH-
leh.

Chamber of Commerce

Please direct (take) me to the Chamber of Commerce.

Per favore, mi indichi la strada per la (mi porti alla)
camera di dommercio.

pehr fah-VOH-*reh,* mee EEN-*dee-kee luh* STRAH-*dah pehr
lah (mee* POHR-*tee* AHL-*lah)* KAH-*meh-rah dee kohm*-
MEHR-*choh.*

Change

Can you change this?

Mi può cambiare questo?

mee PWOH *kahm*-BYAH-*reh* KWEH-*stoh?*

May I have some change?

Potrei avere degli spiccioli?

poh-TRAY *ah*-VEH-*reh* DEH-*lyee* SPEET-*choh-lee?*

Please change the sheets today.

Per favore, cambi le lenzuola oggi.

pehr fah-VOH-*reh,* KAHM-*bee leh lenn*-TSWOH-*lah* OHD-
jee.

Where must I change for _____?
Dove devo cambiare per _____?
DOH-*veh* DEH-*voh* kahm-BYAH-*reh* pehr _____?

Chapel – see Church

Charge
What is this charge for?
Cosa rappresenta questa spesa?
KOH-*sah* rahp-preh-ZENN-*tah* KWEH-*stah* SPEH-*sah*?

Is there a service charge?
C'è una tassa di servizio?
CHEH OON-*ah* TAHSS-*sah* dee sehr-VEE-*tsyoh*?

What is the admission charge?
Qual'è il prezzo d'ingresso?
kwah-LEH *eel* PREHT-*tsoh* deen-GREHS-*soh*?

What is the charge per minute, hour, day, week,
    kilometer?
Qual'è la tariffa per minuto, ora,
    giorno, settimana, chilometro?
kwah-LEH *tah* tah-REEF-*fah* pehr mee-NOO-*toh*, OH-*rah*,
    JOHR-*noh*, sett-tee-MAH-*nah*, kee-LOH-*meh-troh*?

How much per kilometer?
Quanto costa al chilo?
KWAHN-*toh* KOH-*stah* ahl KEE-*loh*?

Cheap
I prefer something cheaper.
Vorrei qualchecosa che costa meno.
vohr-RAY kwahl-keh-KOH-*sah* keh KOH-*stah* MEH-*noh*.

Check
The check please.
Il conto, per favore.
eel KOHN-*toh*, pehr fah-VOH-*reh*.

Clothing check, please.
Lo scontrino, per favore.
loh skohn-TREE-*noh*, pehr fah-VOH-*reh*.

Here is the check for my baggage.
Ecco lo scontrino per i miei bagagli.
EHK-*koh loh skohn*-TREE-*noh pehr ee* MYEH-*ee bah*-GAH-
lyee.

Will you cash a check?
Potete incassare un assegno?
poh-TEH-*teh een-kahss*-SAH-*reh oon ahss*-SEH-*nyoh?*

Is a travelers check acceptable?
Accetta un assegno per viaggiatori?
aht-CHETT-*tah oon ahss*-SEH-*nyoh pehr vyahd-jah-*
TOH-*ree?*

Checkout
What is the checkout time?
A che ora devo liberare la camera?
ah keh OH-*rah* DEH-*voh lee-beh*-RAH-*reh lah* KAH-*meh-*
rah?

Child
Are children allowed?
Sono ammessi i bambini?
SOH-*noh ahm*-MESS-*see ee bahm*-BEE-*nee?*

Chilly — see Cold

Christian
Are you a christian?
Lei è cristiano?
lay EH *kree*-STYAH-*noh?*

I am a christian.
Sono cristiano.
SOH-*noh kree*-STYAH-*noh.*

Church
I would like to attend church services.
Vorrei assistere alle funzioni religiose.
vohr-RAY *ahss*-SEE-*steh-reh* AHL-*leh foon*-TSYOH-*nee*
reh-lee-JOH-*seh.*

When are church services held?
A che ora ci sono le funzioni religiose?
ah keh OH-*rah chee* SOH-*noh leh foon*-TSYOH-*nee reh-lee-*
JOH-*seh?*

Cigarette

A pack of cigarettes, please.
Un pacchetto di sigarette, per favore.
*oon pahk-*KEHT*-toh dee see-gah-*RETT*-teh, pehr fah-*VOH*-reh.*

Citizen

Are you a citizen of Italy (France)?
Lei è cittadino italiano (francese)?
*lay EH cheet-tah-*DEE*-noh ee-tah-*LYAH*-noh (frahn-*CHEH*-seh.)*

I am a citizen of the United States.
Sono cittadino americano.
SOH*-noh cheet-tah-*DEE*-noh ah-meh-ree-*KAH*-noh.*

Clean

This is not clean.
Questo non è pulito.
KWEH*-stoh nohn eh poo-*LEE*-toh.*

I want this cleaned.
Vorrei far pulire questo.
*vohr-*RAY *fahr poo-*LEE*-reh* KWEH*-stoh.*

Clerk

I wish to speak to the room clerk.
Vorrei parlare alla segretaria.
*vohr-*RAY *pahr-*LAH*-reh* AHL*-lah seh-greh-*TAH*-ryah.*

Climate — see Weather

Climb

Can one climb _____ at this time of year?
Si può scalare _____ in questa stagione?
see PWOH *skah-*LAH*-reh* _____ *een* KWEH*-stah stah-*JOH*-neh?*

How long does it take to climb _____?
Quanto tempo ci vuole per scalare _____?
KWAHN*-toh* TEMM*-poh chee* VWOH*-leh pehr skah-*LAH*-reh* _____?

I cannot climb stairs.
Non posso salire le scale.
nohn POHSS*-soh sah-*LEE*-reh leh* SKAH*-leh.*

Close

Are you closed? (When do you open?)
Siete chiusi? (Quando aprite?)
SYEII-*teh* KYOO-*see?* (*KWAHN-doh ah-PREE-teh?*)

When does the store close (open)?
Quando si chiude (si apre) il negozio?
KWAHN-*doh see* KYOO-*deh* (*see* AH-*preh*) *eel neh-*GOH-
tsyoh?

Close the door (window), please.
Chiuda la porta (la finestra), per favore.
KYOO-*dah lah* POHR-*tah* (*lah fee-*NEH-*strah*), *pehr fah-*
VOH-*reh.*

Clothing

What kind of clothing should be worn?
Come bisogna vestirsi?
KOH-*meh bee-*ZOH-*nyoh veh-*STEER-*see?*

Can you recommend a good clothing store?
Mi saprebbe indicare un buon negozio
d'abbigliamento?
*mee sah-*PREHB-*beh een-dee-*KAH-*reh oon bwohn neh-*
GOH-*tsyoh dahb-bee-lyah-*MENN-*toh?*

Coach

Are there any coach seats available?
Ci sono ancora posti sulla corriera?
chee SOH-*noh ahng-*KOH-*rah* POH-*stee sool-la kohr-*
RYEH-*rah?*

Coast

How far is the coast from here?
Quant'è lontana la costa da qui?
*kwahn-*TEH *lohn-*TAH-*nah lah* KOH-*stah dah kwee?*

How long does it take to reach the coast?
Quanto tempo ci vuole per raggiungere la costa?
KWAHN-*toh* TEMM-*poh chee* VWOH-*leh pehr rahd-*JOON-
jeh-reh lah KOH-*stah?*

Coat

Should I wear a coat (and tie)?

Devo mettere la giacca (è la cravatta)?

DEH-*voh* METT-*teh-reh lah* JAHK-*ka (eh la krah-*VAHT-*tah)?*

Cocktail

Do you serve cocktails?

Servite cocktails?

*sehr-*VEE-*teh* KOHK-*tell?*

Would you like a cocktail?

Gradisce un cocktail?

*grah-*DEE-*sheh oon* KOHK-*tell?*

Cold

This is cold.

Questo è freddo.

KWEH-*stoh eh* FREDD-*doh.*

The weather is cold.

Fa freddo.

fah FREDD-*doh.*

I am cold.

Ho freddo.

oh FREDD-*doh.*

Are you cold?

Ha freddo?

ah FREDD-*doh?*

Color

I do not like the color.

Non mi piace il colore.

nohn mee PYAH-*cheh eel koh-*LOH-*reh.*

Do you have other colors?

Avete altri colori?

*ah-*VEH-*teh* AHL-*tree koh-*LOH-*ree?*

Do you have a brighter (darker) color?

Avete un colore più vivace (scuro)?

*ah-*VEH-*teh oon koh-*LOH-*reh pyoo vee-*VAH-*cheh (*SKOO-*roh)?*

Come

Please come back later.
Torni più tardi, per favore.
TOHR-nee pyoo TAHR-*di, pehr fah-*VOH*-reh.*

Come here, please.
Venga qui, per favore.
VENN-*gah kwee, pehr fah-*VOH*-reh.*

Come in.
Avanti.
*ah-*VAHN-*tee.*

Companion

I am traveling with a companion.
Viaggio con un compagno (con una compagna).
VYAHD-*joh kohn oon kohm-*PAH-*nyoh (kohn* OON-*ah
kohm-*PAH-*nyah).*

Have you seen my companion?
Ha visto il mio compagno (la mia compagna)?
ah VEE-*stoh eel* MEE-*oh kohn-*PAH-*nyoh (lah* MEE-*ah
kohm-*PAH-*nyah)?*

Company

I am traveling on company business.
Viaggio per la mia società.
VYAHD-*joh pehr lah*MEE-*ah soh-chyeh-*TAH.

What company are you with?
Per quale società lavora?
pehr KWAH-*leh soh-chyeh-*TAH *lah-*VOH-*rah?*

Compartment

I would like a compartment.
Vorrei uno scompartimento.
*vohr-*RAY OON-*oh skohm-pahr-tee-*MENN-*toh.*

Complaint

I have a complaint.
Vorrei fare un reclamo.
*vohr-*RAY FAH-*reh oon reh-*KLAH-*moh.*

Confirm

Can you confirm my reservation on flight number
_____?

Può confermare la mia prenotazione sul volo numero
_____?

PWOH *kohn-fehr*-MAH-*reh la* MEE-*ah preh-noh-tah*-
TSYOH-*neh sool* VOH-*loh* NOO-*meh-roh* _____?

Consulate

Please direct me to the U. S. Consulate (the U. S.
Embassy).

Per favore, mi indichi la strada per il consolato
Americano (l'Ambasciata Americana).

pehr fah-VOH-*reh, mee* EEN-*dee-kee lah* STRAH-*dah pehr*
eel kohn-soh-LAH-*toh ah-meh-ree*-KAH-*noh (lahm-bah*-
SHAH-*tah ah-meh-ree*-KAH-*nah).*

Contents

What are the contents (ingredients) of this dish?

Quali sono gli ingredienti di questo piatto?

KWAH-*lee* SOH-*noh lyee een-greh*-DYEHN-*tee dee* KWEH-
stoh PYAT-*toh?*

Convention

I am attending a convention.

Partecipo ad un congresso.

pahr-TEH-*chee-poh ahd oon kohn*-GRESS-*soh*

Cook

Can you recommend a good cook?

Può raccomandarmi una buona cuoca (un buon cuoco)?

PWOH *rahk-koh-mahn*-DAHR-*mee* OON-*ah* BWOH-*nah*
KWOH-*kah (oon bwohn* KWOH-*koh)?*

I want it thoroughly cooked.

Lo vorrei molto ben cotto.

loh vohr-RAY MOHL-*toh behn* KOHT-*toh.*

Must this be cooked before being eaten?

Questo si mangia cotto?

KWEH-*stoh see* MAN-*jah* KOHT-*toh?*

Correct
This is (this is not) correct.
È (non è) esatto.
EH *(nohn* EH*)* eh-ZAHT-*toh.*

Correspond
I would like to correspond with you.
Vorrei corrispondere con lei.
*vohr-*RAY *kohr-ree-*SPOHN-*deh-reh kohn* LAY.

May I have your address?
Posso avere il suo indirizzo?
POHSS-*soh ah-*VEH-*reh eel* SOO-*oh een-dee-*REET-*tsoh?*

Cost
How much does it cost (per liter, per kilogram)?
Quanto costa (al litro, al chilo)?
KWAHN-*toh* KOH-*stah (ahl* LEE-*troh, ahl* KEE-*loh)?*

It costs too much.
Costa troppo.
KOH-*stah* TROHP-*poh*

Costly
It is too costly.
È troppo caro.
eh TROHP *poh* KAH-*roh*

Costume
Where do the people wear native costume?
Dove la gente indossa il costume locale?
DOH-*veh lah* JENN-*teh een-*DOHS-*sah eel koh-*STOO-*meh loh-*KAH-*leh?*

Cot – see Bed

Cotton
Do you have any made of cotton?
Ne ha in cotone?
neh AH *een koh-*TOH-*neh?*

Country
What country are you from?
Di dov'è lei?
*dee doh-*VEH *lay?*

Can this be taken out of the country?
Si può esportare questo?
see PWOH *eh-spohr-*TAH-*reh* KWEH-*stoh?*

Credit Card

What credit cards do you honor?
Quali carte credito accetta?
KWAH-*lee kahr-teh* KREH-*dee-toh aht-*CHETT-*tah?*

Cup

Please bring me another cup(ful).
Mi porti un'altra tazza, per favore.
mee POHR-*tee oon-*AHL-*trah* TAHT-*tsah, pehr fah-*VOH-
reh.

Currency

Do you accept U.S. currency?
Accettate valuta americana?
*aht-chett-*TAH-*teh vah-*LOO-*tah ah-meh-ree-*KAH-*nah?*

Where can I exchange currency?
Dove posso cambiare della valuta?
DOH-*veh* POHSS-*soh kahm-*BYAH-*reh* DELL-*lah vah-*LOO-
tah?

Current

Are there any dangerous currents here?
Ci sono correnti pericolose qui?
chee SOH-*noh kohr-*RENN-*tee peh-ree-koh-*LOH-*seh kwee?*

Customhouse

Where is the customhouse?
Dov'è la dogana?
*doh-*VEH *lah doh-*GAH-*nah?*

Do we have to go through customs?
Bisogna fare la dogana?
*bee-*ZOH-*nyah* FAH-*reh la doh-*GAH-*nah?*

Cut – see Accident

Cycle – see also Bicycle, Hostel

We are (I am) cycling to _____.
Andiamo (vado) in bicicletta a _____.
*ahn-dee-*AH-*moh (*VAH-*doh) een bee-chee-*KLETT-*tah ah*

_____.

How long does it take to cycle to _____?
Quanto ci vuole in bicicletta a _____?
KWAHN-*toh chee* VWOH-*leh een bee-chee*-KLETT-*tah*
    ah _____?

Are there accommodations for cyclists along the way?
Ci sono alloggi per ciclisti lungo la strada?
chee SOH-*noh ahl*-LOHD-*jee pehr chee*-KLEE-*stee* LOONG-
    goh lah STRAH-*dah?*

Dance
May I have this dance?
Posso avere questo ballo?
POHSS-*soh ah*-VEH-*reh* KWEH-*stoh* BAHL-*loh?*

Where can we go to dance?
Dove possiamo andare a ballare?
DOH-*veh pohss-see*-AH-*moh ahn*-DAH-*reh ah bahl*-LAH-
    reh?

Dangerous
Is it dangerous?
È pericoloso?
EH *peh-ree-koh*-LOH-*soh?*

Date
What is the date today?
Oggi che data è?
OHD-*jee keh* DAH-*tah* EH?

Do you have a date?
È impegnata (impegnato)?
EH *eem-peh*-NYAH-*luh (eem-peh*-NYAH-*toh)?*

Day
What is the rate per day?
Qual'è la tariffa giornaliera?
kwah-LEH *lah tah*-REEF-*fah johr-nah*-LYEH-*rah?*

Declare
I have nothing to declare.
Non ho nulla da dichiarare.
nohn oh NOOL-*lah dah dee-kyah*-RAH-*reh.*

Deep

Is it very deep?
È molto profondo?
EH MOHL-toh proh-FOHN-doh?

How deep is it?
Quant'è profondo?
kwahn-TEH proh-FOHN-doh?

Delay

Has there been a delay?
C'è stato un ritardo?
CHEH STAH-toh oon ree-TAHR-doh?

Will there be a delay?
Ci sarà un ritardo?
chee sah-RAH oon ree-TAHR-doh?

Deliver

Please deliver this to this address.
Per favore lo consegni a questo indirizzo.
pehr fah-VOH-reh loh kohn-SEH-nyee ah KWEH-stoh een-dee-REET-tsoh.

Dentist

Can you recommend a good (English-speaking) dentist?
Mi saprebbe raccomandare un buon dentista (che parla inglese)?
mee sah-PREHB-beh rahk-koh-mahn-DAH-reh oon bwohn denn-TEE-stah (keh PAHR-lah een-GLEH-seh)?

Can you give me an appointment as soon as possible?
Mi può fissare un appuntamento al più presto?
mee PWOH feess-SAH-reh oon ahp-poon-tah-MENN-toh ahl pyoo PREH-stoh?

I (don't) have an appointment.
Ho (non ho) un appuntamento.
oh (nohn oh) oon ahp-poon-tah-MENN-toh.

I have a terrible toothache.
Ho un fortissimo mal di denti.
oh oon fohr-TEES-see-moh mahl dee DENN-tee.

I have lost a filling.
Ho perso un'otturazione.
oh PEHR-*soh oon-oht-too-rah-*TSYOH-*neh.*

The filling is loose.
L'otturazione si è mossa.
*loht-too-rah-*TSYOH-*neh see* EH MOHS-*sah.*

Can you put in a temporary filling?
Mi può fare un'otturazione provvisoria?
mee PWOH FAH-*reh oon-oht-too-rah-*TSYOH-*neh prohv-
vee-*ZOH-*ryah?*

Please don't pull it unless you must.
Per favore, non mi tolga il dente se non é proprio
    necessario.
*pehr fah-*VOH-*reh, nohn mee* TOHL-*gah eel* DENN-*teh seh
nohn* EH PROH-*pryoh neh-chess-*SAH-RYOH.

Please use (don't use) novocaine.
Per favore, usi (non usi) la novocaina.
*pehr fah-*VOH-*reh,* OO-*zee (nohn* OO-*zee) lah noh-voh-
kah-*EE-*nah.*

When can you give me another appointment?
Quando mi può fissare un altro appuntamento?
KWAHN-*doh mee* PWOH *feess-*SAH-*reh oon* AHL-*troh ahp-
poon tah-*MENN-*toh?*

Deposit
Is a deposit required?
Occorre una caparra?
*ohk-*KOHR-*reh* OON-*ah kah-*PAHR *rah?*

How much deposit is required?
Quanto di caparra?
KWAHN-*toh dee kah-*PAHR-*rah?*

Dessert
What do you have for dessert?
Che dolce avete?
keh DOHL-*cheh ah-*VEH-*teh?*
Is dessert included?
Il dolce è compreso?
eel DOHL-*cheh* EH *kohm-*PREH-*soh?*

Dining Car
Where is the dining car?
Dov'è il vagone ristorante?
doh-VEH *eel vah*-GOH-*neh ree-stoh-*RAHN-*teh?*

Does the train have a dining car?
Il treno ha il vagone ristorante?
eel TREH-*noh ah eel vah-*GOH-*neh ree-stoh-*RAHN-*teh?*

Dining Room
Where is the dining room?
Dov'è la sala da pranzo?
doh-VEH *lah* SAH-*lah dah* PRAHN-*dzoh?*

Dinner
When is dinner served?
A che ora è servito il pranzo?
ah keh OH-*rah* EH *sehr*-VEE-*toh eel* PRAHN-*dzoh?*

Will you have dinner with me?
Vuol pranzare con me?
VWOHL *prahn*-DZAH-*reh kohn* MEH?

Direct
What is the most direct route to _____?
Qual'è la via più diretta per _____?
kwah-LEH-*lah* VEE-*ah pyoo dee-*RETT-*tah pehr* _____ ?

Please direct me to _____?
Per favore mi indichi la strada per _____?
pehr fah-VOH-*reh mee* EEN-*dee-kee lah* STRAH-*dah pehr* _____?

Direction
In which direction is _____?
In che direzione si trova _____?
een keh dee-reh-TSYOH-*neh see* TROH-*vah* _____?

Dirty
This is dirty. (Please bring me another).
Questo è sporco. (Me ne porti un altro, per favore).
KWEH-*stoh* EH SPOHR-*koh (meh neh* POHR-*tee oon* AHL-*troh, pehr fah-*VOH-*reh).*

Discount

Is there a discount for students?

Fate uno sconto per gli studenti?

FAH-*teh* OON-*oh* SKOHN-*toh* pehr lyee stoo-DENN-*tee?*

Dish

What is in this dish?

Cosa c'è in questa pietanza?

KOH-*sah* CHEH *een* KWEH-*stah* pyeh-TAHN-*tsah?*

Which dish do you recommend?

Quale pietanza raccomandate?

KWAH-*leh* pyeh-TAHN-*tsah* rahk-koh-mahn-DAH-*teh?*

Is this dish served hot or cold?

Questa pietanza si serve calda o fredda?

KWEH-*stah* pyeh-TAHN-*tsah* see SEHR-*veh* KAHL-*dah oh*
   FREDD-*dah?*

Disinfected

Please have this disinfected.

Me lo faccia disinfettare, per favore.

meh loh FAHT-*chah dee-seen-fett-*TAH-*reh, pehr fah-*VOH-
   reh.

Distance

What is the distance to _____?

Quant'è lontano _____?

*kwahn-*TEH *lohn-*TAH-*noh* _____?

District

Please take me to the _____ district.

Per favore, me porti al quartiere _____.

*pehr fah-*VOH-*reh, mee* POHR-*tee ahl kwahr-*TYEH-*reh*

   _____.

Disturb

Please do not disturb me until _____.

Per favore, non mi chiami fino a _____.

*pehr fah-*VOH-*reh, nohn mee* KYAH-*mee* FEE-*noh ah*

   _____.

He is disturbing me.

Mi disturba.

*mee dee-*STOOR-*bah.*

Divorced
I am divorced.
Sono divorziato (divorziata).
soh-noh dee-vohr-TSYAH-*toh (dee-vohr*-TSYAH-*tah).*

Dock
When will the ship dock?
Quando attraccherà la nave?
KWAHN-*doh aht-trahk-keh*-RAH *lah* NAH-*veh?*

Is our baggage on the dock?
I nostri bagagli sono sulla banchina?
ee NOHS-*tree bah*-GAH-*lyee* SOH-*noh* SOOL-*lah bahng-*
KEE-*nah?*

Doctor – see also Medical
Can you recommend a good doctor?
Può raccomandare un buon medico?
PWOH *rahk-koh-mahn*-DAH-*reh oon bwohn* MEH-*dee-*
koh?

I would like to see the doctor (the dentist).
Vorrei consultare il medico (il dentista).
vohr-RAY *kohn-sool*-TAH-*reh eel* MEH-*dee-koh (eel denn-*
TEE-*stah).*

Send for a doctor.
Faccia chiamare un medico.
FAHT-*chah kyah*-MAH-*reh oon* MEH-*dee-koh.*

Dog
Are dogs allowed?
Sono ammessi i cani?
SOH-*noh ahm*-MESS-*see ee* KAH-*nee?*

Dollar
How much (how many) can I get for a dollar?
Quanto (quanti) ne posso avere per un dollaro?
KWAHN-*toh (*KWAHN-*tee) neh* POHSS-*soh ah*-VEH-*reh*
pehr oon DOHLL-*lah-roh?*

How many lire for one dollar?
Quante lire per un dollaro?
KWAHN-*teh* LEE-*reh pehr oon* DOHLL-*lah-roh?*

Door

Please open (close) the door.
Per favore apra (chiuda) la porta.
*pehr fah-*VOH*-reh* AH*-prah (*KYOO*-dah) lah* POHR*-tah.*

I cannot unlock my door.
Non riesco a girare la chiave nella serratura.
*nohn ree-*EH*-skoh ah jee-*RAH*-reh la* KYAH*-veh* NELL*-lah
sehr-rah-*TOO*-rah.*

I cannot lock my door.
Non riesco a chiudere la porta a chiave.
*nohn ree-*EH*-skoh ah* KYOO*-deh-reh lah* POHR*-tah ah
KYAH-veh.*

Double Bed

Do you have a room with a double bed?
Avete una camera con letto matrimoniale?
*ah-*VEH*-teh* OON*-ah* KAH*-meh-rah kohn* LETT*-toh mah-
tree-moh-*NYAH*-leh?*

Dozen

How much is a dozen?
Quanto costa una dozzina?
KWAHN*-toh* KOH*-stah* OON*-ah dohd-*DZEE*-nah?*

I'll take a dozen.
Ne prendo una dozzina.
neh PRENN*-doh* OON*-ah dohd-*DZEE*-nah.*

Draft (Current of Air)

There is a draft.
C'è corrente.
CHEH *kohr-*RENN*-teh.*

Dressed

I am not dressed.
Non sono vestito (vestita).
nohn SOH*-noh veh-*STEE*-toh (veh-*STEE*-tah).*

Dresses

I wish to look at dresses.
Vorrei vedere dei vestiti.
*vohr-*RAY *veh-*DEH*-reh day veh-*STEE*-tee.*

Dressing Room

Where is the men's (women's) dressing room?

Dov'è lo spogliatoio per uomini (per donne)?

*doh-*VEH *loh spoh-lyah-*TOH*-yoh pehr* WOH*-mee-nee*
(pehr DOHN*-neh)?*

Dressing (Salad)

A salad with oil and vinegar.

Insalata all'olio e aceto.

*een-sah-*LAH*-tah ahl-*LOH*-lyoh eh ah-*CHEH*-toh.*

A salad with garlic.

Insalata con aglio.

*een-sah-*LAH*-tah kohn* AH*-lyoh.*

Drink

Where can I get something to drink?

Dove posso trovare qualchecosa da bere?

DOH*-veh* POHSS*-soh troh-*VAH*-reh kwahl-keh-*KOH*-sah*
dah BEH*-reh?*

What do you have to drink?

Cosa avete da bere?

KOH*-sah ah-*VEH*-teh dah* BEH*-reh?*

Would you like a drink?

Gradisce bere qualchecosa?

*grah-*DEE*-sheh* BEH*-reh kwal-keh-*KOH*-sah?*

Drive

Please drive me to _____.

Per favore mi porti a _____.

*pehr fah-*VOH*-reh mee* POHR*-tee ah* _____.

Please drive more carefully (slowly).

Per favore guidi più prudentemente (più lentamente).

*pehr fah-*VOH*-reh* GWEE*-dee pyoo proo-denn-teh-*MENN*-*
*teh (pyoo lenn-tah-*MENN*-teh).*

Can you drive?

Sa guidare?

SAH *gwee-*DAH*-reh?*

Driver

I want to hire a driver.

Vorrei prendere un autista.

vohr-RAY PRENN-*deh-reh oon ow-*TEE-*stah.*

I have (I do not have) an international driver's license.

Ho (non ho) la patente internazionale.

*oh (nohn oh) la pah-*TENN-*teh een-tehr-nah-tsyoh-*NAH-*leh.*

Drugstore (Cosmetics)

Please direct (take) me to a drugstore.

Per favore, mi indichi (porti a) una profumeria.

*pehr fah-*VOH-*reh, mee* EEN-*dee-kee (*POHR-*tee ah)* OON-*ah proh-foo-meh-*REE-*ah.*

Drugstore (Pharmacy)

Please direct (take) me to a drugstore.

Per favore, mi indichi (porti a) una farmacia.

*pehr fah-*VOH-*reh, mee* EEN-*dee-kee (*POHR-*tee ah)* OON-*ah fahr-mah-*CHEE-*ah.*

Dry Clean – see Laundry

Duty

Must I pay duty on this?

Devo pagare il dazio su questo?

DEH-*voh pah-*GAH-*reh eel* DAH-*tsyoh soo* KWEH-*stoh?*

What is the duty on this?

Che dazio si paga su questo?

keh DAH-*tsyoh see* PAH-*gah soo* KWEH-*stoh?*

Early

It is too early.

È troppo presto.

EH TROHP-*poh* PREH-*stoh.*

Are we too early?

Siamo arrivati troppo presto?

*see-*AH-*moh ahr-ree-*VAH-*tee* TROHP-*poh* PREH-*stoh?*

Eat
What do you have to eat?
Cosa avete da mangiare?
KOH-*sah ah*-VEH-*teh dah mahn*-JAH-*reh?*

Where can I get something to eat?
Dove posso mangiare qualchecosa?
DOH-*veh* POHSS-*soh mahn*-JAH-*reh kwahl-keh*-KOH-*sah?*

Do you want to eat now?
Vuol mangiare ora?
VWOHL *mahn*-JAH-*reh* OH-*rah?*

Either
Either one will do.
O l'uno o l'altro va bene.
oh LOO-*noh oh* LAHL-*troh vah* BEH-*neh.*

Electricity
Is there an electrical outlet here?
C'è una presa elettrica?
CHEH OON-*ah* PREH-*sah eh*-LETT-*tree-kah?*

Elevator
Is there an elevator here?
C'è l'ascensore qui?
CHEH *lah-shenn*-SOH-*reh kwee?*

Embassy – see Consulate

Emergency
This is an emergency.
È un caso urgente.
EH *oon* KAH-*zoh oor*-JENN-*teh.*

Engaged
I am engaged (busy).
Sono occupato (occupata).
SOH-*noh ohk-koo*-PAH-*toh (ohk-koo*-PAH-*tah).*

I am engaged to be married.
Sono fidanzato (fidanzata).
SOH-*noh fee-dahn*-TSAH-*toh (fee-dahn*-TSAH-*tah).*

English

Do you speak English?
Parlate inglese?
pahr-LAH-teh een-GLEH-seh?

I need an English-speaking guide.
Mi occorre una guida che parla inglese.
mee ohk-KOHR-reh OON-ah GUEE-dah keh PAHR-lah een-GLEH-seh.

I speak only English.
Parlo solo inglese.
PAHR-lo SOH-lo een-GLEH-seh.

Is there a church service in English?
C'è una funzione religiosa in inglese?
CHEH OON-ah foon-TSYOH-neh reh-lee-JOH-sah een een-GLEH-seh?

Enough

That is enough.
Basta così.
BAH-stah koh-SEE.

It isn't hot enough.
Non è abbastanza caldo.
nohn EH-ahb-bah-STAHN-tsah KAHL-doh.

I do not have enough money with me.
Non ho abbastanza soldi con me.
nohn OH ahb-bah-STAHN-tsah SOHL-dee kohn meh.

I've had enough, thank you.
Mi basta, grazie.
mee BAH-stah, GRAH-tsyeh.

Is that enough?
Questo basta?
KWEH-stoh BAH-stah?

Entrance

Where is the entrance to _____?
Dov'è l'ingresso del (della) _____?
doh-VEH leeng-GREHSS-soh dell (DELL-lah) _____?

Envelope

May I have an envelope?
Potrei avere una busta?
poh-TRAY *ah*-VEH-*reh* OON-*ah* BOO-*stah?*

Equipment

Do you rent equipment for _____?
Noleggiate le attrezzature per _____?
noh-ledd-JAH-*teh leh aht-trett-tsah-*TOO-*reh pehr* _____?

Error

There is an error here, I believe.
C'è un errore qui, credo.
CHEH *oon ehr*-ROH-*reh kwee,* KREH-*doh.*

Escort

May I escort you home?
Posso accompagnarla a casa?
POHSS-*soh ahk-kohm-pah*-NYAHR-*la ah* KAH-*sah?*

Evening

See you this evening.
Arrivederci stasera.
ahr-ree-veh-DEHR-*chee stah*-SEH-*rah.*

Excess

What is the rate for excess baggage?
Qual'è la tariffa per il bagaglio in eccesso?
kwahl-EH *lah tah*-REEF-*fah pehr eel bah*-GAH-*lyoh een ett*-CHESS-*soh?*

Is my baggage in excess of the weight allowance?
Ho soprapeso?
oh soh-prah-PEH-*soh?*

Exchange

What is the exchange rate for the dollar?
Qual'è il tasso di cambio per il dollaro?
kwahl-EH *eel* TAHSS-*soh dee* KAHM-*byoh pehr eel* DOHLL-*lah-roh?*

Can I exchange this?
Posso cambiare questo?
POHSS-*soh kahm*-BYAH-*reh* KWEH-*stoh?*

I would like to exchange these dollars for _____.

Vorrei cambiare questi dollari in _____.

vohr-RAY *kahm*-BYAH-*reh* KWEH-*stee* DOHLL-*lah-ree een* _____.

Excursion

I would like to buy an excursion ticket.

Vorrei comprare un biglietto a tariffa ridotta.

vohr-RAY *kohm*-PRAH-*reh* oon *bee*-LYETT-*toh* ah *tah*-REEF-*fah ree*-DOHT-*tah.*

When does the excursion boat run?

A che ora fa servizio il battello per turisti?

ah keh OH-*rah fah sehr*-VEE-*tsyoh eel baht*-TELL-*loh pehr too*-REE-*stee?*

How long does the excursion trip last?

Quanto dura la gita?

KWAHN-*toh* DOO-*rah lah* JEE-*tah?*

Excuse

Excuse me!

Mi scusi!

mee SKOO-*zee!*

Exit

Where is the exit?

Dov'è l'uscita?

doh-VEH *loo*-SHEE-*tah?*

Expensive

It is too expensive.

È troppo caro.

EH TROHP-*poh* KAH-*roh.*

Do you have anything less expensive?

Avete qualchecosa di meno caro?

ah-VEH-*teh kwahl-keh*-KOH-*sah dee* MEN-*noh* KAH-*roh?*

Express

Where do I catch the express to _____?

Dove posso prendere il rapido per _____?

DOH-*veh* POHSS-*soh* PRENN-*deh-reh eel* RAH-*pee-doh pehr* _____?

Is this the express?
È questo il rapido?
EH KWEH-*stoh eel* RAH-*pee-doh?*

Fade

Will this color fade?
Si sbiadisce questo colore?
*see zbyah-*DEE-*sheh* KWEH-*stoh koh-*LOH-*reh?*

Family

Do you have family rates?
Che tariffe fate per le famiglie?
*keh tah-*REEF-*feh* FAH-*teh pehr leh fah-*MEE-*lyeh?*

Far

How far is it to _____?
Quant'è lontano _____?
*kwahn-*TEH *lohn-*TAH-*noh* _____?

Fare

How much is the fare (to _____)?
Quant'è la corsa (per _____)?
*kwahn-*TEH *lah* KOHR-*sah (pehr* _____)?

Fast

Don't go so fast, please.
Non vada così presto, per favore.
nohn VAH-*dah koh-*SEE PREH-*stoh, pehr fah-*VOH-*reh.*

Fat

There is too much fat on this. (Please take it back.)
C'è troppo grasso qui. (Per favore, lo riporti.)
CHEH TROHP-*poh* GRAHSS-*soh kwee. (pehr fah-*VOH-*reh, loh ree-*POHR-*tee.)*

Fee

What is your fee?
Qual'è il suo compenso?
*kwah-*LEH *eel* SOO-*oh kohm-*PENN-*soh?*

What is the admission fee?
Qual'è il prezzo d'ingresso?
*kwah-*LEH *eel* PRETT-*tsoh deeng-*GREHSS-*soh?*

Ferry

Is there a ferry to _____?

C'è il traghetto per _____?

cheh EEL *trah-*GEHTT*-toh pehr* _____?

When does the ferry leave?

A che ora parte il traghetto?

ah keh OH*-rah* PAHR*-teh eel trah-*GEHTT*-toh?*

What is the fare for the ferry?

Qual'è il prezzo del traghetto?

*kwah-*LEH *eel* PRETT*-tsoh dell trah-*GEHTT*-toh?*

Fill

Please fill the glass (the tub, the cup, the tank, the bottle).

Per favore, riempia il bicchiere (la vasca, la tazza, il serbatoio, la bottiglia).

*pehr fah-*VOH*-reh, ree-*EMM*-pyah eel beek-*KYEH*-reh (lah* VAH*-skah, lah* TAHT*-tsah, eel sehr-bah-*TOH*-yoh, lah boht-*TEE*-lyah).*

Filling

I have lost a filling from my tooth.

Ho perso l'otturazione di un dente.

oh PEHR*-soh loht-too-rah-*TSYOH*-neh dee oon* DENN*-teh.*

Film

Please develop this film.

Mi sviluppi questa pellicola, per favore.

*mee zvee-*LOOP*-pee* KWEH*-stah pell-*LEE*-koh-lah, pehr fah-*VOH*-reh.*

When will the film be ready?

Quando sarà pronta la pellicola?

KWAHN*-doh sah-*RAH PROHN*-tah lah pell-*LEE*-koh-lah?*

Do you have film for this camera?

Avete una pellicola per questa macchina?

*ah-*VEH*-teh* OON*-ah pell-*LEE*-koh-lah pehr* KWEH*-stah* MAHK*-kee-nah?*

Find

Please find my _____.
Trovi per favore il mio (la mia, i miei, le mie) _____.
TROH-*vee pehr fah*-VOH-*reh eel* MEE-*oh (lah* MEE-*ah, ee*
   MYEH-*ee, leh* MEE-*eh)* _____.

I cannot find my _____.
Non trovo il mio (la mia, i miei, le mie) _____.
nohn TROH-*voh eel* MEE-*oh (lah* MEE-*ah, ee* MYEH-*ee, leh*
   MEE-*eh)* _____.

Finish

Please wait until I finish.
Aspetti, per favore, finchè finisco.
ah-SPETT-*tee, pehr fah*-VOH-*reh, feen*-KEH *fee*-NEE-*skoh.*

Are you finished?
Ha finito?
ah fee-NEE-*toh?*

Fire

Please light a fire in the fireplace.
Accenda il camino, per favore.
aht-CHENN-*dah eel kah*-MEE-*noh, pehr fah*-VOH-*reh.*

The fire has gone out.
Il fuoco si è spento.
eel FWOH-*koh see eh* SPENN-*toh.*

Fishing

I would like to go fishing.
Vorrei andare a fare della pesca.
vohr-RAY *ahn*-DAH-*reh ah* FAH-*reh* DELL-*lah* PEH-*skah.*

Where can I rent (buy) fishing gear?
Dove posso affittare (comprare) l'occorrente per
   pescare?
DOH-*veh* POHSS-*soh ahf-feet*-TAH-*reh (kohm*-PRAH-*reh)
   lohk-kohr*-RENN-*teh pehr peh*-SKAH-*reh?*

Fit – see also Shopping

It does not fit me.
Non mi sta bene.
nohn mee stah BEH-*neh.*

Fix

Can you fix it?
Lo (la) può aggiustare?
loh (lah) PWOH *ahd-joo-*STAH-*reh?*

Flag

What flag is that?
Che bandiera è quella?
*keh bahn-*DYEH-*rah eh* KWELL-*lah?*

Flat — see also Automobile

Can you fix the flat tire?
Può riparare la gomma a terra?
PWOH *ree-pah-*RAH-*reh lah* GOHM-*mah ah* TEHR-*rah?*

Please (help me) fix the flat tire.
Per favore mi aiuti a riparare la gomma a terra.
*pehr fah-*VOH-*reh mee ah-*YOO-*tee ah ree-pah-*RAH-*reh
lah* GOHM-*mah ah* TEHR-*rah.*

Flight

When does the next flight leave for _____?
A che ora parte il prossimo volo per _____?
ah keh OH-*rah* PAHR-*teh eel* PROHSS-*see-moh* VOH-*loh
pehr* _____?

Could I make a reservation on flight number _____ to
_____?
Posso prenotarmi sul volo numero _____ per _____?
POHSS-*soh preh-noh-*TAHR-*mee sool* VOH-*loh* NOO-*meh-
roh* _____ *pehr* _____?

Are there any seats on flight number _____ to _____?
Ci sono posti sul volo numero _____ per _____?
chee SOH-*noh* POH-*stee sool* VOH-*loh* NOO-*meh-roh* _____
pehr _____?

Is there a connecting flight for _____?
C'è un volo in coincidenza per _____?
CHEH *oon* VOH-*loh een koh-een-chee-*DEHN-*tsah pehr*
_____?

Is a meal served on this flight?
Viene servito un pasto su questo volo?
VYEH-*neh sehr-*VEE-*toh oon* PAH-*stoh soo* KWEH-*stoh*
VOH-*loh?*

Floor

On what floor is my room?
A che piano si trova la mia camera?
ah keh PYAH-noh see TROH-vah lah MEE-ah KAH-meh-rah?

I want to move to a higher (lower) floor.
Vorrei trasferirmi a un piano superiore (inferiore).
vohr-RAY trah-sfeh-REER-mee ah oon PYAH-noh soo-peh RYOH-reh (een-feh-RYOH-reh).

Floor Show

When does the floor show start?
A che ora comincia lo spettacolo?
ah keh OH-rah koh-MEEN-chah loh spett-TAH-koh-loh?

Food – see Meals

Forget

I forgot my money (my key, my passport).
Ho dimenticato i soldi (la chiave, il passaporto).
oh dee-menn-tee-KAH-toh ee SOHL-dee (lah KYAH-veh, eel pahss-sah-POHR-toh).

I am sorry, I have forgotten your name.
Mi dispiace, ho dimenticato il suo nome.
mee dee-SPYAH-cheh, oh dee-menn-tee-KAH-toh eel SOO-oh NOH-meh.

Fork

Please bring me another fork.
Mi porti un'altra forchetta, per favore.
mee POHR-tee oon-AHL-trah fohr-KETT-tah, pehr fah-VOH-reh.

Forward

Please forward all mail to this address.
Per favore, inoltri tutta la corrispondenza a questo indirizzo.
pehr fah-VOH-reh, ee-NOHL-tree TOOT-tah lah kohr-ree-spohn-DENN-tsah ah KWEH-stoh een-dee-REET-tsoh.

Found
Where is lost and found?
Dov'è l'ufficio degli oggetti smarriti?
*doh-*VEH *loof-*FEE-*choh* DEH-*lyee ohd-*JETT-*tee zmahr-*
REE-*tee?*

Fragile
Handle this carefully, please; it is fragile.
Lo tratti con cura, per favore; è fragile.
loh TRAHT-*tee kohn* KOO-*rah, pehr fah-*VOH-*reh;* EH
FRAH-*jee-leh.*

Free
Are you free now?
È libero (libera) ora?
eh LEE-*beh-roh (*LEE-*beh-rah)* OH-*rah?*

Will you be free this afternoon (this evening,
tomorrow)?
Sarà libero (libera) questo pomeriggio (stasera,
domani)?
*sah-*RAH LEE-*beh-roh (*LEE-*beh-rah)* KWEH-*stoh poh-*
*meh-*REED-*joh (stah-*SEH-*rah, doh-*MAH-*nee)?*

Is the admission free?
È gratuito l'ingresso?
EH *grah too* EE *toh loong* GREHSS-*soh?*

Is that table free?
È libera quella tavola?
EH LEE-*beh-rah* KWELL-*lah* TAH-*voh-lah?*

Fresh
Is this fresh?
È fresco (fresca)?
EH FREH-*skoh (*FREH-*skah)?*

Friend
Have you seen my friends?
Ha visto i miei amici?
ah VEE-*stoh ee* MYEH-*ee ah-*MEE-*chee?*

I am with a friend.
Sono con un amico (un'amica).
SOH-*noh kohn oon ah-*MEE-*koh (*OON-*ah-*MEE-*kah).*

Front
I want to sit up front.
Vorrei sedermi in avanti.
vohr-RAY seh-DEHR-mee een ah-VAHN-tee.

Furnished
I want an apartment which is (not) furnished.
Vorrei un appartamento (non) ammobiliato.
vohr-RAY oon ahp-pahr-tah-MENN-toh (nohn) ahm-moh-bee-LYAH-toh.

Is the linen furnished?
Si fornisce la biancheria?
see fohr-NEE-sheh lah byang-keh-REE-ah?

Gamble
Please direct me to a gambling house.
Per favore, mi indichi la strada per il casino.
pehr fah-VOH-reh, mee EEN-dee-kee lah STRAH-dah pehr eel kah-SEE-noh.

Please take me to a gambling house.
Per favore, mi porti al casino.
pehr fah-VOH-reh, mee POHR-tee ahl kah-SEE-noh.

Game
Will you have a game with me?
Vuol giocare con me?
VWOHL joh-KAH-reh kohn MEH?

Garage
Where is the nearest garage?
Dov'è l'autorimessa piu vicina?
doh-VEH low-toh-ree-MESS-sah pyoo vee-CHEE-nah?

Does the hotel have a garage?
C'è un'autorimessa nell'albergo?
CHEH oon-ow-toh-ree-MESS-sah nehl-lahl-BEHR-goh?

Garbage
Where do I dispose of the garbage?
Dove posso buttare dei rifiuti?
DOH-veh POHSS-soh boot-TAH-reh day ree-FYOO-tee?

Will you please take care of the garbage.
Per favore, disponga dei rifiuti.
pehr fah-VOH-*reh, dee*-SPOHN-*gah day ree*-FYOO-*tee.*

Gardens
I would like to see the gardens.
Vorrei visitare i giardini.
vohr-RAY *vee-zee*-TAH-*reh ee jahr*-DEE-*nee.*

Gas, Gasoline – see Automobile

Gate
What gate does it leave from.
Da quale uscita si parte?
dah KWAH-*leh oo*-SHEE-*tah see* PAHR-*teh?*

Where is gate number _____?
Dov'è l'uscita numero _____?
doh-VEH *loo*-SHEE-*tah* NOO-*meh-roh* _____?

Get
How do I get to _____?
Come posso recarmi a _____?
KOH-*meh* POHSS-*soh reh*-KAHR-*mee ah* _____?

Will you tell me where to get off?
Mi dica, per favore, dove devo scendere?
mee DEE-*kah, pehr fah*-VOH-*reh,* DOH-*veh* DEH-*voh*
SHENN-*deh-reh.*

Where can I get _____?
Dove posso ottenere _____?
DOH-*veh* POHSS-*soh oht-teh*-NEH-*reh* _____?

Glass
Please bring me a glass of water (milk, wine).
Per favore, mi porti un bicchiere di acqua (latte, vino).
pehr fah-VOH-*reh, mee* POHR-*tee oon beek*-KYEH-*reh dee*
AHK-*kwah (*LAHT-*teh,* VEE-*noh).*

Please bring me another glass.
Per favore mi porti un altro bicchiere.
pehr fah-VOH-*reh mee* POHR-*tee oon* AHL-*troh beek-*
KYEH-*reh.*

Glasses

I have lost my glasses.
Ho perso gli occhiali.
oh PEHR-*soh lyee ohk*-KYAH-*lee*.

Can you repair my glasses?
Mi può riparare gli occhiali?
mee PWOH *ree-pah*-RAH-*reh lyee ohk*-KYAH-*lee?*

Here is (I do not have) the prescription for my glasses.
Ecco (non ho) la prescrizione per gli occhiali.
EHK-*koh (nohn oh) lah preh-skree*-TSYOH-*neh pehr lyee*
    ohk-KYAH-*lee*.

Go

I want to go to _____.
Vorrei andare a _____.
vohr-RAY *ahn*-DAH-*reh ah* _____.

How do I go to _____?
Come posso andare a _____?
KOH-*meh* POHSS-*soh ahn*-DAH-*reh ah* _____?

I am going to _____.
Vado a _____.
VAH-*doh ah* _____.

Golf

Do you play golf?
Gioca a golf?
JOH-*kah ah* GOHLF?

Where is the nearest (the best) golf course?
Dov'è il più vicino (il migliore) campo di golf?
doh-VEH *eel pyoo vee*-CHEE-*noh (eel mee*-LYOH-*reh)*
    KAHM-*poh dee* GOHLF?

Good

It is (not) very good.
È (non è) molto buono.
EH *(nohn* EH) MOHL-*toh* BWOH-*noh*.

Goodbye

Goodbye. (formal)
Arrivederla.
*ahr-ree-veh-*DEHR-*lah*.

Goodbye. (friendly)
Arrivederci.
*ahr-ree-veh-*DEHR-*chee.*

Good Evening
Good evening.
Buona sera.
BWOH-*nah* SEH-*rah.*

Good Morning
Good morning.
Buon giorno.
bwohn JOHR-*noh.*

Good Night
Good night.
Buona notte.
BWOH-*nah* NOHT-*teh.*

Grateful
I am very grateful to you.
Le sono molto grato (grata).
leh SOH-*noh* MOHL-*toh* GRAH-*toh (*GRAH-*tah).*

Grocery
Where is there a grocery store?
Dov'è un negozio di generi alimentari?
*doh-*VEH *oon neh-*GOH-*tsyoh dee* JEH-*neh-ree ah-lee-menn-*TAH-*ree?*

Guest
This lady (this gentleman) is my guest.
Questa signora (questo signore) è mia (mio) ospite.
KWEH-*stah see-*NYOH-*rah (*KWEH-*stoh see-*NYOH-*reh) eh* MEE-*ah (*MEE-*oh)* OH-*spee-teh.*

Will you be my guest?
Posso averla come ospite?
POHSS-*soh ah-*VEHR-*lah* KOH-*meh* OH-*spee-teh?*

Guide
Where can we get a guide?
Dove posso trovare una guida?
DOH-*veh* POHSS-*soh troh-*VAH-*reh* OON-*ah* GWEE-*dah?*

I want an English-speaking guide.
Vorrei una guida che parla inglese.
vohr-RAY OON-*ah* GWEE-*dah keh* PAHR-*lah een*-GLEH-
seh.

Do you sell guide books?
Vendete le guide?
venn-DEH-*teh leh* GWEE-*deh?*

Hair – see also Barber and Beauty Parlor
Where can I get my hair cut?
Dove posso farmi tagliare i capelli?
DOH-*veh* POHSS-*soh* FAHR-*mee tah*-LYAH-*reh ee kah-*
PELL-*lee?*

Hanger
Please bring me some hangers.
Per favore, mi porti degli attaccapanni.
pehr fah-VOH-*reh,* mee POHR-*tee* DEH-*lyee aht-tahk-kah-*
PAHN-*nee.*

Happy
I am happy to meet you.
Sono lieto (lieta) di conoscerla.
SOH-*noh* LYEH-*toh* (LYEH-*tah) dee koh*-NOH-*shehr-lah.*

Harbor
Is swimming permitted in the harbor?
È permesso nuotare nel porto?
eh pehr-MESS-*soh nwoh*-TAH-*reh nell* POHR-*toh?*

Hat
Is this your hat?
È suo questo cappello?
eh SOO-*oh* KWEH-*stoh kahp*-PELL-*loh?*

Have you seen my hat?
Ha visto il mio cappello?
ah VEE-*stoh eel* MEE-*oh kahp*-PELL-*loh?*

Have
Have you any _____?
Avete del (della, dello) _____?
ah-VEH-*teh dell* (DELL-*lah,* DELL-*loh)* _____?

Headwaiter

Please ask the headwaiter to come over here.

Per favore, mi mandi il capo cameriere.

pehr fah-VOH-reh, mee MAHN-dee eel KAH-poh kah-meh-RYEH-reh.

Health

My health has been poor.

Non sono stato (stata) bene.

nohn SOH-noh STAH-toh (STAH-tah) BEH-neh.

How is your health?

Come sta di salute?

KOH-meh stah dee sah-LOO-teh?

To your health!

Salute!

sah-LOO-teh!

Hear

I did not hear you; please repeat.

Non l'ho sentita; ripeta, per favore.

nohn loh senn-TEE-tah; ree-PEH-tah, pehr fah-VOH-reh.

Heater

Please show me how to operate the heater.

Per favore, mi faccia vedere come funziona il riscaldamento.

pehr fah-VOH-reh, mee FAHT-chah veh-DEH-reh KOH-meh foon-TSYOH-nah eel ree-skahl-dah-MENN-toh.

Heavy

It is very (too) heavy.

È molto (troppo) pesante.

EH MOHL-toh (TROHP-poh) peh-SAHN-teh.

Heel

Please replace the heels.

Per favore, rifaccia i tacchi.

pehr fah-VOH-reh, ree-FAHT-chah ee TAHK-kee.

Help − see also Accident

Help!

Aiuto!

ah-YOO-toh!

Can you help me?
Mi potrebbe aiutare?
*mee poh-*TREHB-*beh ah-yoo-*TAH-*reh?*

Here
Come here, please.
Venga qui, per favore.
VENG-*gah kwee, pehr fah-*VOH-*reh.*

When will it be here?
Quando arriverà?
KWAHN-*doh ahr-ree-veh-*RAH?

Here is my _____.
Ecco il mio (la mia) _____.
EHK-*koh eel* MEE-*oh (lah* MEE-*ah)* _____.

High
The price is too high.
Il prezzo è troppo alto.
eel PRETT-*tsoh eh* TROHP-*poh* AHL-*toh.*

Hire
How much would it cost to hire _____?
Quanto costerebbe noleggiare _____?
KWAHN-*toh koh-steh-*REHB-*beh noh-ledd-*JAH-*reh* _____

Hitchhiking
Is hitchhiking allowed?
È permesso fare l'autostop?
EH *pehr-*MESS-*soh* FAH-*reh* LOW-*toh-stohp?*

Holiday
When is the next holiday?
Quando è la prossima festa?
KWAHN-*doh* EH *lah* PROHSS-*see-mah* FEH-*stah?*

Is today a holiday?
È festa oggi?
EH FEH-*stah* OHD-*jee?*

Home
May I take you home?
Posso riportarla a casa?
POHSS-*soh ree-pohr-*TAHR-*lah ah* KAH-*sah?*

Honeymoon

We are on our honeymoon.

Siamo in luna di miele.

*see-*AH-*moh een* LOO-*nah dee* MYEH-*leh.*

Horse

Where can I get a horse?

Dove posso procurarmi un cavallo?

DOH-*veh* POHSS-*soh proh-koo-*RAHR-*mee oon kah-*VAHL-*loh?*

Would you like to go horseback riding with me?

Vorrebbe andare a cavallo con me?

*vohr-*REHB-*beh ahn-*DAH-*reh ah kah-*VAHL-*loh kohn meh?*

Is there any horse racing here?

Ci sono corse ippiche qui?

CHEE SOH-*noh* KOHR-*seh* EEP-*pee-keh* KWEE?

Hospital — see also Accident, Medical

Where is the hospital?

Dov'è l'ospedale?

*doh-*VEH *loh-speh-*DAH-*leh?*

Please take me to the hospital.

Per favore, mi porti all'ospedale.

*pehr fah-*VOH-*reh, mee* POHR-*tee ahl-loh-speh-*DAH-*leh.*

Please direct me to the hospital.

Per favore, mi indichi la strada per l'ospedale.

*pehr fah-*VOH-*reh, mee* EEN-*dee-kee lah* STRAH-*dah pehr loh-speh-*DAH-*leh.*

Hostel

Is there a youth hostel nearby?

C'è un ostello per studenti qui vicino?

CHEH *oon oh-*STELL-*loh pehr stoo-*DENN-*tee kwee vee-*CHEE-*noh?*

May I have a list of the member hostels?

Potrei avere un elenco degli ostelli affiliati?

*poh-*TRAY *ah-*VEH-*reh oon eh-*LEN-*koh* DEH-*lyee oh-*STELL-*lee ahf-fee-*LYAH-*tee?*

I am staying at the hostel.
Sono alloggiato all'ostello.
SOH-*noh ahl-lohd*-JAH-*toh ahl-loh*-STELL-*loh.*

Hot

May I have some hot water?
Potrei avere dell'acqua calda?
poh-TRAY *ah*-VEH-*reh dell*-LAHK-*kwah* KAHL-*dah?*

This is not hot enough; please take it back.
Non è abbastanza caldo; lo riporti, per favore.
nohn eh ahb-bah-STAHN-*tsah* KAHL-*doh;* loh *ree*-POHR-
tee, pehr fah-VOH-*reh.*

There is no hot water.
Non c'è acqua calda.
nohn CHEH AHK-*kwah* KAHL-*dah.*

Hotel

Can you recommend a good hotel?
Mi saprebbe raccomandare un buon albergo?
mee sah-PREHB-*beh rahk-koh-mahn*-DAH-*reh oon bwohn*
ahl-BEHR-*goh?*

Where is the _____ hotel?
Dov'è l'albergo _____?
doh-VEH *lahl*-BEHR-*goh* _____?

Please send it to my hotel.
Per favore, lo spedisca al mio albergo.
pehr fah-VOH-*reh, loh speh*-DEES-*kah ahl* MEE-*oh ahl-*
BEHR-*goh.*

Hour

What is the charge per hour?
Qual'è la tariffa all'ora?
kwahl-EH *lah tah*-REEF-*fah ahl*-LOH-*rah?*

At what hour should we meet?
A che ora dobbiamo incontrarci?
a keh OH-*rah dohb*-BYAH-*moh een-kohn*-TRAHR-*chee?*

At what hour should I come?
A che ora devo venire?
a keh OH-*rah* DEH-*voh veh*-NEE-*reh?*

How

How long?
Per quanto tempo?
pehr KWAHN-*toh* TEMM-*poh?*

How far?
Quanto lontano?
KWAHN-*toh lohn*-TAH-*noh?*

How many?
Quanti (quante)?
KWAHN-*tee (*KWAHN-*teh)?*

How much?
Quanto?
KWAHN-*toh?*

How long will it take?
Quanto tempo ci vorrà?
KWAHN-*toh* TEMM-*poh chee vohr*-RAH?

How do you say _____ in _____?
Come si dice _____ in _____?
KOH-*meh see* DEE-*cheh* _____ *een* _____?

Hungry

I am (I am not) hungry.
Ho (non ho) fame.
oh (nohn oh) FAH-*meh.*

Hurry

Please hurry.
Per favore, faccia presto.
pehr fah-VOH-*reh,* FAHT-*chah* PREH-*stoh.*

Hurt

Does it hurt?
Fa male?
fah MAH-*leh?*

Are you hurt?
Si è fatto (fatta) male?
see EH FAHT-*toh (*FAHT-*tah)* MAH-*leh?*

Ice

Please bring me some ice.
Per favore, mi porti del ghiaccio.
*pehr fah-*VOH-*reh, mee* POHR-*tee dell* GYAHT-*choh.*

Do you have an ice bag?
Ha una borsa per il ghiaccio?
ah OON-*ah* BOHR-*sah pehr eel* GYAHT-*choh?*

Identification

Here is my identification.
Ecco la mia carta d'identità.
EHK-*koh lah* MEE-*ah* KAHR-*tah dee-denn-tee-*TAH.

Ill — see also Accident, Medical

I am ill.
Sono ammalato (ammalata).
SOH-*noh ahm-mah-*LAH-*toh (ahm-mah-*LAH-*tah).*

Immediately

Call a doctor immediately.
Chiami immediatamente un medico.
KYAH-*mee eem-meh-dyah-tah-*MEN-*teh oon* MEH-*dee-koh.*

Please do it immediately.
Per favore, lo faccia subito.
*pehr fah-*VOH-*reh, loh* FAHT-*chah* SOO-*bee-toh.*

I want to leave immediately.
Voglio partire immediatamente.
VOH-*lyoh pahr-*TEE-*reh eem-meh-dyah-tah-*MEN-*teh.*

I need it immediately.
Mi occorre immediatamente.
*mee ohk-*KOHR-*reh eem-meh-dyah-tah-*MEN-*teh.*

Important

It is very important.
È molto importante.
EH MOHL-*toh eem-pohr-*TAHN-*teh.*

Include

Are all meals included?
Sono compresi tutti i pasti?
SOH-*noh kohm-*PREH-*see* TOOT-*tee ee pah-stee?*

Is breakfast (lunch, supper) included?

È compresa la prima colazione (la colazione, la cena)?

EH *kohm*-PREH-*sah lah* PREE-*mah koh-lah*-TSYOH-*neh (lah koh-lah*-TSYOH-*neh, lah* CHEH-*nah)?*

Is the tip included?

E compresa la mancia?

EH *kohm*-PREH-*sah lah* MAHN-*chah?*

Is coffee (dessert) included?

È compreso il caffè (il dolce)?

EH *kohm*-PREH-*soh eel kahf*-FEH *(eel* DOHL-*cheh)?*

Incorrect

This is incorrect.

Questo è sbagliato.

KWEH-*stoh eh zbah*-LYAH-*toh.*

Indigestion

I have indigestion; please bring me a _____.

Ho digerito male; per favore, mi porti un (una, uno) _____.

oh dee-jeh-REE-*toh* MAH-*leh;* pehr fah-VOH-*reh, mee* POHR-*tee oon (*OON-*ah,* OON-*oh)* _____.

Indoors

I will stay indoors today (this morning, this evening, this afternoon).

Rimarrò in casa oggi (stamane, stasera, questo pomeriggio).

ree-mahr-ROH *een* KAH-*sah* OHD-*jee (stah*-MAH-*neh, stah*-SEH-*rah, kweh-stoh poh-meh*-REED-*joh).*

Inexpensive

Can you recommend an inexpensive restaurant?

Mi saprebbe indicare un ristorante a buon prezzo?

mee sah-PREHB-*beh een-dee-*KAH-*reh oon ree-stoh*-RAHN-*teh ah bwohn* PRETT-*tsoh?*

I want something inexpensive.

Desidero qualchecosa a buon prezzo.

deh-SEE-*deh-roh kwahl-keh* KOH-*sah ah bwohn* PRETT-*tsoh.*

Informal
Can I dress informally?
Posso vestirmi alla buona?
POHSS-*soh veh*-STEER-*mee ahl-lah* BWOH-*nah?*

Information
I would like some information.
Vorrei delle informazioni.
vohr-RAY DELL-*leh een-fohr-mah*-TSYOH-*nee.*

Where is the information desk (window)?
Dov'è l'ufficio (lo sportello) informazioni?
doh-VEH *loof*-FEE-*choh (loh spohr*-TELL-*loh) een-fohr-mah*-TSYOH-*nee?*

Please direct me to the information bureau.
Per favore, mi indichi l'ufficio informazioni.
pehr fah-VOH-*reh, mee* EEN-*dee-kee loof*-FEE-*choh een-fohr-mah*-TSYOH-*nee.*

Inland
What is the best route inland?
Qual'è la strada migliore all'interno?
kwahl-EH *lah* STRAH-*dah mee*-LYOH-*reh ahl-leen*-TEHR-*noh?*

Inn
Can you recommend a good inn?
Mi saprebbe indicare una buona pensione?
mee sah-PREHB-*beh een-dee*-KAH-*reh* OON-*ah* BWOH-*nah penn*-SYOH-*neh?*

Insect
Have you any insect repellent?
Avete un repellente per gli insetti?
ah-VEH-*teh oon reh-pell*-LENN-*teh pehr lyeen*-SETT-*tee?*

Interpreter
I want to hire an interpreter.
Vorrei prendere un interprete.
vohr-RAY PRENN-*deh-reh oon een*-TEHR-*preh-teh.*

Where can I find an interpreter?
Dove posso trovare un interprete?
DOH-*veh* POHSS-*soh troh*-VAH-*reh oon een*-TEHR-*preh-teh?*

Introduce

May I introduce _____?
Posso presentare _____?
POHSS-*soh* preh-zenn-TAH-*reh* _____?

Invite

Thank you for the invitation.
Grazie dell'invito.
GRAH-*tsyeh* dell-leen-VEE-*toh*.

I invite you to come with me (be my guest).
La invito a venire con me (a essere mio (mia) ospite).
lah een-VEE-*toh* *ah* veh-NEE-*reh* *kohn* MEH (*ah* ESS-*seh-reh* MEE-*oh* (MEE-*ah*) OH-*spee-teh*).

Jacket

Do I need to wear a jacket?
Devo portare la giacca?
DEH-*voh* pohr-TAH-*reh* *lah* JAHK-*kah*?

Jewelry

I would like to leave my jewelry in your safe.
Vorrei depositare i miei gioielli nella vostra cassaforte.
vohr-RAY deh-poh-zee-TAH-*reh* *ee* mee-EH-*ee* joh-YELL-*lee* NELL-*lah* VOH-*strah* kahss-sah-FOHR-*teh*.

Jewish

I am Jewish.
Sono israelita.
SOH-*noh* ee-zrah-eh-LEE-*tah*.

Are you Jewish?
È israelita, lei?
EH ee-zrah-eh-LEE-*tah*, LAY?

Job

What is your job?
Che cosa fa lei?
keh KOH-*sah* FAH LAY?

Key

I have lost my key.
Ho perso la chiave.
oh PEHR-*soh* *lah* KYAH-*veh*.

May I have another key?
Potrei avere un'altra chiave?
poh-TRAY ah-VEH-reh oon AHL-trah KYAH-veh?

Kilogram

How much per kilogram for excess baggage?
Qual'è la tariffa per ogni chilo di soprapeso?
*kwahl-EH lah tah-REEF-fah pehr OH-nyee KEE-loh dee
    soh-prah-PEH-soh?*

Kilometer (= 3/5 of a mile)

How many kilometers to _____?
Quanti chilometri ci sono per _____?
KWAHN-tee kee-LOH-meh-tree chee SOH-noh pehr _____?

How many kilometers from _____ to _____?
Quanti chilometri ci sono da _____ a _____?
*KWAHN-tee kee-LOH-meh-tree chee SOH-noh dah _____
    ah _____?*

Knife

Please bring me a (another) knife.
Per favore, mi porti un (un altro) coltello.
*pehr fah-VOH-reh, mee POHR-tee oon (oon AHL-troh)
    kohl-TELL-loh.*

Know

Do you know where _____ is?
Mi sa dire dov'è _____?
mee sah DEE-reh doh-VEH _____?

I (I don't) know how.
So (non so).
SOH (nohn SOH).

Please let me know when we get to _____.
Per favore, mi dica quando arriviamo a _____.
*pehr fah-VOH-reh, mee DEE-kah KWAHN-doh ahr-ree-
    VYAH-moh ah _____.*

Kosher

Do you serve (sell) kosher food?
Servite (vendete) il cibo kosher?
sehr-VEE-teh (ven-DEH-teh) eel CHEE-boh KOH-shehr?

Laundry and Dry Cleaning

Do you have overnight laundry and dry-cleaning service?

Avete un servizio di lavanderia e tintoria in ventiquattro ore?

ah-VEH-teh oon sehr-VEE-tsyoh dee lah-vahn-deh-REE-ah eh teen-toh-REE-ah een venn-tee-KWAH-troh OH-reh?

I want this (these) washed (cleaned, pressed).

Vorrei far lavare (pulire a secco, stirare) questo (questi).

vohr-RAY fahr lah-VAH-reh (poo-LEE-reh ah SEKK-koh, stee-RAH-reh) KWEH-stoh (KWEH-stee).

Can you remove this spot (stain)?

Può togliere questa macchia?

PWOH TOH-lyeh-reh kweh-STAH mahk-KYAH?

Don't wash this in hot water.

Non lo lavi in acqua calda.

nohn lah LAH-vee een AHK-kwah KAHL-dah.

No starch, please.

Niente amido, per favore.

NYENN-teh AH-mee-doh, pehr fah-VOH-reh.

I would like this button sewn on, please.

Mi faccia attaccare questo bottone, per favore.

mee FAHT-chah aht-tahk-KAH-reh KWEH-stoh boht-TOH-neh, pehr fah-VOH-reh.

I would like this mended.

Vorrei farlo rammendare.

vohr-RAY FAHR-loh rahm-menn-DAH-reh.

When can I have it (have them) back?

Quando potrò riaverlo (riaverla, riaverli, riaverle)?

KWAHN-doh poh-TROH ree-ah-VEHR-loh (ree-ah-VEHR-lah, ree-ah-VEHR-lee, ree-ah-VEHR-leh)?

Will it be ready today (tonight, tomorrow)?

Sarà pronto (pronta) oggi (stasera, domani)?

sah-RAH PROHN-toh (PROHN-tah) OHD-jee (stah-SEH-rah, doh-MAH-nee)?

Will they be ready today (tonight, tomorrow)?
Saranno pronti (pronte) oggi (stasera, domani)?
sah-RAHN-*noh* PROHN-*tee (*PROHN-*teh)* OHD-*jee (stah-*
SEH-*rah, doh-*MAH-*nee)?*

A button (the belt) is missing.
Manca un bottone (la cintura).
MAHN-*kah oon boht-*TOH-*neh (lah cheen-*TOO-*rah).*

Less – see also Shopping
Do you have anything less expensive?
Avete qualchecosa di meno costoso?
ah-VEH-*teh kwahl-keh-*KOH-*sah dee* MEH-*noh koh-*STOH-
soh?

Let
Let me know when we get to _____.
Mi dica quando arriviamo a _____.
mee DEE-*kah* KWAHN-*doh ahr-ree-*VYAH-*moh ah* _____.

Letters – see also Post Office
Are there any letters for me?
Ci sono lettere per me?
chee SOH-*noh* LETT-*teh-reh pehr* MEH?

Where can I mail some letters?
Dove posso imbucare delle lettere?
DOH-*veh* POHSS-*soh eem-boo-*KAH-*reh* DELL-*leh* LETT-*teh-*
reh?

Please mail these letters for me.
Per favore, mi imbuchi queste lettere.
*pehr fah-*VOH-*reh, mee eem-*BOO-*kee* KWEH-*steh* LETT-
teh-reh.

Library
Please take me to the library.
Per favore, mi porti alla biblioteca.
*pehr fah-*VOH-*reh, mee* POHR-*tee* AHL-*lah bee-blyoh-*TEH-
kah.

Please direct me to the library.
Per favore, mi indichi la strada per la biblioteca.
*pehr fah-*VOH-*reh, mee* EEN-*dee-kee lah* STRAH-*dah pehr*
*lah bee-blyoh-*TEH-*kah.*

License — see Driver

Lifeboats
Where are the lifeboats?
Dove sono le barche di salvataggio?
DOH-veh SOH-noh leh BAHR-keh dee sahl-vah-TAHD-joh?

Life Preservers
Where are the life preservers?
Dove sono i salvagenti?
DOH-veh SOH-noh ee sahl-vah-JENN-tee?

How do you use the life preservers?
Come si usano i salvagenti?
KOH-meh see OO-zah-noh ee sahl-vah-JENN-tee?

Light
May I have a light?
Potrei avere del fuoco?
poh-TRAY ah-VEH-reh dell FWOH-koh?

Like — see also Shopping
I like (I don't like) _____.
Mi piace (non mi piace) _____.
mee PYAH-cheh (nohn mee PYAH-cheh) _____.

Limit
What is the speed limit?
Qual'è il limite di velocità?
kwahl-EH eel LEE-mee-teh dee veh-loh-chee-TAH?

What is the weight limit?
Qual'è il limite di peso?
kwahl-EH eel LEE-mee-teh dee PEH-soh?

Limousine
Is there limousine service to the airport?
C'è un servizio di pullman per l'aeroporto?
CHEH oon sehr-VEE-tsyoh dee POOL-mahn pehr lah-eh-roh-POHR-toh?

When does the limousine leave for the airport?
Quando parte il pullman per l'aeroporto?
KWAHN-doh PAHR-teh eel POOL-mahn pehr lah-eh-roh-POHR-toh?

I want to hire a car.
Vorrei noleggiare un'automobile.
vohr-RAY *nol-ledd*-JAH-*reh* oon *ow-toh*-MOH-*bee-leh.*

Liquor
Where can I buy some liquor?
Dove posso comprare delle bevande alcooliche?
DOH-*veh* POHSS-*soh kohm*-PRAH-*reh* DELL-*leh beh*-VAHN-*deh ahl*-KOH-*lee-keh?*

How much liquor can I take out?
Quanto alcool posso portare con me?
KWAHN-*toh* AHL-*kohl* POHSS-*soh pohr*-TAH-*reh kohn* MEH?

Little
I want just a little, please.
Solo un poco, per favore.
SOH-*loh* oon POH-*koh, pehr fah*-VOH-*reh.*

A little more (less), please.
Ancora un poco (un poco meno), per favore.
ahng-KOH-*rah* oon POH-*koh* (oon POH-*koh* MEH-*noh), pehr fah*-VOH-*reh.*

Live
Where do you live?
Dove abita?
DOH-*veh* AH-*bee-tah?*

Lobby
I'll meet you in the lobby.
Incontriamoci nell'atrio.
een-kohn-TRYAH-*moh-chee nehl*-LAH-*tree-oh.*

Local
Where do I get the local train?
Dove posso prendere l'accelerato?
DOH-*veh* POHSS-*soh* PRENN-*deh-reh laht-cheh-leh*-RAH-*toh?*

Is this the local?
È questo l'accelerato?
eh KWEH-*stoh laht-cheh-leh*-RAH-*toh?*

Lock

Please lock my door.
Chiuda la mia porta a chiave, per favore.
KYOO-*dah lah* MEE-*ah* POHR-*tah ah* KYAH-*veh, pehr fah-*
VOH-*reh.*

The lock does not work.
La serratura non funziona.
*lah sehr-rah-*TOO-*rah nohn foon-*TSYOH-*nah.*

How does the lock work?
Come funziona la serratura?
KOH-*meh foon-*TSYOH-*nah lah sehr-rah-*TOO-*rah?*

I have lost the key for the lock.
Ho perso la chiave della serratura.
oh PEHR-*soh lah* KYAH-*veh* DELL-*lah sehr-rah-*TOO-*rah.*

Locker

Where can I rent a locker?
Dove posso prendere a nolo una cassetta di sicurezza?
DOH-*veh* POHSS-*soh* PRENN-*deh-reh ah* NOH-*loh oon-ah*
*kahss-*SETT-*tah dee see-koo-*RETT-*tsah?*

Long

How long will it last?
Quanto tempo durerà?
KWAHN-*toh* TEMM-*poh doo-reh-*RAH?

How long will it take?
Quanto tempo prenderà?
KWAHN-*toh* TEMM-*poh prenn-deh-*RAH?

How long is the stop at _____?
Quanto dura la fermata a _____?
KWAHN-*toh* DOO-*rah lah fehr-*MAH-*tah ah* _____?

How long must I wait?
Quanto devo aspettare?
KWAHN-*toh* DEH-*voh ah-spett-*TAH-*reh?*

How long does it stay open?
Fino a che ora rimane aperto?
FEE-*noh ah keh* OH-*rah ree-*MAH-*neh ah-*PEHR-*toh?*

Lost

I am lost.
Ho perso la via.
oh PEHR-*soh lah* VEE-*ah.*

Where is _____?
Dov'è _____?
*doh-*VEH _____?

I have lost my passport (my wallet).
Ho perso il passaporto (il portafoglio).
oh PEHR-*soh eel pahss-sah-*POHR-*toh (eel pohr-tah-*FOH-*lyoh).*

Love

I love you.
Ti amo.
tee AH-*moh.*

I love my wife (my husband).
Amo mia moglie (mio marito).
AH-*moh* MEE-*ah* MOH-*lyeh (*MEE-*oh mah-*REE-*toh).*

I love _____.
Amo _____.
AH-*moh* _____.

Lower

I want a lower berth.
Vorrei una cucetta in basso.
*vohr-*RAY OON-*ah koo-*CHETT-*tah een* BAHSS-*soh.*

I want a room on a lower floor.
Vorrei una camera su un piano inferiore.
*vohr-*RAY OON-*ah* KAH-*meh-rah soo oon* PYAH-*noh een-feh-*RYOH-*reh.*

Lunch

Can we have lunch now?
Possiamo far colazione ora?
*pohss-see-*YAH-*moh fahr koh-lah-*TSYOH-*neh* OH-*rah?*

When is lunch served?
A che ora è servita la colazione?
ah keh OH-*rah eh sehr-*VEE-*tah lah koh-lah-*TSYOH-*neh?*

How late (early) do you serve lunch?
A che ora finite (cominciate) di servire la colazione?
ah keh OH-rah fee-NEE-teh (koh-meen-CHAH-teh) dee sehr-VEE-reh lah koh-lah-TSYOH-neh?

Will you have lunch with me?
Vuol far colazione con me?
VWOHL-fahr koh-lah-TSYOH-neh kohn MEH?

Does that include lunch?
La colazione è compresa?
lah koh-lah-TSYOH-neh eh kohm-PREH-sah?

Magazine
Where are magazines sold?
Dove si vendono le riviste?
DOH-veh see VENN-doh-noh leh ree-VEE-steh?

Maid
Please send the maid to my room.
Per favore, mi mandi la cameriera.
pehr fah-VOH-reh, mee MAHN-dee lah kah-meh-RYEH-rah.

Mail – see also Post Office
Is there any mail for me?
C'è posta per me?
CHEH POH-stah pehr MEH?

When is the mail delivered?
A che ora arriva la posta?
ah keh OH-rah ahr-REE-vah lah POH-stah?

Please mail this for me.
Per favore, m'imbuchi questo.
pehr fah-VOH-reh, meem-BOO-kee KWEH-stoh.

Mailbox
Where is a mailbox, please?
Per favore, dov'è la buca delle lettere?
pehr fah-VOH-reh, doh-VEH lah BOO-kah DELL-leh LETT-teh-reh?

Make

Please make the bed.
Per favore, faccia il letto.
*pehr fah-*VOH-*reh,* FAHT-*chah eel* LETT-*toh.*

Man – see also Men's Room

Who is that man?
Chi è quell'uomo?
kee EH *kwell-*LWOH-*moh?*

Manager

I want to see the manager.
Vorrei parlare con il direttore.
*vohr-*RAY *pahr-*LAH-*reh kohn eel dee-rett-*TOH-*reh.*

Are you the manager?
Lei è il direttore?
lay EH *eel dee-rett-*TOH-*reh?*

Manicure – see Beauty Parlor

Map

(carta geographica = map of a country; pianta = map of a city or town)

Do you have a map of _____?
Avete una carta geographica (una pianta) di _____?
*ah-*VEH-*teh* OON-*ah* KAHR-*tah jeh-oh-*GRAH-*fee-kah*
    (OON-*ah* PYAN-*tah) dee* _____?

I need a map of _____, please.
Mi occorre una carta geographica (una pianta) di
    _____, per favore.
*mee ohk-*KOHR-*reh* OON-*ah* KAHR-*tah jeh-oh-*GRAH-*fee-*
    kah (OON-*ah* PYAN-*tah) dee* _____, *pehr fah-*VOH-*reh.*

Married

I am (I am not) married.
Sono (non sono) sposato (sposata).
SOH-*noh (nohn* SOH-*noh) spoh-*ZAH-*toh (spoh-*ZAH-*tah).*

Are you married?
È sposato (sposata)?
*eh spoh-*ZAH-*toh (spoh-*ZAH-*tah)?*

Mass
What time is mass?
A che ora è la messa?
ah keh OH-*rah* EH *lah* MESS-*sah?*

Massage
I would like to have a massage.
Vorrei un massaggio, per favore.
*voh-*RAY *oon mahss-*SAHD-*joh, pehr fah-*VOH-*reh.*

Match
Excuse me, do you have a match?
Per favore, potrebbe darmi un fiammifero?
*pehr fah-*VOH-*reh, poh-*TREBB-*beh* DAHR-*mee oon fyam-*
    MEE-*feh-roh?*

Matinee
Is there a matinee today?
C'è una matinee oggi?
CHEH OON-*ah mah-tee-*NAY OHD-*jee?*

Matter
What is the matter?
Cosa c'è?
KOH-*sah* CHEH*?*

Mattress
I would like another mattress.
Vorrei un altro materasso.
*vohr-*RAY *oon* AHL-*troh mah-teh-*RAHSS-*soh.*

This mattress is too hard (soft).
Questo materasso è troppo duro (soffice).
KWEH-*stoh mah-teh-*RAHSS-*soh eh* TROHP-*poh* DOO-*roh*
    (SOHF-*fee-cheh).*

This mattress is lumpy.
Questo materasso fa le gobbe.
KWEH-*stoh mah-teh-*RAHSS-*soh fah leh* GOHB-*beh.*

Meals
When are meals served?
A che ora sono serviti i pasti?
ah keh OH-*rah* SOH-*noh sehr-*VEE-*tee ee* PAH-*stee?*

Does that include meals?
Sono compresi i pasti?
SOH-*noh kohm*-PREH-*see ee* PAH-*stee?*

What meals are included?
Quali pasti sono compresi?
KWAH-*lee* PAH-*stee* SOH-*noh kohm*-PREH-*see?*

Mean

What do you mean?
Cosa vuol dire lei?
KOH-*sah vwohl* DEE-*reh lay?*

That is (that is not) what I mean.
È (non è) quello che voglio dire.
EH *(nohn* EH*)* KWELL-*loh keh* VOH-*lyoh* DEE-*reh.*

What does _____ mean?
Cosa significa _____?
KOH-*sah see*-NYEE-*fee-kah* _____?

Medical

Is there a (an English-speaking) doctor near here (in the hotel)?
C'è un medico (che parla inglese) nelle vicinanze (nell'albergo)?
CHEH *oon* MEH-*dee-koh (keh* PAHR-*lah een*-GLEH-*seh)* NELL-*leh vee-chee*-NAHN-*tseh (nell-lahl*-BEHR-*goh)?*

Can you recommend a good (English-speaking) doctor?
Mi saprebbe raccomandare un buon medico (che parla inglese)?
mee sah-PREHB-*beh rahk-koh-mahn*-DAH-*reh oon bwohn* MEH-*dee-koh (keh* PAHR-*lah een*-GLEH-*seh)?*

Can you give me an appointment as soon as possible?
Mi può dare un appuntamento appena possible?
mee PWOH DAH-*reh oon ahp-poon-tah*-MENN-*toh ahp*-PEH-*nah pohss*-SEE-*bee-leh?*

Can I come right now?
Posso venire subito?
POHSS-*soh veh*-NEE-*reh* SOO-*bee-toh?*

I have (I don't have) an appointment.
Ho (non ho) un appuntamento.
oh (nohn oh) oon ahp-poon-tah-MENN-toh.

I am having trouble breathing (sleeping).
Ho difficoltà a respirare (dormire).
oh deef-fee-kohl-TAH ah reh-spee-RAH-reh (dohr-MEE-reh).

I have a stomachache (nausea, cramps).
Ho mal di stomaco (nausea, dei crampi).
oh mahl dee STOH-mah-koh (NOW-seh-ah, day KRAHM-pee).

I have food poisoning.
Ho un avvelenamento da cibo.
oh oon ahv-veh-leh-nah-MENN-toh dah CHEE-boh.

I have diarrhea (dysentery).
Ho diarrea (la dissenteria).
oh dee-ahr-REH-ah (lah dees-sen-teh-REE-ah).

I am constipated.
Soffro di stitichezza.
SOHF-froh dee stee-tee-KEDD-dzah.

I have a pain in my chest (my back, my arm, my leg, my hand, my foot).
Ho un dolore al petto (alla schiena, al braccio, alla gamba, alla mano, al piede).
oh oon doh-LOH-reh ahl PETT-toh (ahl-lah SKYEH-nah, ahl BRAHT-choh, ahl-lah GAHM-bah, ahl-lah MAH-noh, ahl PYEH-deh).

I have an earache.
Ho male all'orecchio.
oh MAH-leh ahl-loh-REKK-kyoh.

I have a bad cough.
Ho molta tosse.
oh MOHL-tah TOHSS-seh.

I have a sore throat.
Ho mal di gola.
oh MAHL dee GOH-lah.

I have a splitting headache.
Ho un forte mal di testa.
oh oon FOHR-*teh* MAHL *dee* TEH-*stah.*

I have a bad sunburn.
Mi sono scottato (scottata) al sole.
mee SOH-*noh skoht-*TAH-*toh (skoht-*TAH-*tah) ahl* SOH-
   leh.

I have sunstroke.
Ho un'insolazione.
*oh oon-een-soh-lah-*TSYOH-*neh.*

I have a fever.
Ho la febbre.
oh lah FEBB-*breh.*

I have chills.
Ho preso freddo.
oh PREH-*soh* FREDD-*doh.*

I have sprained my wrist (my ankle).
Mi sono slogato (slogata) il polso (la caviglia).
mee SOH-*noh sloh-*GAH-*toh (sloh-*GAH-*tah) eel* POHL-*soh*
   *(lah kah-*VEE-*lyah).*

Are you going to take X-rays?
Mi fa una radiografia?
mee fah OON-*ah rah-dyoh-grah-*FEE-*ah?*

Do I have to go to the hospital?
Devo essere ricoverato (ricoverata)?
DEH-*voh* ESS-*seh-reh ree-koh-veh-*RAH-*toh (ree-koh-veh-*
   RAH-*tah)?*

I have something in my eye.
Ho qualcosa nell'occhio.
*oh kwahl-*KOH-*sah nell-*LOHK-*kyoh.*

I am allergic to _____.
Sono allergico a _____.
SOH-*noh ahl-*LEHR-*jee-koh ah* _____.

Please use (don't use) anesthesia.
Per favore, usi (non usi) un anestetico.
*pehr fah-*VOH-*reh,* OO-*zee (nohn* OO-*zee) oon ah-neh-*
   STEH-*tee-koh.*

Can I have a sedative (an aspirin, a sleeping pill)?
Potrei avere un sedativo (un'aspirina, un sonnifero)?
*poh-*TRAY *ah-*VEH*-reh oon seh-dah-*TEE*-voh (oon-ah-*
   *spee-*REE*-nah, oon sohn-*NEE*-feh-roh)?*

Do I have to stay in bed?
Devo rimanere a letto?
DEH*-voh ree-mah-*NEH*-reh ah* LETT*-toh?*

For how long?
Per quanto tempo?
pehr KWAHN*-toh* TEMM*-poh?*

When do you think I will be better?
Quando pensa che starò meglio?
KWAHN*-doh* PENN*-sah keh stah-*ROH MEH*-lyoh?*

Where can I have this prescription filled?
Dove posso far eseguire questa ricetta?
DOH*-veh* POHSS*-soh fahr eh-zeh-*GWEE*-reh* KWEH*-stah*
   *ree-*CHETT*-tah?*

When should I see you again?
Quando dovrei tornare per la visita?
KWAHN*-doh doh-*VRAY *tohr-*NAH*-reh pehr lah* VEE*-see-*
   tah?

Medium

I like my meat medium (medium rare).
Vorrei la carne a media cottura (al sangue).
*vohr-*RAY *lah* KAHR*-neh ah* MEH*-dyah koht-*TOO*-rah (ahl*
   SAHNG*-gweh).*

Meet

Let's meet at _____.
Incontriamoci a (in) _____.
*een-kohn-tree-*AH*-moh-chee ah (een)* _____.

I am meeting my husband (my wife, a friend).
Devo incontrare il mio marito (la mia moglie, un
   amico, un'amica).
DEH*-voh een-kohn-*TRAH*-reh eel* MEE*-oh mah-*REE*-*
   toh (lah MEE*-ah* MOH*-lyeh, oon ah-*MEE*-koh, oon-ah-*
   MEE*-kah).*

I am very pleased to meet you.
Sono lieto di conoscerla.
SOH-*noh* LYEH-*toh dee koh*-NOH-*shehr-lah.*

I would like to meet him (meet her).
Vorrei conoscerlo (conoscerla).
vohr-RAY *koh*-NOH-*shehr-loh (koh*-NOH-*shehr-lah).*

Mend – see Laundry

Men's Roon

Where is the men's room?
Dove sono i gabinetti per uomini?
DOH-*veh* SOH-*noh ee gah-bee*-NETT-*tee pehr* WOH-*mee-nee?*

Menu

The menu, please.
La carta, per favore.
lah KAHR-*tah, pehr fah*-VOH-*reh.*

Is _____ on the menu?
Potrei avere un (una, un') _____?
poh-TRAY *ah*-VEH-*reh oon (*OON-*ah, oon)* _____?

Message

I would like to leave a message for _____?
Vorrei lasciare un messaggio per _____?
vohr-RAY *lah*-SHAH-*reh oon mess*-SAHD-*joh pehr* _____?

Are these any messages for me?
Ci sono messaggi per me?
chee SOH-*noh mess*-SAHD-*jee pehr* MEH?

Milk

May I have a glass of milk, please.
Vorrei un bicchiere di latte, per favore.
vohr-RAY *oon beek*-KYEH-*reh dee* LAHT-*teh, pehr fah*-VOH-*reh.*

Is the milk pasteurized?
E pastorizzato il latte?
EH *pah-stoh-reed*-DZAH-*toh eel* LAHT-*teh?*

Mind

Do you mind if I smoke?

La disturbo se fumo?

lah dee-STOOR-boh seh FOO-*moh?*

Mine

That is mine.

È mio (mia).

EH MEE-*oh* (MEE-*ah).*

Minister

Where can I find a (an English-speaking) minister?

Dove posso trovare un pastore (che parla inglese)?

DOH-*veh* POHSS-*soh troh*-VAH-*reh oon pah*-STOH-*reh (keh*
    PAHR-*lah eeng*-GLEH-*seh)?*

Minutes

I'll see you in _____ minutes.

La vedrò fra _____ minuti.

lah veh-DROH *frah* _____ *mee*-NOO-*tee.*

Miss

I missed my plane (my train); when is the next one?

Ho perso l'aereo (il treno); quando ce ne sarà un altro?

oh PEHR-*soh lah*-EH-*reh-oh (eel* TREH-*noh);* KWAHN-*doh
    cheh neh suh*-RAH *oon* AHL *troh?*

Mistake

Is there a mistake?

C'è un errore?

CHEH *oon ehr*-ROH-*reh?*

There must be some mistake.

Ci dev'essere un errore.

chee deh-VESS-*seh-reh oon ehr*-ROH-*reh.*

Moderate

Can you recommend a moderate-priced hotel
    (restaurant)?

Mi saprebbe indicare un albergo (un ristorante) a
    prezzi moderati?

mee sah-PREBB-*beh een-dee*-KAH-*reh oon ahl*-BEHR-*goh
    (oon ree-stoh*-RAHN-*teh) ah* PRETT-*tsee moh-deh*-RAH-
    tee?

Moment

Wait a moment.
Aspetti un momento, per favore.
*ah-*SPETT*-tee oon moh-*MENN*-toh, pehr fah-*VOH*-reh.*

Stop here a moment, please.
Si fermi qui un momento, per favore.
see FEHR*-mee* KWEE *oon moh-*MENN*-toh, pehr fah-*VOH*-reh.*

I'll see you in a moment.
La vedrò fra un momento.
*lah veh-*DROH *frah oon moh-*MENN*-toh.*

Money – see also Bank

I need some _____ money.
Mi occorre del denaro _____.
*mee ohk-*KOHR*-reh dell deh-*NAH*-roh* _____.

Will you accept American money?
Accettate denaro americano?
*aht-chett-*TAH*-teh deh-*NAH*-roh ah-meh-ree-*KAH*-noh?*

I have no money with me.
Non ho denaro con me.
*nohn oh deh-*NAH*-roh kohn* MEH.

Money Order

I wish to send a money order.
Vorrei mandare un vaglia.
*vohr-*RAY *mahn-*DAH*-reh oon* VAH*-lyah.*

More

I would like some more, please.
Ne vorrei ancora, per favore.
*neh vohr-*RAY *ahng-*KOH*-rah, pehr fah-*VOH*-reh.*

Please speak more slowly.
Parli più lentamente, per favore.
PAHR*-lee pyoo lenn-tah-*MENN*-teh, pehr fah-*VOH*-reh.*

Morning

We will leave tomorrow morning.
Partiremo domani mattina.
*pahr-tee-*REH*-moh doh-*MAH*-nee maht-*TEE*-nah.*

I'll see you in the morning.
La vedrò domani mattina.
*lah veh-*DROH *doh-*MAH*-nee maht-*TEE*-nah.*

Most
What is the most I can take?
Qual'è la quantità massima concessa?
*kwah-*LEH *lah kwahn-tee-*TAH MAHSS*-see-mah kohn-*CHESS*-sah?*

Motor – see also Automobile
There is something wrong with the motor.
C'è un guasto al motore.
CHEH *oon* GWAH*-stoh all moh-*TOH*-reh.*

Move
I want to move to another room (to another hotel).
Vorrei trasferirmi in un'altra stanza (in un altro albergo).
*vohr-*RAY *trah-sfeh-*REER*-mee een oon* AHL*-trah* STAHN*-tsah (een oon* AHL*-troh ahl-*BEHR*-goh).*

Movie
What movie is being shown?
Che film c'è?
keh FEELM CHEH*?*

Would you like to go to a movie with me?
Posso invitarla al cinema?
POHSS*-soh een-vee-*TAHR*-lah ahl* CHEE*-neh-mah?*

Much
How much is it?
Quanto costa?
KWAHN*-toh* KOH*-stah?*

That is too much.
Costa troppo.
KOH*-stah* TROHP*-poh.*

I like you very much.
Lei è molto simpatico (simpatica).
lay EH MOHL*-toh seem-*PAH*-tee-koh (seem-*PAH*-tee-kah).*

I like it very much.
Mi piace moltissimo.
mee PYAH-*cheh mohl*-TEES-*see-moh.*

Museum

Where is the _____ museum, please?
Dov'è il museo _____, per favore?
doh-VEH *eel moo*-ZEH-*oh* _____, *pehr fah*-VOH-*reh?*

Music

Where can we hear some good music?
Dove possiamo ascoltare della buona musica?
DOH-*veh pohss-see*-AH-*moh ah-skohl*-TAH-*reh* DELL-*lah*
   BWOH-*nah* MOO-*zee-kah?*

Must

I must leave now.
Devo partire ora.
DEH-*voh pahr*-TEE-*reh* OH-*rah.*

Name

What is your name?
Come si chiama?
KOH-*meh see* KYAH-*mah?*

My name is _____.
Mi chiamo _____.
mee KYAH-*moh* _____.

Napkin

May I have a napkin, please.
Mi dia un tovagliolo, per favore.
mee DEE-*ah oon toh-vah*-LYOH-*loh,* **pehr** *fah*-VOH-*reh.*

National

What is the national dish?
Qual'è il piatto nazionale?
kwah-LEH *eel* PYAT-*toh nah-tsyoh*-NAH-*leh?*

Near

Are we near it?
Siamo vicini?
see-AH-*moh vee*-CHEE-*nee?*

How near are we?
Quanto vicini siamo?
KWAHN-*toh* vee-CHEE-*nee see*-AH-*moh?*

Necessary

It is (it is not) necessary.
È (non è) necessario.
EH *(nohn* EH) *neh-chess*-SAH-*ryoh.*

Need

I need _____.
Mi occorre _____.
mee ohk-KOHR-*reh* _____.

Do I need tokens?
Occorrono dei gettoni?
ohk-KOHR-*roh-noh day* jett-TOH-*nee?*

Do I need reservations?
Occorrono delle prenotazioni?
ohk-KOHR-*roh-noh dell-leh preh-noh-tah*-TSYOH-*nee?*

How much do you need?
Quanto le occorre?
KWAHN-*toh leh* ohk-KOHR-*reh?*

How many do you need?
Quanti (quanto) gliono occorrono?
KWAHN-*tee* (KWAHN-*teh*) LYEH-*neh* ohk-KOHR-*roh-
noh?*

Needle

I would like to buy some needles and thread.
Vorrei comprare degli aghi e del filo.
vohr-RAY *kohm*-PRAH-*reh deh-lyee* AH-*gee eh dell* FEE-
loh.

New

This is something new to me.
Questo mi risulta nuovo.
KWEH-*stoh mee ree*-SOOL-*tah* NWOH-*voh.*

Newspaper

Where can I buy an American (English) newspaper?
Dove posso comprare un giornale americano (inglese)?
DOH-*veh* POHSS-*soh* kohm-PRAH-*reh* oon johr-NAH-*leh*
   *ah-meh-ree-*KAH-*noh* (eeng-GLEH-*seh*)?

Next

What is the next town (stop)?
Qual'è la prossima città (fermata)?
kwah-LEH *lah* PROHSS-*see-mah* cheet-TAH (fehr-MAH-
   tah)?

When is the next boat (train, plane)?
Quando parte il prossimo battello (treno, aereo)?
KWAHN-*doh* PAHR-*teh* eel PROHSS-*see-moh* baht-TELL-
   loh (TREH-*noh,* ah-EH-*reh-oh*)?

Next stop, please.
La prossima fermata, per favore.
lah PROHSS-*see-mah* fehr-MAH-*tah, pehr fah-*VOH-*reh.*

Nice

It is nice to meet you.
Sono lieto di conoscerla.
SOH-*noh* LYEH-*toh dee koh-*NOH-*shehr-la.*

That is very nice of you.
È molto gentile da parte sua.
EH MOHL-*toh jenn-*TEE-*leh dah* PAHR-*teh* SOO-*ah.*

She is very nice.
È molto simpatica.
EH MOHL-*toh seem-*PAH-*tee-kah.*

He is very nice.
È molto simpatico.
EH MOHL-*toh seem-*PAH-*tee-koh.*

Nightclub

Can you recommend a good nightclub?
Mi saprebbe indicare un buon locale notturno?
*mee sah-*PREBB-*beh een-dee-*KAH-*reh* oon BWOHN loh-
   KAH-*leh* noht-TOOR-*noh*?

Noisy

My room is too noisy; I want to change it.

La mia camera è troppo rumorosa; vorrei cambiarla.

lah MEE-*ah* KAH-*meh-rah* eh TROHP-*poh roo-moh-*ROH-*sah;* vohr-RAY *kahm-*BYAHR-*lah.*

Noon

We are leaving at noon.

Partiamo a mezzogiorno.

*pahr-*TYAH-*moh ah medd-dzoh-*JOHR-*noh.*

Nothing

I have nothing to declare.

Non ho nulla da dichiarare.

nohn oh NOOL-*lah dah dee-kyah-*RAH-*reh.*

Nothing, thank you.

Nulla, grazie.

NOOL-*lah,* GRAH-*tsyeh.*

Number

What is your telephone number?

Qual'è il suo numero di telefono?

*kwah-*LEH-*eel* SOO-*oh* NOO-*meh-roh dee teh-*LEH-*foh-noh?*

What is your room number?

Qual'è il suo numero di camera?

*kwah-*LEH *eel* SOO-*oh* NOO-*meh-roh dee* KAH-*meh-rah?*

What is my room number?

Qual'è il numero della mia camera?

*kwah-*LEH *eel* NOO-*meh-roh* DELL-*lah* MEE-*ah* KAH-*meh-rah?*

What number bus do I take to _____?

Che numero d'autobus devo prendere per _____?

keh NOO-*meh-roh dow-toh-*BOOSS DEH-*voh* PRENN-*deh-reh pehr* _____?

I am in number _____.

Sono al numero _____.

SOH-*no ahl* NOO-*meh-roh* _____.

Nurse – see also Accident, Medical

Is there a doctor or a nurse aboard?
C'è un medico o un'infermiera a bordo?
CHEH *oon* MEH-*dee-koh oh* oon-ee-fehr-MYEH-*rah ah*
    BOHR-*doh?*

Obtain

Where can I obtain _____?
Dove posso ottenere _____?
DOH-*veh* POHSS-*soh* oht-teh-NEH-*reh* _____?

Occupation

What is your occupation?
Di che cosa si occupa?
dee keh KOH-*sah see* OHK-*koo-pah?*

Occupy

Is this _____ occupied?
È occupato (occupata) questo (questa) _____?
EH *ohk-koo-*PAH-*toh (ohk-koo-*PAH-*tah) kweh-stoh
    (kweh-stah)* _____.

Off

How do you turn it off?
Come si spegne?
KOH-*me see* SPEH-*nyeh?*

Please tell me when (where) to get off.
Per favore, mi dica quando (dove) devo scendere.
*pehr fah-*VOH-*reh, mee* DEE-*kah* KWAHN-*doh* (DOH-*veh*)
    DEH-*voh* SHENN-*deh-reh.*

I want to get off at the next stop, please.
Per favore, vorrei scendere alla prossima fermata.
*pehr fah-*VOH-*reh, vohr-*RAY SHENN-*deh-reh* AHL-*lah*
    PROHSS-*see-mah fehr-*MAH-*tah.*

Often

How often do you come here?
Quanto spesso viene qui?
KWAHN-*toh* SPESS-*soh* VYEH-*neh* KWEE?

How often do the buses (the trains, the planes, the boats) run?

Quanto spesso fanno servizio gli autobus (i treni, gli aerei, i battelli)?

KWAHN-toh SPESS-soh FAHN-noh sehr-VEE-tsyoh lyee ow-toh-BOOSS (ee TREH-nee, lyee ah-EH-reh-ee, ee baht-TELL-lee)?

Do you come here often?

Viene qui spesso?

VYEH-neh kwee SPESS-soh?

I come (I don't come) here often.

Vengo (non vengo) qui spesso.

VEHN-goh (nohn VEHN-goh) kwee SPESS-soh.

Old

How old are you?

Quanti anni ha lei?

KWAHN-tee AHN-nee ah lay?

I am _____ years old.

Ho _____ anni.

oh _____ AHN-nee.

Is this an old building?

È antico questo edificio?

eh ahn-TEE-koh KWEH-stoh eh-dee-FEE-choh?

It is (it is not) old.

È (non è) vecchio (vecchia).

EH (nohn EH) VEKK-kyoh (VEKK-ryah).

On

How do you turn it on?

Come si accende?

KOH-meh see aht-CHENN-deh?

What flight are you on?

Qual'è il suo volo?

kwah-LEH eel SOO-oh VOH-loh?

One-Way

A one-way ticket to _____, please.
Per favore, un biglietto di andata per _____.
*pehr fah-*VOH*-reh, oon bee-*LYETT*-toh dee ahn-*DAH*-tah
   pehr _____.*

Is this street one-way?
Questa strada è a senso unico?
KWEH-*stah* STRAH-*dah* EH *ah* SENN-*soh* OO-*nee-koh?*

Only

I speak only English.
Parlo solo inglese.
PAHR-*loh* SOH-*loh een-*GLEH-*seh.*

Open

May I open the door (the window)?
Posso aprire la porta (la finestra)?
POHSS-*soh ah-*PREE-*reh lah* POHR-*tah (lah fee-*NEH-
   stra)?

Please open (don't open) the door (the window).
Per favore apra (non apra) la porta (la finestra).
*pehr fah-*VOH*-reh* AH-*prah (nohn* AH-*prah) lah* POHR-*tah
   (lah fee-*NEH-*strah).*

Is it still open?
È ancora aperto?
*eh ahng-*KOH-*rah ah-*PEHR-*toh?*

When do you open?
A che ora si apre?
a keh OH-*rah see* AH-*preh?*

I cannot get it open.
Non riesco ad aprirlo (aprirla).
*nohn ree-*EH-*skoh ahd ah-*PREER-*loh (ah-*PREER-*lah).*

How long does it stay open?
Quanto tempo rimane aperto?
KWAHN-*toh* TEMM-*poh ree-*MAH-*neh ah-*PEHR-*toh?*

Opener

Excuse me, do you have a can opener (bottle opener)?

Ha, per favore, un apriscatole (un cavaturaccioli)?

*ah, pehr fah-*VOH-*reh, oon ah-pree-*SKAH-*toh-leh (oon kah-vah-too-*RAHT-*choh-lec)?*

Opera

Where is the opera house?

Dov'è il teatro dell'opera?

*doh-*VEH *eel teh-*AH-*troh dell-*LOH-*peh-rah?*

What opera is being given tonight?

Quale opera si dà stasera?

KWAH-*leh* OH-*peh-rah see* DAH *stah-*SEH-*rah?*

Would you like to go to the opera with me?

Gradirebbe andare all'opera con me?

*grah-dee-*REHBB-*beh ahn-*DAH-*reh ahl-*LOH-*peh-rah kohn* MEH?

Operator – see Telephone

Opposite

What is that building opposite _____?

Che edificio è quello dirimpetto a _____?

*keh eh-dee-*FEE-*choh* EH KWELL-*loh dee-reem-*PETT-*toh ah _____?*

Orchestra

Is the orchestra playing tonight?

Ci sarà un concerto orchestrale stasera?

*chee sah-*RAH *oon kohn-*CHEHR-*toh ohr-keh-*STRAH-*leh stah-*SEH-*rah?*

Order

May I order, please?

Posso ordinare, per favore?

POHSS-*soh ohr-dee-*NAH-*reh, pehr fah-*VOH-*reh?*

Where can I cash a money order?

Dove posso incassare un vaglia?

DOH-*veh* POHSS-*soh een-kahss-*SAH-*reh oon* VAH-*lyah?*

I did not order this.

Non ho ordinato questo.

*nohn oh ohr-dee-*NAH-*toh* KWEH-*stoh.*

This is (this is not) what I ordered.
È (non è) quello che ho ordinato.
EH *(nohn* EH*)* KWELL-*loh keh oh ohr-dee-*NAH-*toh.*

Outlet
Where is the electrical outlet?
Dov'è la presa elettrica?
*doh-*VEH *lah* PREH-*sah eh-*LETT-*tree-kah?*

Overcooked
This is overcooked; please take it back.
È troppo cotto; lo riporti, per favore.
EH TROHP-*poh* KOHT-*toh; loh ree-*POHR-*tee pehr fah-*
VOH-*reh.*

Overnight
We will be staying overnight.
Pernotteremo qui.
*pehr-noht-teh-*REH-*moh* KWEE.

May I leave the car here overnight?
Posso lasciare la macchina qui durante la notte?
POHSS-*soh lah-*SHAH-*reh lah* MAHK-*kee-nah* KWEE *doo-*
RAHN-*teh lah* NOHT-*teh?*

Overtime
What is the charge for overtime?
Qual'è la tariffa per lo straordinario?
*kwah-*LEH *lah tah-*REEF-*fah pehr loh strah-ohr-dee-*
NAH-*ryoh?*
Is there a charge for overtime?
C'è una tariffa per lo straordinario?
cheh OON-*ah tah-*REEF-*fah pehr loh strah-ohr-dee-*NAH-
ryoh?

Owe
How much do I owe?
Quanto le devo?
KWAHN-*toh leh* DEH-*voh?*

Owner
May I see the owner, please?
Vorrei parlare con il proprietario, per favore.
*vohr-*RAY *pahr-*LAH-*reh kohn eel proh-pryeh-*TAH-*ryoh,*
*pehr fah-*VOH-*reh.*

Are you the owner?
È lei il proprietario?
EH *lay eel proh-pryeh-*TAH-*ryoh?*

Pack
Pack this carefully.
Ne faccia un pacco solido.
neh FAHT-*chah oon* PAHK-*koh* SOH-*lee-doh.*

Package
Has a package arrived for me?
È arrivato un pacco per me?
EH *ahr-ree-*VAH-*toh oon* PAHK-*koh pehr* MEH?

Page
Please page _____.
Per favore, chiami _____.
*pehr fah-*VOH-*reh,* KYAH-*mee* _____.

Pain
Do you feel any pain?
Ha dolore?
*ah doh-*LOH-*reh?*

Paper
Where can I buy a paper?
Dove posso comprare un giornale?
DOH-*veh* POHSS-*soh kohm-*PRAH *roh oon johr-*NAH-*leh?*

May I have some writing paper?
Vorrei della carta da lettere.
*vohr-*RAY DELL-*lah* KAHR-*tah dah* LETT-*teh-reh.*

Parcel
What will it cost to send this parcel?
Quanto costa spedire questo pacco?
KWAHN-*toh* KOH-*stah speh-*DEE-*reh* KWEH-*stoh* PAHK-
  koh?

Parcel Post — see Post Office

Pardon
I beg your pardon.
Mi scusi.
mee SKOO-*zee.*

Park

May I park here for a while?
Posso parcheggiare qui un momento?
POHSS-*soh pahr-kehd*-JAHR-*reh* KWEE *oon moh*-MENN-*toh?*

Where can I park?
Dove posso parcheggiare?
DOH-*veh* POHSS-*soh pahr-keh*-JAHR-*reh?*

Pass

Do I need a pass?
Mi occore un permesso?
mee ohk-KOHR-*reh oon pehr*-MESS-*soh?*

May I have a pass?
Potrei avere un permesso?
poh-TRAY *ah*-VEH-*reh oon pehr*-MESS-*soh?*

Passport

Here is my passport.
Ecco il mio passaporto.
EHK-*koh eel* MEE-*oh pahss-sah*-POHR-*toh.*

I don't have my passport with me.
Non ho il passaporto con me.
nohn oh eel pahss-sah-POHR-*toh kohn* MEH.

I have lost my passport.
Ho perso il passaporto.
oh PEHR-*soh eel pahss-sah*-POHR-*toh.*

Pastry

What kind of pastry do you have?
Che tipo di paste avete?
keh TEE-*poh dee* PAH-*steh ah*-VEH-*teh?*

Pawn

I would like to pawn this.
Vorrei dare questo in pegno.
vohr-RAY DAH-*reh* KWEH-*stoh een* PEH-*nyoh.*

Pawnshop

Could you direct me to a pawnshop?
Potrebbe indicarmi un'agenzia di prestiti su pegno?
poh-TREBB-*beh een-dee*-KAHR-*mee oon-ah-jenn*-TSEE-*ah dee* PREH-*stee-tee soo* PEH-*nyoh?*

Pay

Who do I pay?
Chi pago?
KEE PAH-*goh?*

How much must I pay?
Quanto devo pagare?
KWAHN-*toh* DEH-*voh pah*-GAH-*reh?*

Do I pay now or later?
Pago ora o dopo?
PAH-*goh* OH-*rah oh* DOH-*poh?*

Did you already pay?
Ha già pagato?
ah JAH *pah*-GAH-*toh?*

I have already paid.
Ho già pagato.
oh JAH *pah*-GAH-*toh.*

I have not paid yet.
Non ho ancora pagato.
nohn oh ahng-KOH-*rah pah*-GAH-*toh.*

Pen

Do you have a pen (a pencil) I could borrow for a
  moment?
Per favore, mi potrebbe prestare un memento una
  penna (una matita)?
pehr fah-VOH-*reh, mee poh*-TREBB-*beh preh*-STAH-*reh
  oon moh*-MENN-*toh* OON-*ah* PENN-*nah (*OON-*ah mah*-
  TEE-*tah)?*

Pepper

May I have the pepper, please?
Vorrei il pepe, per favore.
vohr-RAY *eel* PEH-*peh, pehr fah*-VOH-*reh.*

Performance

When does the performance begin?
A che ora comincia lo spettacolo?
ah keh OH-*rah koh*-MEEN-*chah loh spett*-TAH-*koh-loh?*

Permit
Do I need a permit?
Mi occorre un permesso?
*mee ohk-*KOH-*reh oon pehr-*MESS-*soh?*

Personal
This is for my personal use.
È per mio uso personale.
eh pehr MEE-*oh* OO-*zoh pehr-soh-*NAH-*leh.*

Will you accept a personal check?
Potete accettare un assegno personale?
*poh-*TEH-*teh aht-chett-*TAH-*reh oon ahss-*SEH-*nyoh pehr-*
   *soh-*NAH-*leh?*

Phone – see also Telephone
I would like to make a phone call to _____.
Vorrei fare una telefonata a _____.
*vohr-*RAY FAH-*reh* OON-*ah teh-leh-foh-*NAH-*tah ah*

   _____.

Photograph
Excuse me, would you take a photograph of me?
Mi scusi, può farmi una fotografia?
mee SKOO-*zee,* PWOH FAHR-*mee* OON-*ah foh-toh-grah-*
   FEE-*ah?*

Piano
I play the piano.
Suono il pianoforte.
SWOH-*noh eel pyah-noh-*FOHR-*teh.*

Do you play the piano?
Suona il pianoforte?
SWOH-*nah eel pyah-noh-*FOHR-*teh?*

Picnic
Let's have a picnic.
Facciamo un picnic.
*faht-*CHAH-*moh oon* PEEK-*neek.*

Pillow
Please bring me a (another) pillow.
Per favore, mi porti un (un altro) cuscino.
*pehr fah-*VOH-*reh, mee* POHR-*tee oon (oon* AHL-*troh)*
   *koo-*SHEE-*noh.*

Plane – see Flight

Plate

May I have a plate (a clean plate), please?

Per favore, vorrei un piatto (un piatto pulito).

pehr fah-VOH-reh, vohr-RAY oon PYAHT-toh (oon PYAHT-toh poo-LEE-toh).

Platform

At which platform is the train for _____?

Da quale binario parte il treno per _____?

dah KWAH-leh bee-NAH-ryoh PAHR-teh eel TREH-noh pehr _____?

Play

I want to see a play tonight.

Stasera vorrei andare a teatro.

stah-SEH-rah vohr-RAY ahn-DAH-reh ah teh-AH-troh.

Which play would you suggest?

Quale spettacolo mi suggerisce?

KWAH-leh spett-TAH-koh-loh mee sood-jeh-REE-sheh?

Will you attend the play with me?

Vuol venire a teatro con me?

VWOHL veh-NEE-reh ah teh-AH-troh kohn MEH?

When does the play begin?

A che ora comincia lo spettacolo?

ah keh OH-rah koh-MEEN-chah loh spett-TAH-koh-loh?

Do you play golf (tennis, chess, bridge)?

Gioca a golf (tennis, scacchi, bridge)?

JOH-koh ah GOHLF (TENN-nees, SKAHK-kee, breej)?

Would you like to play golf (tennis, chess, bridge)?

Vuole giocare a golf (tennis, scacchi, bridge)?

VWOH-leh joh-KAH-reh ah GOHLF (TENN-nees, SKAHK-kee, breej)?

I don't play (very well).

Non so giocare (molto bene).

nohn SOH joh-KAH-reh (MOHL-toh BEH-neh).

Please

Please don't do that.
La prego di non farlo.
lah PREH-goh dee nohn FAHR-loh.

Please pass the _____.
Mi passi il (la, l', lo) _____.
mee PAHSS-see eel (lah, l, loh) _____.

Plenty

I have plenty, thanks.
Grazie, ne ho abbastanza.
GRAH-tsyeh neh oh ahb-bah-STAHN-tsah.

Point

Please point the way to _____.
Per favore, mi indichi la strada per _____.
pehr fah-VOH-reh, mee EEN-dee-kee lah STRAH-dah pehr

_____.

Please point to the phrase in this book.
Per favore, mi indichi la frase in questo libro.
pehr fah-VOH-reh, mee EEN-dee-kee lah FRAH-zeh in
  KWEH-stoh LEE-broh.

Police

Call the police!
Chiami la polizia!
KYAH-mee lah poh-lee-TSEE-ah!

Where is the police station?
Dov'è il commissariato?
doh-VEH eel kohm-mees-sahr-YAH-toh?

Policeman

Call a policeman!
Chiami un poliziotto!
KYAH-mee oon poh-lee-tsee-OHT-toh!

Polish

Would you polish my shoes, please?
Per favore, mi lucidi le scarpe.
pehr fah-VOH-reh, mee LOO-chee-dee leh SKAHR-peh.

Pool

Where is the pool?
Dov'è la piscina?
doh-VEH *lah pee*-SHEE-*nah?*

Is there a charge for the pool?
Si paga per la piscina?
see PAH-*gah pehr lah pee*-SHEE-*nah?*

Port

What is the next port?
Qual'è il prossimo porto?
kwah-LEH *eel* PROHSS-*see-moh* POHR-*toh?*

When do we reach port?
Quando arriveremo in porto?
KWAHN-*doh ahr-ree-veh-*REH-*moh een* POHR-*toh?*

Porter

I need a porter.
Mi occorre un facchino.
mee ohk-KOHR-*reh oon fahk*-KEE-*noh.*

Possible

As soon as possible.
Appena possibile.
ahp-PEH-*nah pohss*-SEE-*bee-leh.*

Postage — see also Post Office

What is the postage on this?
Che affrancatura ci vuole per questo?
*keh ahf-frahn-kah-*TOO-*rah chee* VWOH-*leh pehr* KWEH-*stoh?*

Postcards

Do you sell postcards?
Vendete cartoline illustrate?
venn-DEH-*teh kahr-toh-*LEE-*neh eel-loo-*STRAH-*teh?*

Do you have postcards of _____?
Avete delle cartoline illustrate di _____?
ah-VEH-*teh* DELL-*leh kahr-toh-*LEE-*neh eel-loo-*STRAH-*teh dee* _____?

Please mail these postcards for me.
Per favore, mi imbuchi queste cartoline.
pehr fah-VOH-reh, mee eem-BOO-kee KWEH-steh kahr-toh-LEE-neh.

Postman

When does the postman arrive?
A che ora arriva il postino?
ah keh OH-rah ahr-REE-vah eel poh-STEE-noh?

Please give this to the postman.
Per favore, dia questo al postino.
pehr fah-VOH-reh, DEE-ah KWEH-stoh ahl poh-STEE-noh.

Post Office

Where is the post office?
Dov'è l'ufficio postale?
doh-VEH loof-FEE-choh poh-STAH-leh?

Where can I buy airmail stamps?
Dove posso comprare francobolli per posta aerea?
DOH-veh POHSS-soh kohm-PRAH-reh frahng-koh-BOHL-lee pehr POH-stah ah-EH-reh-ah?

How many stamps do I need for _____?
Quanti francobolli occorrono per _____?
KWAHN-tee frahng-koh-BOHL-lee ohk-KOHR-roh-noh pehr _____?

How much is the postage?
Qual'è la tariffa postale?
kwah-LEH lah tah-REEF-fah poh-STAH-leh?

How long will it take to get to _____?
Quanto ci metterà ad arrivare a _____?
KWAHN-toh chee mett-teh-RAH ahd ahr-ree-VAH-reh ah _____?

Will it arrive within _____ days (weeks)?
Arriverà entro _____ giorni (settimane)?
ahr-ree-veh-RAH enn-troh _____ JOHR-nee (sett-tee-MAH-neh)?

Please send this (these) by airmail (parcel post,
   registered mail, insured mail, special delivery).
Per favore, spedisca questo (questi) per posta aerea
   (come pacco postale, raccomandata, assicurata,
   expresso con ricevuta).
*pehr fah-*VOH-*reh, speh-*DEES-*kah* KWEH-*stoh* (KWEH-
   stee) pehr POH-*stah ah-*EH-*reh-ah* (KOH-*meh* PAHK-
   *koh poh-*STAH-*leh, rahk-koh-mahn-*DAH-*tah, ahss-see-
   koo-*RAH-*tah, eh-*SPRESS-*soh kohn ree-cheh-*VOO-*tah).*

Would you wrap this package for me?
Per favore, mi imballi questo pacco.
*pehr fah-*VOH-*reh, mee eem-*BAHL-*lee* KWEH-*stoh* PAHK-
   koh?

Will the receiver have to pay duty?
Il destinatario dovrà pagare il dazio?
*eel deh-stee-nah-*TAH-*ryoh doh-*VRAH *pah-*GAH-*reh eel*
   DAH-*tsyoh?*

Pounds (1 kilogram = 2.2 pounds)
How many pounds of baggage per person?
Quanti chili di bagaglio a testa?
KWAHN-*tee* KEE-*lee dee bah-*GAH-*lyoh ah* TEH-*stah?*

How many pounds of overweight baggage do I have?
Quanti chili ho di soprapeso?
KWAHN-*tee* KEE-*lee oh dee soh-prah-*PEH-*soh?*

Prefer
I prefer something cheaper (better).
Preferisco qualcosa di meno caro (di meglio).
*preh-feh-*REE-*skoh kwahl-*KOH-*sah dee* MEH-*noh* KAH-*roh*
   (dee MEH-*lyoh).*

Pregnant
I am pregnant.
Sono incinta.
SOH-*noh een-*CHEEN-*tah.*

Prescription — see also Medical
Can you fill this prescription?
Mi può preparare questa ricetta?
mee PWOH *preh-pah-*RAH-*reh* KWEH-*stah ree-*CHETT-
   tah?

Press – see Laundry

Priest

Where can I find a priest (who speaks (English)?

Dove posso trovare un sacerdote (che parla inglese)?

DOH-*veh* POHSS-*soh* troh-VAH-*reh oon sah-chehr*-DOH-*teh (keh* PAHR-*lah een*-GLEH-*seh)?*

Private

I want a private room with a bath (a private compartment).

Vorrei una camera singola con bagno (uno scompartimento privato).

vohr-RAY OON-*ah* KAH-*meh-rah* SEENG-*goh-lah kohn* BAH-*nyoh* (OON-*ah skohm-pahr-tee*-MENN-*toh pree-*VAH-*toh).*

Profession

What is your profession?

Qual'è la sua professione?

kwah-LEH *lah* SOO-*ah proh-fess*-SYOH-*neh?*

Program

Where can I get a program?

Dove posso avere un programma?

DOH-*veh* POHSS-*soh ah*-VEH-*reh oon proh*-GRAHM-*mah?*

Is there a charge for the program?

Si paga il programma?

see PAH-*gah eel proh*-GRAHM-*mah?*

When does the program begin?

A che ora comincia il programma?

ah keh OH-*rah koh*-MEEN-*chah eel proh*-GRAHM-*mah?*

Pronounce

How do you pronounce this?

Come se pronuncia questo?

KOH-*meh see proh*-NOON-*chah* KWEH-*stoh?*

Protestante

I am a Protestant.

Sono protestante.

SOH-*noh proh-teh*-STAHN-*teh.*

Can you direct me to the nearest Protestant church?
Mi saprebbe indicare la chiesa protestante piú vicina?
*mee sah-*PREBB-*beh een-dee-*KAH-*reh lah* KYEH-*zah proh-
teh-*STAHN-*teh pyoo vee-*CHEE-*nah?*

Public
Is this open to the public?
È aperto (aperta) al pubblico?
EH *ah-*PEHR-*toh (ah-*PEHR-*tah) ahl* POOB-*blee-koh?*

Push
Can you give me a push?
Mi può dare una spinta?
mee PWOH DAH-*reh* OON-*ah* SPEEN-*tah?*

Put
Please put this in the safe (in my room).
Per favore, lo metta nella cassaforte (in camera).
*pehr fah-*VOH-*reh, loh* METT-*tah* NELL-*lah kahss-sah-
FOHR-*teh (een* KAH-*meh-rah).*

Quality
I want the best quality.
Vorrei la qualità migliore.
*vohr-*RAY *lah kwah-lee-*TAH *mee-*LYOH-*reh.*

Quantity
What quantity may I take (have)?
Quanto ne posso prendere (avere)?
KWAHN-*toh neh* POHSS-*soh* PRENN-*deh-reh (ah-*VEH-
reh)?

Question
I have a question.
Vorrei fare una domanda.
*vohr-*RAY FAH-*reh* OON-*ah doh-*MAHN-*dah.*

Quickly
Call a doctor quickly!
Chiami subito un medico!
KYAH-*mee* SOO-*bee-toh oon* MEH-*dee-koh!*

Call the police quickly!
Chiami subito la polizia!
KYAH-*mee* SOO-*bee-toh la poh-lee-*TSEE-*ah!*

Come here quickly!

Venga subito qui!

VENG-*gah* SOO-*bee-toh* KWEE*!*

Quiet

Can you recommend a nice quiet restaurant (a nice quiet hotel)?

Mi saprebbe indicare un buon ristorante tranquillo (un buon albergo tranquillo)?

*mee sah-*PREHB-*beh een-dee-*KAH-*reh oon bwohn ree-stoh-*RAHN-*teh trahng-*KWEEL-*loh (oon bwohn ahl-*BEHR-*goh trahng-*KWEEL-*loh)?*

Quiet, please.

Silenzio, per favore.

*see-*LENN-*tsyoh, pehr fah-*VOH-*reh.*

Rabbi

Where can I find a rabbi (who speaks English)?

Dove posso trovare un rabbino (che parla inglese)?

DOH-*veh* POHSS-*soh troh-*VAH-*reh oon rahb-*BEE-*noh (keh* PAHR-*lah een-*GLEH-*seh)?*

Radio

May I have a radio for my room, please?

Potrei avere una radio in camera, per favore?

*poh-*TRAY *ah-*VEH-*reh* OON-*ah* RAH-*dyoh een* KAH-*meh-rah, pehr fah-*VOH-*reh?*

The radio in my room does not work.

La radio in camera non funziona.

lah RAH-*dyoh een* KAH-*meh-rah nohn foon-*TSYOH-*nah.*

Railroad – see also Train

Where is the railroad station?

Dov'è la stazione ferroviaria?

*doh-*VEH *lah stah-*TSYOH-*neh fehr-roh-vee-*AH-*ryah?*

Can you take me to the railroad station?

Mi può portare alla stazione ferroviaria?

mee PWOH *pohr-*TAH-*reh* AHL-*lah stah-*TSOYH-*neh fehr-roh-vee-*AH-*ryah?*

Rain

It's going to rain this morning (this afternoon, this evening).

Pioverà stamane (questo pomeriggio, stasera).

pyoh-veh-RAH stah-MAH-neh (KWEH-stoh poh-meh-REED-joh, stah-SEH-rah).

Is it raining?

Piove?

PYOH-veh?

Rare

I want my meat rare (medium rare), please.

Vorrei la carne al sangue (poco cotta), per favore.

vohr-RAY lah KAHR-neh ahl SAHNG-gweh (POH-koh KOHT-tah), pehr fah-VOH-reh.

I ordered this rare; please take it back.

L'ho ordinata al sangue; la riporti, per favore.

loh ohr-dee-NAH-tah ahl SAHNG-gweh; lah ree-POHR-tee, pehr fah-VOH-reh.

This is too rare; please take it back.

Non è abbastanza cotta; la riporti per favore.

nohn EH ahb-bah-STAHN-tsah KOHT-tah; lah ree-POHR-tee, pehr fah-VOH-reh.

Rate — see also Bank

What is the rate per kilometer (per minute, per hour, per day, per week, per month, per word)?

Qual'è la tariffa al chilometro (al minuto, all'ora, al giorno, alla settimana, al mese, per parola)?

kwah-LEH lah tah-REEF-fah ahl kee-LOH-meh-troh (ahl mee-NOO-toh, ahl-LOH-rah, ahl JOHR-noh, ahl-lah sett-tee-MAH-nah, ahl MEH-seh, pehr pah-ROH-lah)?

What is your rate to _____?

Quanto costa fino a _____?

KWAHN-toh KOH-stah FEE-noh ah _____?

What is the rate of exchange?

Qual'è il tasso di cambio?

kwah-LEH eel TAHSS-soh dee KAHM-byoh?

Rather

I would rather see _____ than _____.
Preferirei vedere _____ anzichè _____.
preh-feh-ree-RAY veh-DEH-reh _____ *ahn-zee-KEH*
_____.

I would rather not.
Preferirei di no.
preh-feh-ree-RAY dee NOH.

Raw

I like my meat nearly raw.
Mi piace la carne quasi cruda.
mee PYAH-cheh lah KAHR-neh KWAH-zee KROO-dah.

This is raw; please take it back.
È crudo; lo riporti, per favore.
EH KROO-doh; loh ree-POHR-tee, pehr fah-VOH-reh.

Razor

Where is the electrical outlet for the razor?
Dov'è la presa elettrica per il rasoio?
doh-VEH lah PREH-sah eh-LETT-tree-kah pehr eel rah-ZOH-yoh?

Where can I buy razor blades?
Dove posso comprare delle lamette?
DOH-veh POHSS-soh kohm-PRAH-reh DELL-leh lah-METT-teh?

Ready

When will it be ready?
Quando sarà pronto (pronta)?
KWAHN-doh sah-RAH PROHN-toh (PROHN-tah)?

When will you be ready?
Quando sarà pronto (pronta) lei?
KWAHN-doh sah-RAH PROHN-toh (PROHN-tah) lay?

When will they be ready?
Quando saranno pronti (pronte)?
KWAHN-doh sah-RAHN-noh PROHN-tee (prohn-teh)?

Are you ready?
È pronto (pronta)?
EH PROHN-toh (PROHN-tah)?

Are they ready?
Sono pronti (pronte)?
SOH-*noh* PROHN-*tee (PROHN-teh)*?

I am (I am not) ready.
Sono (non sono) pronto (pronta).
SOH-*noh (nohn* SOH-*noh)* PROHN-*toh (PROHN-tah)*.

Reasonable
Can you recommend a hotel with reasonable rates?
Mi saprebbe indicare un albergo con prezzi
   ragionevoli?
*mee sah-*PREHB-*beh een-dee-*KAH-*reh oon ahl-*BEHR-*goh
   kohn* PRETT-*tsee rah-joh-*NEH-*voh-lee?*

Receipt
Give me a receipt, please.
Mi dia una ricevuta, per favore.
mee DEE-*ah* OON-*ah ree-cheh-*VOO-*tah, pehr fah-*VOH-*reh.*

Recipe
Would you give me the recipe for this dish?
Mi vuol dare la ricetta di questo piatto?
mee vwohl DAH-*reh lah ree-*CHETT-*tah dee* KWEH-*stoh*
   PYATT-*toh?*

Recommend
Can you recommend a good restaurant (hotel)?
Mi può raccomandare un buon ristorante (albergo)?
mee PWOH *rahk-koh-mahn-*DAH-*reh oon bwohn ree-stoh-*
   RAHN-*teh (ahl-*BEHR-*goh)?*

What do you recommend?
Cosa mi raccomanda?
KOH-*sah mee rahk-koh-*MAHN-*dah?*

Record
Can you tell me where phonograph records are sold?
Mi saprebbe dire dove si vendono dischi?
*mee sah-*PREHB-*beh* DEE-*reh* DOH-*veh see* VENN-*doh-noh*
   DEE-*skee?*

Reduce
I am trying to reduce.
Cerco di dimagrire.
CHEHR-*koh dee dee-mah-*GREE-*reh.*

Refrigerator

I would like a room with a refrigerator.
Vorrei una camera con frigorifero.
vohr-RAY OON-ah KAH-meh-rah kohn free-goh-REE-feh-roh.

Refund

Will you give me a refund?
Mi da un rimborso?
mee dah oon reem-BOHR-soh?

Refuse (Garbage)

Where does one dispose of refuse?
Dove posso buttare i rifiuti?
DOH-veh POHSS-soh boot-TAH-reh ee ree-FYOO-tee?

Register

Where do I register?
Dove devo fare la registrazione?
DOH-veh DEH-voh FAH-reh lah reh-jee-strah-TSYOH-neh?

Remember

I do not remember the address.
Non ricordo l'indirizzo.
nohn ree-KOHR-doh leen-dee-REET-tsoh.

I do not remember your name.
Non ricordo il suo nome.
nohn ree-KOHR-doh eel SOO-oh NOH-meh.

Rent

Where can I rent _____?
Dove posso affittare _____?
DOH-veh POHSS-soh ahf-feet-TAH-reh _____?

How much would it cost to rent _____?
Quanto costa affittare _____?
KWAHN-toh KOH-stah ahf-feet-TAH-reh _____?

Repair

Can you repair this?
Me lo può riparare?
meh loh PWOH ree-pah-RAH-reh?

Do you know who can repair this?
Chi me lo potrebbe riparare?
kee meh loh poh-TREBB-beh ree-pah-RAH-reh?

Repeat

Repeat it, please.
Lo ripeta, per favore.
*loh ree-*PEH-*tah, pehr fah-*VOH-*reh.*

Request

I have a request.
Ho una richiesta.
oh OON-*ah ree-*KYEH-*stah.*

Reservation

I want to confirm (cancel) my reservation to _____.
Vorrei confermare (annullare) la mia prenotazione per
_____.
*vohr-*RAY *kohn-fehr-*MAH-*reh (ahn-nool-*LAH-*reh) lah*
MEE-*ah preh-noh-tah-*TSYOH-*neh pehr* _____.

Do I need a reservation?
Occorre la prenotazione?
*ohk-*KOH-*reh lah preh-noh-tah-*TSYOH-*neh.*

I have (I don't have) a reservation.
Ho (non ho) la prenotazione.
*oh (nohn oh) lah preh-noh-tah-*TSYOH-*neh.*

Should we make a reservation?
Dobbiamo prenotare?
*dohb-*BYAH-*moh preh-noh-*TAH-*reh?*

Could I make a reservation on the flight to _____?
Vorrei prenotarmi sul volo per _____?
*vohr-*RAY *preh-noh-*TAHR-*mee sool* VOH-*loh pehr* _____?

Can I reserve a seat (in the front, near a window)?
Vorrei prenotare un posto (in avanti, vicino al
  finestrino)?
*vohr-*RAY *preh-noh-*TAH-*reh oon* POHS-*toh (een ah-*
  VAHN-*tee, vee-*CHEE-*noh ahl fee-neh-*STREE-*noh)?*

Is this reserved?
È prenotato?
EH *preh-noh-*TAH-*toh?*

Resident

Are you a resident of _____?

Lei è domiciliato a _____?

lay eh doh-mee-chee-LYAH-toh ah _____?

Resort

Can you recommend a good resort?

Mi saprebbe raccomandare un buon posto di villeggiatura?

mee sah-PREBB-beh rah-koh-mahn-DAH-reh oon bwohn POH-stoh dee veel-lehd-jah-TOO-rah?

Restaurant

Can you recommend a good restaurant?

Mi saprebbe indicare un buon ristorante?

mee sah-PREBB-beh een-dee-KAH-reh oon bwohn ree-stoh-RAHN-teh?

Return

I want to return on _____.

Vorrei tornare _____.

vohr-RAY tohr-NAH-reh _____.

When will he return?

Quando tornerà?

KWAHN-doh tohr-neh-RAH?

Reverse

I would like to reverse the charges.

Vorrei trasferire l'importo al destinatario.

vohr-RAY trah-sfeh-REE-reh leem-POHR-toh ahl deh-stee-nah-TAH-ryoh.

Reward

I am offering a reward of _____.

Offro una ricompensa di _____.

OHF-froh OON-ah ree-kohm-PENN-sah dee _____.

Ride

May I have a ride?

Posso avere un passaggio?

POHSS-soh ah-VEH-reh oon pahss-SAHD-joh?

Let's go for a ride.
Facciamo una corsa in automobile.
faht-CHAH-*moh* OON-*ah* KOHR-*sah een ow-toh*-MOH-*bee-leh*.

River

What river is this?
Quale fiume è questo?
KWAH-*leh* FYOO-*meh eh* KWEH-*stoh?*

Road

Is this the road to _____?
È questa la strada per _____?
EH KWEH-*stah lah* STRAH-*dah pehr* _____?

Which is the road to _____?
Qual'è la strada per _____?
kwah-LEH *lah* STRAH-*dah pehr* _____?

Which road should I take?
Quale strada devo prendere?
KWAH-*leh* STRAH-*dah* DEH-*voh* PRENN-*deh-reh?*

Where does that road go?
Dove porta quella strada?
DOH-*veh* POHR-*tah* KWELL-*lah* STRAH-*dah?*

Is the road paved or bumpy?
La strada è a fondo buono o cattivo?
lah STRAH-*dah* EH *ah* FOHN-*doh* BWOH-*noh oh kaht*-TEE-*voh?*

Robbed

I have been robbed!
Mi hanno derubato (derubata)!
mee AHN-*noh deh-roo*-BAH-*toh (deh-roo*-BAH-*tah)!*

Call the manager!
Chiami il direttore!
KYAH-*mee eel dee-rett*-TOH-*reh!*

Room

I want a room with a double bed (with twin beds) and bath.

Vorrei una camera con letto matrimoniale (a due letti) con bagno.

vohr-RAY OON-*ah* KAH-*meh-rah* kohn LETT-*toh mah-tree-moh*-NYAH-*leh (ah* DOO-*eh* LETT-*tee)* kohn BAH-*nyoh*.

I want a room with a single bed and bath.

Vorrei una camera singola con bagno.

vohr-RAY OON-*ah* KAH-*meh-rah* SEENG-*goh-lah* kohn BAH-*nyoh*.

Do you have a room?

Avete una camera?

ah-VEH-*teh* OON-*ah* KAH-*meh-rah?*

Is there room for us?

C'è posto per noi?

CHEH POHS-*toh pehr noy?*

I am in room _____.

Sono alla camera _____.

SOH-*noh* AHL-*lah* KAH-*meh-rah* _____.

Room service, please.

Servizio, per favore.

sehr-VEE-*tsyoh, pehr fah*-VOH-*reh*.

Round Trip

A round-trip ticket to _____, please.

Per favore, un biglietto di andata e ritorno per _____.

pehr fah-VOH-*reh*, oon *bee*-LYETT-*toh dee ahn*-DAH-*tah eh ree*-TOHR-*noh pehr* _____.

How much is a round-trip ticket?

Quanto costa il biglietto di andata e ritorno?

KWAHN-*toh* KOH-*stah eel bee*-LYETT-*toh dee ahn*-DAH-*tah eh ree*-TOHR-*noh?*

Route

Which is the best route to _____?

Qual'è la migliore strada per _____?

kwah-LEH *lah mee*-LYOH-*reh* STRAH-*dah pehr* _____?

Rubbish

Please take care of this rubbish.

Porti via questi rifiuti, per favore.

POHR-*tee* VEE-*ah* KWEH-*stee* ree-FYOO-*tee, pehr fah*-VOH-*reh.*

Ruins

Is there a tour of the ruins?

Si possono visitare le rovine?

see POHSS-*soh-noh vee-zee*-TAH-*reh leh roh*-VEE-*neh?*

Which way are the ruins?

Come si va alle rovine?

KOH-*meh see vah* AHL-*leh roh*-VEE-*neh?*

Safe

Is it unsafe?

C'è pericolo?

CHEH *peh*-REE-*koh-loh?*

Please keep these in the safe for me.

Per favore, li (le) metta nella cassaforte.

pehr fah-VOH-*reh, lee (leh)* METT-*tah* NELL-*lah kahss-
sa*-FOHR-*teh.*

Sale

Is this for sale?

È in vendita?

eh een VENN-*dee-tah?*

Salt

May I have the salt, please.

Il sale, per favore.

eel SAH-*leh, pehr fah*-VOH-*reh.*

Please cook it without salt.

Lo (la) cucini senza sale, per favore.

loh (lah) koo-CHEE-*nee* SENN-*tsah* SAH-*leh, pehr
fah*-VOH-*reh.*

Sandwiches

Do you have sandwiches?

Avete dei panini imbottiti?

ah-VEH-*teh day pah*-NEE-*nee eem-boht*-TEE-*tee?*

Say

How do you say _____ in _____?
Come si dice _____ in _____?
KOH-*meh see* DEE-*cheh* _____ *een* _____?

What did you (he, she) say?
Cosa ha detto?
KOH-*sah ah* DETT-*toh?*

Schedule

May I have a schedule?
Posso avere un orario?
POHSS-*soh ah*-VEH-*reh oon oh*-RAH-*ryoh?*

School

Are you in school?
Lei va a scuola?
lay vah ah SKWOH-*lah?*

Where do you go to school?
Dove va a scuola?
DOH-*veh vah ah* SKWOH-*lah?*

Seasick

I am seasick.
Ho il mal di mare.
oh eel MAHL *dee* MAH-*reh.*

Seat

Is this seat taken?
È occupato questo posto?
*eh ohk-koo-*PAH-*toh* KWEH-*stoh* POH-*stoh?*

I want a window seat, please.
Vorrei un posto vicino al finestrino.
*vohr-*RAY *oon* POH-*stoh vee-*CHEE-*noh ahl fee-neh-*STREE-*noh.*

Are there any seats available?
Ci sono posti disponibili?
chee SOH-*noh* POH-*stee dee-spoh-*NEE-*bee-lee?*

See

May I see you tonight?
Posso vederla stasera?
POHSS-*soh veh-*DEHR-*lah stah-*SEH-*rah?*

Have you seen my _____?
Ha visto il mio (la mia, i miei, le mie) _____?
ah VEE-*stoh eel* MEE-*oh (lah* MEE-*ah, ee* MYEH-*ee, leh*
MEE-*eh)* _____?

I want to see _____.
Vorrei vedere _____.
vohr-RAY *veh*-DEH-*reh* _____.

Sell
Would you sell this?
Lo venderebbe?
loh venn-deh-REBB-*beh?*

Separate
We want separate rooms.
Vorremmo delle camere separate.
vohr-REHM-*moh* DELL-*leh* KAH-*meh-reh seh-pah*-RAH-
teh.

Servant
I would like to advertise for a servant.
Vorrei mettere un annuncio per una domestica.
vohr-RAY METT-*teh-reh oon ahn*-NOON-*choh pehr* OON-*ah
doh*-MEH-*stee-kah.*

Service
Is the service charge included?
Il servizio è compreso?
eel sehr-VEE-*tsyoh* EH *kohm*-PREH-*soh?*

Room service, please.
Servizio, per favore.
sehr-VEE-*tsyoh, pehr fah*-VOH-*reh.*

Is there bus service (limousine service) to the airport
(the hotel)?
C'è il servizio d'autobus (il servizio in automobile) per
l'aeroporto (per l'albergo)?
CHEH *eel sehr*-VEE-*tsyoh dow-toh*-BOOSS *(eel sehr*-VEE-
tsyoh een ow-toh-MOH-*bee-leh) pehr lah-eh-roh*-POHR-
toh (pehr lahl-BEHR-*goh)?*

When is the church service?
A che ora è la funzione religiosa?
ah keh OH-*rah* EH *lah foon*-TSYOH-*neh reh-lee*-JOH-*sah?*

Sew – see Laundry

Share

I do not want to share a bath.

Non desidero avere il bagno in comune.

nohn deh-SEE-deh-roh ah-VEH-reh eel BAH-nyoh een koh-MOO-neh.

Sharp

This knife is not sharp enough.

Questo coltello non è abbastanza affilato.

KWEH-*stoh kohl*-TELL-*loh nohn* EH *ahb-bah*-STAHN-*tsah ahf-fee*-LAH-*toh.*

Shave – see Barber

Shaver

Where can I plug in an electric shaver?

Dove posso innestare il rasoio elettrico?

DOH-*veh* POHSS-*soh een-neh*-STAH-*reh eel rah*-ZOH-*yoh eh*-LETT-*tree-koh?*

Sheets

Please change the sheets.

Per favore, cambi le lenzuola.

pehr fah-VOH-*reh,* KAHM-*bee leh lenn*-TSWOH-*lah.*

Shine

Please shine my shoes.

Per favore, mi lucidi le scarpe.

pehr fah-VOH-*reh, mee* LOO-*chee-dee leh* SKAHR-*peh.*

Ship

When does the ship arrive?

A che ora arriva la nave?

ah keh OH-*rah ahr*-REE-*vah lah* NAH-*veh?*

When does the ship leave?

A che ora parte la nave?

ah keh OH-*rah* PAHR-*teh lah* NAH-*veh?*

Shoe

Where can I get my shoes repaired?

Dove posso far riparare le scarpe?

DOH-*veh* POHSS-*soh fahr ree-pah*-RAH-*reh leh* SKAHR-*peh?*

Shopping

Where is the shopping center?
Dov'è il centro?
doh-VEH *eel* CHENN-*troh?*

Is there a salesman (a salesgirl) who speaks English?
C'è un commesso (una commessa) che parla inglese?
CHEH *oon kohm*-MESS-*soh (*OON-*ah kohm*-MESS-*sah) keh*
   PAHR-*lah een*-GLEH-*seh?*

Do you speak English?
Parla inglese?
PAHR-*lah een*-GLEH-*seh?*

May I help you?
Posso aiutarla?
POHSS-*soh ah-yoo*-TAHR-*lah?*

Can you help me?
Può aiutarmi?
PWOH *ah-yoo*-TAHR-*mi?*

I am just looking, thank you.
Grazie, voglio solo guardare.
GRAH-*tsyeh,* VOH-*lyoh* SOH-*loh gwahr*-DAH-*reh.*

I want to buy _____.
Vorrei comprare _____.
vohr-RAY *kohm*-PRAH-*reh* _____.

Do you sell _____?
Vendete _____?
venn-DEH-*teh* _____?

Can I see _____?
Potrei vedere _____?
poh-TRAY *veh*-DEH-*reh* _____?

I want to spend about _____.
Vorrei spendere circa _____.
vohr-RAY SPENN-*deh-reh* CHEER-*kah* _____.

What else do you have?
Che altro avete?
keh AHL-*troh ah*-VEH-*teh?*

How much is it?
Quanto costa?
KWAHN-*toh* KOH-*stah?*

It is too expensive.
È troppo caro.
EH TROHP-*poh* KAH-*roh.*

Can I see something else?
Potrei vedere qualcos'altro?
poh-TRAY *veh*-DEH-*reh kwahl-koh*-SAHL-*troh?*

Can I see something better (less expensive)?
Potrei vedere qualcosa di meglio (di meno caro)?
poh-TRAY *veh*-DEH-*reh kwahl*-KOH-*sah dee* MEH-*lyoh*
   (*dee* MEH-*noh* KAH-*roh*)?

I prefer this one.
Preferisco questo (questa).
preh-fehr-REE-*skoh* KWEH-*stoh (*KWEH-*stah).*

I'll take this one.
Prendo questo (questa).
PRENN-*doh* KWEH-*stoh (*KWEH-*stah).*

May I try it on?
Posso provarmelo (provarmela)?
POHSS-*soh proh*-VAHR-*meh-loh (proh*-VAHR-*meh-lah)?*

It doesn't fit.
Non mi va bene.
nohn mee vah BE-*neh.*

Do you do alterations here?
Fate le alterazioni qui?
FAH-*teh leh ahl-teh-rah*-TSYOH-*nee* KWEE?

Can you take it in?
Può stringerlo (stringerla)?
PWOH STREEN-*jehr-loh (*STREEN-*jehr-lah)?*

Can you let it out?
Può allargarlo (allargarla)?
PWOH *ahl-lahr*-GAHR-*loh (ahl-lahr*-GAHR-*lah)?*

Can you shorten it?
Può accorciarlo (accorciarla)?
PWOH *ahk-kohr*-CHAHR-*loh (ahk-kohr*-CHAHR-*lah)?*

Can you lengthen it?
Può allungarlo (allungarla)?
PWOH *ahl-loong*-GAHR-*loh (ahl-loong*-GAHR-*lah)?*

Will you take my measurements?
Mi prenda le misure?
mee PRENN-*dah leh mee*-ZOO-*reh?*

My size in the United States is _____.
La mia misura negli Stati Uniti è _____.
lah MEE-*ah mee*-ZOO-*rah* NEH-*lyee* STAH-*tee oo*-NEE-*tee*
EH _____.

Does it come in other colors?
Lo (la) avete in altri colori?
loh (lah) ah-VEH-*teh een* AHL-*tree koh*-LOH-*ree?*

Do you accept this credit card (American money,
   travelers' checks, personal checks)?
Accetta questa carta credito (denaro americano,
   assegni per viaggiatori, un assegno personale)?
aht-CHETT-*tah* KWEH-*stah* KAHR-*tah* KREH-*dee-toh
   (deh*-NAH-*roh ah-meh-ree*-KAH-*noh, ahss*-SEH-*nyee
   pehr vyahd-jah*-TOH-*ree, oon ahss*-SEH-*nyoh pehr-soh-*
   NAH-*leh)?*

Do you accept returns?
Posso restituirlo (restituirla)?
POHSS *ooh reh-stee-too*-WEER *loh (reh-stee-too*-WEER-
   lah)?

I bought it here.
L'ho comprato qui.
loh kohm-PRAH-*toh* KWEE.

I would like to exchange it for the next size.
Vorrei cambiarlo (cambiarla) con una misura più
   grande.
vohr-RAY *kahm*-BYAHR-*loh (kahm*-BYAHR-*lah) kohn
   OON-*ah mee*-ZOO-*rah pyoo* GRAHN-*deh.*

Will you wrap this, please.
Mi lo avvolga, per favore.
mee loh ahv-VOHL-*gah, pehr fah*-VOH-*reh.*

Do you deliver?
Fate la consegna a domicilio?
FAH-*teh lah kohn*-SEH-*nyah ah doh-mee*-CHEE-*lyoh?*

Please deliver it to my hotel.
Me lo (la) consegni all'albergo, per favore.
meh loh (lah) kohn-SEH-*nyee ahl-lahl*-BEHR-*goh, pehr fah*-VOH-*reh.*

Please send it to _____.
Per favore, lo (la) mandi a _____.
pehr fah-VOH-*reh, loh (lah)* MAHN-*dee ah* _____.

How much will it cost to insure it?
Quanto costa assicurarlo (assicurarla)?
KWAHN-*toh* KOH-*stah ahss-see-koo*-RAHR-*loh (ahss-see-koo*-RAHR-*lah)?*

I want to send it as a gift.
Vorrei mandarlo (mandarla) come regalo.
vohr-RAY *mahn*-DAHR-*loh (mahn*-DAHR-*lah)* KOH-*meh reh*-GAH-*loh.*

Will the receiver have to pay duty?
Il destinatario dovrà pagare il dazio?
eel deh-stee-nah-TAH-*ryoh doh*-VRAH *pah*-GAH-*reh eel* DAH-*tsyoh?*

Give me a receipt, please.
Mi dia una ricevuta, per favore.
mee DEE-*ah* OON-*ah ree-cheh*-VOO-*tah, pehr fah*-VOH-*reh.*

Show
Please show me the way to _____.
Per favore, mi indichi la strada per _____.
pehr fah-VOH-*reh, mee* EEN-*dee-kee lah* STRAH-*dah pehr* _____.

When is the next show?
Quand'è il prossimo spettacolo?
kwahn-DEH *eel* PROHSS-*see-moh spett*-TAH-*koh-loh?*

Shower

I want a room with a shower, please.

Vorrei una camera con doccia, per favore.

*vohr-*RAY OON-*ah* KAH-*meh-rah kohn* DOHT-*chah, pehr
    fah-*VOH-*reh.*

Shut

Please shut the door (the window).

Chiuda, per favore, la porta (la finestra).

KYOO-*dah, pehr fah-*VOH-*reh, lah* POHR-*tah (lah fee-*
    NEH-*strah).*

Sick

I am sick.

Sono ammalato.

*soh-noh ahm-mah-*LAH-*toh.*

Side Dish

May I have a side dish of _____, please?

Vorrei una porzione di _____, per favore.

*vohr-*RAY OON-*ah pohr-*TSYOH-*neh dee* _____, *pehr fah-*
    VOH-*reh.*

Sights

I would like to make a tour of the sights.

Vorrei fare il giro della città.

*vohr-*RAY FAH-*reh eel* GEE-*roh* DELL-*lah chee-*TAH.

Sightseeing

I want to go sightseeing.

Vorrei fare una gita turistica.

*vohr-*RAY FAH-*reh* OON-*ah* JEE-*tah too-*REES-*tee-kah.*

What tours can you arrange?

Che gite può organizzare?

keh JEE-*teh* PWOH *ohr-gah-need-*DZAH-*reh?*

Sign

What does that sign mean?

Cosa significa quel cartello?

KOH-*sah see-*NYEE-*fee-kah kwell kahr-*TELL-*loh?*

Signal

What is the signal for _____?

Qual'è la segnalazione per _____?

*kwah-*LEH *lah seh-nyah-lah-*TSYOH-*neh pehr* _____?

Single

I want a single room with a bath.
Vorrei una camera singola con bagno.
vohr-RAY OON-*ah* KAH-*meh-rah* SEENG-*goh-lah kohn*
  BAH-*nyoh.*

I am single. (masc.)
Sono scapolo.
soh-noh SKAH-*poh-loh.*

I am single. (fem.)
Non sono sposata.
nohn SOH-*noh spoh-*SAH-*tah.*

Are you single (masc.)?
È scapolo?
EH SKAH-*poh-loh?*

Sit

I would like to sit down for a while.
Vorrei sedermi un momento.
vohr-RAY *seh-*DEHR-*mee oon moh-*MENN-*toh.*

Size

What size is it?
Che misura è?
*keh mee-*ZOO-*rah* EH?

It is (it is not) the right size.
È (non è) la misura giusta.
EH *(nohn* EH*) lah mee-*ZOO-*rah* JOO-*stah.*

Skate

Do you like to skate?
Le piace pattinare?
leh PYAH-*cheh paht-tee-*NAH-*reh?*

I cannot skate.
Non so pattinare.
*nohn soh paht-tee-*NAH-*reh.*

Where can I find a skating rink?
Dove posso trovare una pista di pattinaggio?
DOH-*veh* POHSS-*soh troh-*VAH-*reh* OON-*ah* PEE-*stah dee*
  *paht-tee-*NAHD-*joh?*

Ski
Do you like to ski?
Le piace sciare?
leh PYAH-*cheh shee-*AH-*reh?*

Where is the best place to ski?
Dov'è il posto migliore per sciare?
*doh-*VEH *eel* POH-*sto mee-*LYOH-*reh pehr shee-*AH-*reh?*

Skin Dive
Do you like to skin dive?
Le piace la pesca subacquea?
leh PYAH-*cheh lah* PEH-*skah soob-*AHK-*kweh- ah?*

I don't know how to skin dive.
Non so fare la pesca subacquea.
nohn soh FAH-*reh lah* PEH-*skah soob-*AHK-*kweh-ah.*

Where is the best place for skin diving?
Qual'è il posto migliore per la pesca subacquea?
*kwah-*LEH *eel* POH-*stoh mee-*LYOH-*reh pehr lah* PEH-*skah soob-*AHK-*kweh-ah?*

Sleep
I am going to sleep.
Vado a dormire.
VAH-*doh ah dohr* MEE *reh.*

Sleeping
My wife (my husband) is sleeping.
Mia moglie (mio marito) dorme.
MEE-*ah* MOH-*lyeh (*MEE-*oh mah-*REE-*toh)* DOHR-*meh.*

Does the train have sleeping accommodations?
Il treno ha il vagone letto?
eel TREH-*noh ah eel vah-*GOH-*neh* LETT-*toh?*

Slope
Where is the best place to ski?
Dov'è il posto migliore per sciare?
DOH-*veh* SOH-*noh ee mee-*LYOH-*ree* KAHM-*pee pehr loh* SHEE?

Slow
Slow down!
Rallenti!
*rahl-*LENN-*tee!*

Slower
Please speak slower.
Per favore, parli più lentamente.
*pehr fah-*VOH*-reh,* PAHR-*lee pyoo len-tah-*MENN*-teh.*

Small
This is too small.
È troppo piccolo (piccola).
EH TROHP-*poh* PEEK-*koh-loh* (PEEK-*koh-lah*).

This is not small enough.
Non è abbastanza piccolo (piccola).
nohn EH *ahb-bah-*STAHN*-tsah* PEEK-*koh-loh* (PEEK-*koh-lah*).

Smoke
Do you smoke?
Fuma?
FOO-*mah?*

Do you mind if I smoke?
Le dispiace se fumo?
*leh dee-*SPYAH*-cheh seh* FOO-*moh?*

Smoking
Where is the smoking car?
Dov'è lo scompartimento fumatori?
*doh-*VEH *loh skohm-pahr-tee-*MENN*-toh foo-mah-*TOH*-ree?*

Snack
Where can I get a snack?
Dove posso fare uno spuntino?
DOH-*veh* POHSS-*soh* FAH-*reh oon-oh spoon-*TEE*-noh?*

Soap
Please bring me some soap.
Per favore, mi porti del sapone.
*pehr fah-*VOH*-reh, mee* POHR-*tee dell sah-*POH-NEH.

Soil
My _____ is soiled.
Il mio (la mia) _____ è sporco (sporca).
eel MEE-*oh (lah* MEE-*ah)* _____ EH SPOHR-*koh* (SPOHR-*kah*).

Sole

A new pair of soles, please.

Per favore, rifaccia le suole.

pehr fah VOH-*reh,* *ree-*FAHT-*chah leh* SWOH-*leh.*

Something

Can we get something to eat (to drink)?

Possiamo avere qualcosa da mangiare (da bere)?

*pohss-see-*AH-*moh ah-*VEH-*reh kwahl-*KOH-*sah dah*
    *mahn-*JAH-*reh (dah* BEH-*reh)?*

Soon

I'll see you soon.

La vedrò tra poco.

*lah veh-*DROH *trah* POH-*koh.*

How soon does the bus (the plane, the boat, the train)
    leave?

Tra quanto tempo parte l'autobus (l'aereo, il battello,
    il treno)?

trah KWAHN-*toh* TEMM-*poh* PAHR-*teh low-toh-*BOOSS
    *(lah-*EH-*reh-oh, eel baht-*TELL-*loh, eel* TREH-*noh)?*

How soon does the bus (the plane, the boat, the train)
    arrive?

Tra quanto tempo arriva l'autobus (l'aereo, il battello,
    il treno)?

trah KWAHN-*toh* TEMM-*poh ahr-*REE-*vah low-toh-*BOOSS
    *(lah-*EH-*reh-oh, eel baht-*TELL-*loh, eel* TREH-*noh)?*

Sorry

I am sorry.

Mi dispiace.

*mee dee-*SPYAH-*cheh.*

Sound

What is that sound?

Cos'è quel rumore?

*koh-*SEH *kwehl roo-*MOH-*reh?*

Souvenir

Where can I find a souvenir shop?

Dove posso trovare un negozio per i ricordi?

DOH-*veh* POHSS-*soh troh-*VAH-*reh oon neh-*GOH-*tsyoh*
    *pehr ee ree-*KOHR-*dee?*

Speak

Do you speak English?
Parla inglese?
PAHR-*lah een*-GLEH-*seh?*

I speak only English.
Parlo soltanto inglese.
PAHR-*loh sohl*-TAHN-*toh een*-GLEH-*seh.*

Please speak more slowly.
Per favore, parli più lentamente.
pehr fah-VOH-*reh,* PAHR-*lee pyoo len-tah*-MENN-*teh.*

May I please speak with _____?
Per favore, vorrei parlare con _____.
pehr fah-VOH-*reh, vohr*-RAY *pahr*-LAH-*reh kohn* _____.

I don't speak _____ very well.
Non parlo _____ molto bene.
nohn PAHR-*loh* _____ MOHL-*toh* BEH-*neh.*

I want a guide (a driver) who speaks English.
Vorrei una guida (un autista) che parla inglese.
vohr-RAY OON-*ah* GWEE-*dah (oon ow*-TEE-*stah) keh*
  PAHR-*lah een*-GLEH-*seh.*

Special Delivery — see Post Office

Spectacles — see Glasses

Speed

What is the speed limit?
Qual'è il limite di velocità?
kwah-LEH *eel* LEE-*mee-teh dee veh-loh-chee*-TAH?

Spoon

Please bring me a spoon.
Per favore, mi porti un cucchiaio.
pehr fah-VOH-*reh, mee* POHR-*tee oon kook*-KYAH-*yoh.*

Stables

Where are the stables?
Dove sono le scuderie?
DOH-*veh* SOH-*noh leh skoo-deh*-REE-*eh?*

Stamps — see Post Office

Standby

Please put me on standby.

Per favore, mi metta in lista d'attesa.

*pehr fah-*VOH*-reh, mee* METT*-tah een* LEE*-stah daht-*TEH*-sah.*

Stateroom

Where is stateroom _____?

Dov'è la cabina _____?

*doh-*VEH *lah kah-*BEE*-nah* _____?

I am in stateroom _____.

Sono nella cabina _____.

SOH*-noh* NELL*-lah kah-*BEE*-nah* _____.

Which stateroom are you in?

In che cabina è?

*een keh kah-*BEE*-nah* EH?

Station

Can you direct me to the railroad station (to the bus station)?

Mi saprebbe indicare la stazione farroviaria (la stazione degli autobus)?

*mee sah-*PREBB*-beh een-dee-*KAH*-reh lah stah-*TSYOH*-neh fehr-roh-vee-*AH*-ryah (lah stah* TOYOII *noh doh lyoo ow-toh-*BOOSS*)?*

Can you take me to the railroad station (to the bus station)?

Può portarmi alla stazione ferroviaria (alla stazione degli autobus)?

PWOII *pohr-*TAHR*-mee* AHL*-lah stah-*TSYOH*-neh fehr-roh-vee-*AH*-ryah (ahl-lah stah-*TSYOH*-neh deh-lyee ow-toh-*BOOSS*)?*

Stay

I am going to stay for _____ days (weeks).

Mi tratterrò per _____ giorni (settimane).

*mee traht-teh-*ROH *pehr* _____ JOHR*-nee (sett-tee-*MAH*-neh).*

How long are you planning to stay?
Quanto tempo conta di trattenersi?
KWAHN-*toh* TEMM-*poh* KOHN-*tah dee traht-teh*-NEHR-*see?*

Where are you staying?
Dov'è alloggiato (alloggiata)?
doh-VEH *ahl-lohd*-JAH-*toh (ahl-lohd*-JAH-*tah)?*

I am staying at _____.
Sono alloggiato al _____.
soh-noh ahl-lohd-JAH-*toh ahl* _____.

Stolen

My _____ has been stolen!
Mi hanno rubato il (la, i, le, gli) _____!
mee AHN-*noh roo*-BAH-*toh eel (lah, ee, leh, lyee)* _____!

Call the police (the manager)!
Chiami la polizia (il direttore)!
KYAH-*mee lah poh-lee*-TSEE-*ah (eel dee-rett*-TOH-*reh)!*

Stop

Stop here, please.
Si fermi qui, per favore.
see FEHR-*mee kwee, pehr fah*-VOH-*reh.*

Next stop, please.
La prossima fermata, per favore.
lah PROHSS-*see-mah fehr*-MAH-*tah, pehr fah*-VOH-*reh.*

Do we stop at _____?
Ci fermiamo a _____?
chee fehr-MYAH-*moh ah* _____?

Stop!
Si fermi!
see FEHR-*mee!*

Stranger

I am a stranger here.
Sono un estraneo (un'estranea) qui.
soh-noh oon eh-STRAH-*neh-oh (oon eh*-STRAH-*neh-ah) kwee.*

Street

What street is this?
Che strada è questa?
keh STRAH-*dah eh* KWEH-*stah?*

What street comes after _____?
Qual'è la strada dopo _____?
*kwah-*LEH *lah* STRAH-*dah* DOH-*poh* _____?

It is on _____ street.
Si trova in via _____.
see TROH-*vah een* VEE-*ah* _____.

Student

I am a student.
Sono studente.
SOH-*noh stoo-*DENN-*teh.*

Are you a student?
Lei è studente?
*lay eh stoo-*DENN-*teh?*

Do you give student rates?
Fate uno sconto agli studenti?
FAH-*teh oon-oh* SKOHN-*toh* AH-*lyee stoo-*DENN-*tee?*

Subtitles

Does the movie have English subtitles!
Il film ha le didascalie in inglese?
*eel feelm ah leh dee-deh-skah-*LEE-*eh een een-*GLEH-*seh?*

Subway

What subway do I take to _____?
Quale metropolitana devo prendere per _____?
KWAH-*leh meh-troh-poh-lee-*TAH-*nah* DEH-*voh* PRENN-*deh-reh pehr* _____?

Where can I find the subway for _____?
Dove posso trovare la metropolitana per _____?
DOH-*veh* POHSS-*soh troh-*VAH-*reh lah meh-troh-poh-lee-*TAH-*nah pehr* _____?

Sugar

May I have some sugar, please?
Vorrei dello zucchero, per favore.
*vohr-*RAY DELL-*loh* TSOOK-*keh-roh, pehr fah-*VOH-*reh.*

Suit

Where can I have a suit made (cleaned, pressed)?
Dove posso farmi fare (pulire, stirare) un vestito?
DOH-*veh* POHSS-*soh* FAHR-*mee* FAH-*reh* (*poo*-LEE-*reh*,
stee-RAH-*reh*) *oon veh*-STEE-*toh?*

Please clean (press) this suit.
Per favore mi pulisca (mi stiri) questo vestito.
pehr fah-VOH-*reh mee poo*-LEE-*skah (mee* STEE-*ree*)
KWEH-*stoh veh*-STEE-*toh.*

Suitcase

This is my suitcase.
Questa è la mia valigia.
KWEH-*stah eh lah* MEE-*ah vah*-LEE-*jah.*

Would you carry my suitcase, please?
Mi porti la valigia, per favore.
mee POHR-*tee lah vah*-LEE-*jah, pehr fah*-VOH-*reh.*

Sunburn

What do you have for sunburn?
Cosa mi consiglia per una scottatura?
KOH-*sah mee kohn*-SEE-*lyah pehr* OON-*ah skoht-tah*-TOO-
rah.

Sweet

This is too sweet.
È troppo dolce.
EH TROHP-*poh* DOHL-*cheh.*

This is not sweet enough.
Non è abbastanza dolce.
nohn EH *ahb-bah*-STAHN-*tsah* DOHL-*cheh.*

Swim

Where can I go swimming?
Dove posso andare a nuotare?
DOH-*veh* POHSS-*soh ahn*-DAH-*reh ah nwoh*-TAH-*reh?*

I don't know how to swim.
Non so nuotare.
nohn soh nwoh-TAH-*reh.*

Synagogue

Can you direct me to the nearest synagogue?

Per favore, mi può indicare la sinagoga più vicina?

*pehr fah-*VOH*-reh, mee pwoh een-dee-*KAH*-reh lah seen-
ah-*GOH*-gah pyoo vee-*CHEE*-nah?*

Can you take me to the nearest synagogue?

Per favore, mi può portare alla sinagoga più vicina?

*pehr fah-*VOH*-reh, mee* PWOH *pohr-*TAH*-reh* AHL*-lah
seen-ah-*GOH*-gah pyoo vee-*CHEE*-nah?*

Table

A table near the window, please.

Per favore, una tavola vicino alla finestra.

*pehr fah-*VOH*-reh,* OON*-ah* TAH*-voh-lah vee-*CHEE*-noh*
AHL*-lah fee-*NEH*-strah.*

A table for two (for three, for four, for just myself),
please.

Per favore, una tavola per due (per tre, per quattro,
per me solo).

*pehr fah-*VOH*-reh,* OON*-ah* TAH*-voh-lah pehr* DOO*-eh
(pehr treh, pehr* KWAHT*-troh, pehr meh* SOH*-loh).*

Take

How long will it take?

Quanto ci vorrà?

KWAHN*-toh chee vohr-*RAH*?*

Take me to the _____.

Mi porti al (alla) _____.

mee POHR*-tee ahl (*AHL*-lah) _____.*

Please take my bags.

Per favore, prenda le mie valigie.

*pehr fah-*VOH*-reh,* PRENN*-dah leh* MEE*-eh vah-*LEE*-jeh.*

Please take my order.

Per favore, prenda il mio ordine.

*pehr fah-*VOH*-reh,* PRENN*-dah eel* MEE*-oh* OHR*-dee-neh.*

Take it away, please.

Lo porti via, per favore.

loh POHR*-tee* VEE*-ah, pehr fah-*VOH*-reh.*

Is this taken?
È occupato?
EH *ohk-koo-*PAH*-toh?*

Taste

This has a strange taste.
Ha un sapore strano.
*ah oon sah-*POH*-reh* STRAH*-noh.*

It does not taste right.
Non ha buon sapore.
*nohn ah bwohn sah-*POH*-reh.*

May I taste it?
Posso assaggiarlo?
*pohss-soh ahss-sah-*JAHR*-loh?*

Tax

Is the tax included?
La tassa è compresa?
lah TAHSS*-sah eh kohm-*PREH*-sah?*

How much is the tax?
Quant'è la tassa?
*kwahn-*TEH *lah* TAHSS*-sah?*

Taxi

Please get me a taxi.
Per favore, mi chiami un tassì.
*pehr fah-*VOH*-reh, mee* KYAH*-mee oon tahss-*SEE.

Tea

May I please have some tea?
Per favore, vorrei del tè.
*pehr fah-*VOH*-reh, vohr-*RAY *dell teh.*

Tea with lemon (with milk).
Tè al limone (con latte).
*teh ahl lee-*MOH*-neh (kohn* LATT*-teh).*

Iced tea.
Tè ghiacciato.
*teh gyaht-*CHAH*-toh.*

Teach

Will you teach me _____?

Mi può insegnare _____?

mee PWOH *een-seh-*NYAH*-reh* _____?

Telegram

Where can I go to send a telegram?

Dove posso andare per spedire un telegramma?

DOH-*veh* POHSS-*soh* ahn-DAH-*reh pehr speh-*DEE-*reh oon teh-leh-*GRAHM-*mah?*

I want to send a telegram to _____ at _____.

Vorrei spedire un telegramma al _____ a _____.

*vohr-*RAY *speh-*DEE-*reh oon teh-leh-*GRAHM-*mah ahl* _____ *ah* _____.

What is the cost per word to _____?

Qual'è la tariffa per parola per _____?

*kwah-*LEH *lah tah-*REEF-*fah pehr pah-*ROH-*lah pehr* _____?

What is the night rate to _____?

Qual'è la tariffa notturna per _____?

*kwah-*LEH *lah tah-*REEF-*fah noht-*TOOR-*nah pehr* _____?

It is urgent; when will it be delivered to _____?

È urgente; quando verrà consegnato a _____?

*eh oor-*JENN-*teh; kwahn-doh vehr-*RAH *kohn-seh-*NYAH-*toh ah* _____?

I want to pay for the answer.

Vorrei spedirlo con risposta pagata.

*vohr-*RAY *speh-*DEER-*loh kohn ree-*SPOH-*stah pah-*GAH-*tah.*

Please read it back to me.

Me lo rilegga, per favore.

*meh loh ree-*LEHG-*gah, pehr fah-*VOH-*reh.*

Telephone

Where can I make a telephone call?

Dove posso fare una telefonata?

DOH-*veh* POHSS-*soh* FAH-*reh* OON-*ah teh-leh-foh-*NAH-*tah?*

Do I need tokens?
Mi occorrono dei gettoni?
*mee ohk-*KOHR*-roh-noh day jett-*TOH*-nee?*

Where can I get some tokens?
Dove posso ottenere dei gettoni?
DOH-*veh* POHSS-*soh oht-teh-*NEH*-reh day jett-*TOH*-nee?*

Will you telephone for me?
Per favore, vuol telefonare per me?
*pehr fah-*VOH*-reh, vwohl teh-leh-foh-*NAH*-reh pehr meh?*

A local call, number _____.
Una telefonata urbana, al numero _____.
*oon-ah teh-leh-foh-*NAH*-tah oor-*BAH*-nah, ahl* NOO-*meh-roh* _____.

Long distance operator, please.
Servizio interurbano, per favore.
*sehr-*VEE*-tsyoh een-tehr-oor-*BAH*-noh, pehr fah-*VOH*-reh.*

Overseas operator, please.
La comunicazione con l'estero, per favore.
*lah koh-moo-nee-kah-*TSYOH*-neh kohn* LEH-*steh-roh,
pehr fah-*VOH*-reh.*

How much is a call to _____?
Quanto costa una telefonata a _____?
KWAHN-*toh* KOH-*stah* OON-*ah teh-leh-foh-*NAH*-tah ah*
_____?

I want a number _____ in _____.
Vorrei il numero _____ a _____.
*vohr-*RAY *eel* NOO-*meh-roh* _____ *ah* _____.

Information, please.
Informazioni, per favore.
*een-fohr-mah-*TSYOH*-nee, pehr fah-*VOH*-reh.*

Operator, that's the wrong number.
Signorina, è il numero sbagliato.
*see-nyoh-*REE*-nah, eh eel* NOO-*meh-roh zbah-*LYAH*-toh.*

There is no answer.
Non risponde.
*nohn ree-*SPOHN*-deh.*

The line is busy.
La linea è occupata.
lah LEE-neh-ah eh ohk-koo-PAH-tah.

Hold the line, please.
Rimanga in linea, per favore.
ree-MAHN-gah een LEE-neh-ah, pehr fah-VOH-reh.

May I speak with _____?
Potrei parlare con _____?
poh-TRAY pahr-LAH-reh kohn _____?

When can I reach him.
Quando posso raggiungerlo?
KWAHN-doh POHSS-soh rahd-JOON-jehr-lo?

Where can I reach him?
Dove posso raggiungerlo?
DOH-veh POHSS-soh rahd-JOON-jehr-lo?

This is _____ speaking.
È _____ che parla.
EH _____ keh PAHR-la.

Please take a message for _____.
Per favore, prenda un messaggio per _____.
pehr fah-VOH-reh, PRENN-dah oon mess-SAHD-joh pehr

    _____.

Have him call _____ at number _____.
Lo preghi di chiamare _____ al numero _____.
loh PREH-ghee dee kyah-MAH-reh _____ ahl NOO-meh-
    roh _____.

I'll call back later.
Richiamerò
ree-kyah-meh-ROH.

Television

Is there a television in the room?
C'è la televisione in camera?
CHEH lah teh-leh-vee-ZYOH-neh een KAH-meh-rah?

Can I have a television in my room?
Potrei avere la televisione in camera?
poh-TRAY ah-VEH-reh lah teh-leh-vee-ZYOH-neh een KAH-
    meh-rah?

The television in my room isn't working.
La televisione in camera non funziona.
lah teh-leh-vee-ZYOH-neh een KAH-meh-rah nohn foon-
TSYOH-nah.

Tell

Please tell me when to get off.
Per favore, mi dica quando devo scendere.
pehr fah-VOH-reh, mee DEE-kah KWAHN-doh DEH-voh
SHENN-deh-reh.

Please tell me where to get off.
Per favore, mi dica dove devo scendere.
pehr fah-VOH-reh, mee DEE-kah DOH-veh DEH-voh
SHENN-deh-reh.

Temple – see Synagogue

Tennis

Let's play tennis.
Giochiamo a tennis.
joh-KYAH-moh ah TENN-neess.

Where can we play tennis?
Dove possiamo giocare a tennis?
DOH-veh pohss-see-AH-moh joh-KAH-reh ah TENN-neess.

Thank You

Thank you very much.
Grazie mille.
GRAH-tsyeh MEEL-leh.

No, thank you.
No, grazie.
noh, GRAH-tsyeh.

That

What is that?
Cos'è quello?
koh-SEH KWELL-loh?

What is that in _____?
Cos'è quello nel (nella) _____?
koh-SEH KWELL-loh nell (NELL-lah) ___?

That will be all.
Bene così.
BEH-*neh koh*-SEE.

Theater

I want to go to the theater tonight; what do you
   recommend?
Stasera vorrei andare a teatro; cosa mi raccomanda?
stah-SEH-*rah vohr*-RAY *ahn*-DAH-*reh ah teh*-AH-*troh;*
   KOH-*sah mee rahk koh*-MAHN-*dah?*

Can you direct me to the theater, please?
Per favore, mi può portare al teatro?
pehr fah-VOH-*reh, mee* PWOH *een-dee*-KAH-*reh eel teh*-
   AH-*troh?*

Can you take me to the theater, please?
Per favore, mi può portare al teatro?
pehr fah-VOH-*reh, mee* PWOH *pohr*-TAH-*reh ahl teh*-AH-
   troh?

Would you like to go to the theater with me?
Vorrebbe andare a teatro con me?
vohr-REBB-*beh ahn*-DAH-*reh ah teh*-AH-*troh kohn meh?*

Thermometer

Where is the thermometer?
Dov'è il termometro?
doh-veh eel tehr-MOH-*meh-troh?*

Things

Where are your things?
Dov'è la sua roba?
doh-VEH *lah soo-ah* ROH-*bah?*

These are my things.
Questa è roba mia.
KWEH-*stah eh* ROH-*bah* MEE-*ah.*

Thirsty

I am (I am not) thirsty.
Ho (non ho) sete.
oh (nohn oh) SEH-*teh.*

This

What is this in _____?
Cos'è questo nel (nella) _____?
koh-SEH KWEH-stoh nell (NELL-lah) _____?

What street is this?
Che strada è questa?
keh STRAH-dah eh KWEH-stah?

What city is this?
Che città è questa?
keh cheet-TAH eh KWEH-stah?

Is this the way?
È questa la via?
EH KWEH-stah lah VEE-ah?

Through

I want to check this through to _____.
Vorrei farlo proseguire fino a _____.
vohr-RAY FAHR-loh proh-seh-GWEE-reh FEE-noh ah

_____.

What city are we passing through?
Quale città stiamo attraversando?
KWAH-leh cheet-TAH stee-AH-moh aht-trah-vehr-SAHN-doh?

Ticket

A one way ticket to _____, please.
Un biglietto di andata per _____, per favore.
oon bee-LYETT-toh dee ahn-DAH-tah pehr _____, pehr fah-VOH-reh.

A round-trip ticket to _____, please.
Un biglietto di andata e ritorno per _____, per favore.
oon bee-LYETT-toh dee ahn-DAH-tah eh ree-TOHR-noh pehr _____, pehr fah-VOH-reh.

How much is a ticket to _____?
Quanto costa il biglietto per _____?
KWAHN-toh KOH-stah eel bee-LYETT-toh pehr _____?

Do you have any tickets for tonight?
Avete dei biglietti per stasera?
ah-VEH-teh day bee-LYETT-tee pehr stah-SEH-rah?

Where is the ticket window?
Dov'è lo sportello?
doh-VEH *loh spohr*-TELL-*loh?*

Tide

When is high tide?
Quando c'è alta marea?
KWAHN-*doh* CHEH *ahl-tah* mah-REH-*ah?*

When is low tide?
Quando c'è bassa marea?
KWAHN-*doh* CHEH BAHSS-*sah* mah-REH-*ah?*

Time

What time is it?
Che ora è?
keh OH-*rah* EH?

What time is breakfast (lunch, dinner)?
A che ora è servita la prima colazione (la colazione, il pranzo)?
ah keh OH-*rah eh sehr*-VEE-*tah lah* PREE-*mah koh-lah*-TSYOH-*neh (lah koh-lah*-TSYOH-*neh, eel* PRAHN-*dzoh)?*

Timetable

Please give me a timetable.
Per favore, mi dia l'orario.
pehr fah-VOH-*reh, mee* DEE-*ah loh*-RAH-*ryoh.*

Tip

Is the tip included?
La mancia è compresa?
lah MAHN-*chah* EH *kohm*-PREH-*sah?*

How much tip should I leave?
Che mancia dovrei lasciare?
keh MAHN-*chah doh*-VRAY *lah--*SHAH-*reh?*

Tired

I am (I am not) tired.
Sono (non sono) stanco (stanca).
SOH-*noh (nohn* SOH-*noh)* STAHNG-*koh (*STAHNG-*kah).*

Tissues

Please bring me some tissues.

Per favore, mi porti dei fazzoletti di carta.

pehr fah-VOH-reh, mee POHR-tee day faht-tsoh-LETT-tee dee kahr-tah.

Tobacco

Where can I buy some tobacco?

Dove posso comprare del tabacco?

DOH-*veh* POHSS-*soh kohm-*PRAH-*reh dell tah-*BAHK-*koh?*

Today

We are leaving today.

Partiamo oggi.

pahr-tee-AH-moh OHD-jee.

I need it today.

Mi occorre oggi.

mee ohk-KOHR-reh OHD-jee.

Toilet Paper

Please bring me some toilet paper.

Per favore, mi porti della carta igienica.

pehr fah-VOH-reh, mee POHR-tee DELL-lah KAHR-tah ee-JEH-nee-kah.

Token

Do I need a token?

Mi occorre un gettone?

mee ohk-KOHR-reh oon jett-TOH-neh?

Where can I buy some tokens?

Dove posso comprare dei gettoni?

DOH-*veh* POHSS-*soh kohm-*PRAH-*reh day jett-*TOH-*nee?*

Tomorrow

We are leaving tomorrow.

Partiamo domani.

pahr-tee-AH-moh doh-MAH-nee.

I would like a reservation for tomorrow.

Vorrei una prenotazione per domani.

vohr-RAY oon-ah preh-noh-tah-TSYOH-neh pehr doh-MAH-nee.

May I see you tomorrow?
Potrei vederla domani?
poh-TRAY *veh*-DEHR-*lah* *doh*-MAH-*nee?*

I need it tomorrow.
Mi occorre domani.
mee ohk KOHR-*reh* *doh*-MAH-*nee.*

Tonight

A room for tonight only, please.
Una camera solo per stanotte, per favore.
OON-*ah* KAH-*meh-rah* SOH-*loh* pehr *stah*-NOHT-*teh*, pehr
   fah-VOH-*reh.*

May I see you tonight?
Potrei vederla stasera?
poh-TRAY *veh*-DEHR-*lah* *stah*-SEH-*rah?*

Toothache – see also Dentist

I have a toothache.
Ho mal di denti.
oh mahl dee DENN-*tee.*

Tough

This meat is too tough; please take it back.
La carne è troppo dura; per favore, la riporti.
lah KAHR-*neh* EH TROHP-*poh* DOO-*rah; pehr fah*-VOH-*reh*,
   lah ree-POHR-*tee.*

Tour

We would like a tour of the city.
Vorremmo fare un giro della città.
vohr-REHM-*moh* FAH-*reh oon* JEE-*roh* DELL-*lah cheet-*
   TAH.

Can you arrange a tour for this morning (this
   afternoon, this evening)?
Può organizzare un giro per stamane (questo
   pomeriggio, stasera)?
PWOH *ohr-gah-need*-DZAH-*reh oon* JEE-*roh pehr sta-*
   MAH-*neh* (KWEH-*stoh poh-meh*-REED-*joh, stah-*SEH-
   rah)?

Where can we get a tour to _____?
Vorremmo visitare _____.
vohr-REHM-moh vee-zee-TAH-reh _____?

Do any tours leave from this hotel?
Ci sono dei giri che partono dell'albergo?
chee SOH-noh day JEE-ree keh PAHR-toh-noh dahl ahl-BEHR-goh?

When do they leave?
A che ora si parte?
ah keh OH-rah see PAHR-teh?

Tourist

A ticket in tourist class, please.
Un biglietto classe turistica, per favore.
oon bee-LYETT-toh KLAHSS-seh too-REE-stee-kah, pehr fah-VOH-reh.

Towels

Please bring me some towels.
Per favore, mi porti degli asciugamani.
pehr fah-VOH-reh, mee POHR-tee DEH-lyee ah-shoo-gah-MAH-nee.

Town

What town is this?
Che città è questa?
keh cheet-TAH eh KWEH-stah?

What is the next town?
Qual'è la prossima città?
kwah-LEH lah PROHSS-see-mah cheet-TAH?

May I have a ride to town?
Può portarmi in città?
PWOH pohr-TAHR-mee een cheet-TAH?

Track

What track does it leave from?
Da quale binario parte?
dah KWAH-leh bee-NAH-ryoh PAHR-teh?

Where is track _____?
Dov'è il binario _____?
doh-VEH eel bee-NAH-ryoh _____?

Trade
Will you trade me that for this?

Posso cambiare quello con questo?

POHSS-*soh kahm*-BYAH-*reh* KWELL-*loh kohn* KWEH-*stoh?*

Train
When does the train arrive (leave)?

A che ora arriva (parte) il treno?

ah keh OH-*rah ahr*-REE-*vah (*PAHR-*teh) eel* TREH-*noh?*

Does this train stop at _____?

Questo treno si ferma a _____?

KWEH-*stoh* TREH-*noh see* FEHR-*mah ah* _____?

Is this the train for _____?

È questo il treno per _____?

EH KWEH-*stoh eel* TREH-*noh pehr* _____?

Does the train have sleeping cars?

Il treno porta vagoni letto?

eel TREH-*noh* POHR-*tah vah*-GOH-*nee* LETT-*toh?*

Does the train have a dining car?

Il treno porta il vagone ristorante?

eel TREH-*noh* POHR-*tah eel vah*-GOH-*neh ree-stoh*-RAHN-*toh?*

Transfer
Where do I transfer?

Dove faccio la coincidenza?

DOH-*veh* FAHT-*choh lah koh-een-chee*-DENN-*tsah?*

Transportation
What kind of transportation is there to _____?

Quali mezzi di trasporto ci sono per _____?

KWAH-*lee* MEDD-*dzee dee trah*-SPOHR-*toh chee* SOH-*noh pehr* _____?

Travel Agency
Where is the nearest travel agency?

Dov'è la più vicina agenzia di viaggi?

doh-VEH *lah pyoo vee*-CHEE-*nah ah-jenn*-TSEE-*ah dee* VYAHD-*jee?*

Travelers Checks — see also Bank

I have travelers checks.

Ho degli assegni viaggiatori.

oh DEH-*lyee ahss*-SEH-*nyee vyahd-jah*-TOH-*ree.*

Do you accept travelers checks?

Accettate gli assegni viaggiatori?

aht-chett-TAH-*teh lyee ahss*-SEH-*nyee vyahd-jah*-TOH-
ree?

Do you cash travelers checks?

Incassate gli assegni viaggiatori?

een-kahss-SAH-*teh lyee ahss*-SEH-*nyee vyahd-jah*-TOH-
ree?

Trip

How long does the trip take?

Quanto dura la gita?

KWAHN-*toh* DOO-*rah lah* JEE-*tah?*

This is my (our) first (second, third) trip.

Questo è el mio (il nostro) primo (secondo, terzo)
viaggio.

KWEH-*ston eh eel* MEE-*oh (eel* NOH-*stroh)* PREE-*moh
(seh*-KOHN-*doh,* TEHR-*tsoh)* VYAHD-*joh.*

Trouble

What is the trouble?

Cos'è successo?

koh-SEH *soot*-CHESS-*soh?*

True

That is (that is not) true.

È (non è) vero.

EH *(nohn* EH) VEH-*roh.*

Trunk

That is my trunk.

Ecco il mio baule.

EHK-*koh eel* MEE-*oh bah*-OO-*leh.*

Please take my trunk to the hotel (to the airport, to
my room, to the railroad station).

Per favore, porti il mio baule all'albergo (all'aeroporto,
nella mia camera, alla stazione ferroviaria).

*pehr fah-VOH-reh, POHR-tee eel MEE-oh bah-OO-leh ahl
ahl-BEHR-goh (ahl-lah-eh-roh-POHR-toh, NELL-lah
MEE-ah KAH-meh-rah, AHL-la stah-TSYOH-neh fehr-
roh-VYAH-ree-ah).*

Try
May I try this on.

Posso provarlo (provarla)?

POHSS-soh proh-VAHR-loh (proh-VAHR-lah)?

Tub
I would like a bath with a tub.

Vorrei una stanza da bagno con vasca.

*vohr-RAY OON-ah STAHN-tsah dah BAH-nyoh kohn VAH-
skah.*

Turn
Where should I turn?

Dove devo voltare?

DOH-veh DEH-voh vohl-TAH-reh?

Typewriter
Where can I rent a typewriter?

Dove posso noleggiare una macchina da scrivere?

*DOH-veh POHSS-soh noh-ledd-JAH-reh OON-ah MAHK-
kee-nah dah SKREE-veh-reh?*

Umbrella
Where can I buy an umbrella?

Dove posso comprare un ombrello?

*DOH-veh POHSS-soh kohm-PRAH-reh oon ohm-BRELL-
loh?*

Undercooked
This is undercooked; please take it back.

Non è abbastanza cotto; lo riporti, per favore.

*nohn EH ahb-bah-STAHN-tsah KOHT-toh; loh ree-POHR-
tee, pehr fah-VOH-reh.*

Understand

I understand.
Capisco.
*kah-*PEE*-skoh.*

I don't understand.
Non capisco.
*nohn kah-*PEE*-skoh.*

Do you understand?
Ha capito?
*ah kah-*PEE*-toh?*

Undertow

Is there an undertow?
C'è corrente?
CHEH *kohr-*RENN*-teh?*

United States

I am from the United States.
Vengo dagli Stati Uniti.
VENN*-goh* DAH*-lyee* STAH*-tee oo-*NEE*-tee.*

Have you ever been to the United States?
Ha mai visitato gli Stati Uniti?
*ah my vee-zee-*TAH*-toh lyee* STAH*-tee oo-*NEE*-tee?*

University

Which is the best way to the university?
Qual'è la strada migliore per andare all'università?
*kwah-*LEH *lah* STRAH*-dah mee-*LYOH*-reh pehr ahn-*DAH*-*
   *reh ahl oo-nee-vehr-see-*TAH*?*

Upper

I want an upper berth.
Vorrei una cuccetta superiore.
*vohr-*RAY *oon-ah koo-*CHETT*-tah soo-peh-*RYOH*-reh.*

Urgent

It is urgent.
È urgente.
EH *oor-*JENN*-teh.*

Use

I don't know how to use this.
Non so come usarlo (usarla).
nohn soh KOH-meh oo-ZAHR-loh (oo-ZAHR-lah).

That is for my own use.
È per mio uso personale.
eh pehr MEE-oh OO-zoh pehr-soh-NAH-leh.

Vacancies

Have you any vacancies?
Avete delle camere disponibili?
ah-VEH-teh DELL-leh KAH-meh-reh dee-spoh-NEE-bee-lee?

Vacation

I am on my vacation.
Sono in vacanze.
SOH-noh een vah-KAHN-tse.

Vaccinate

I have been vaccinated for _____.
Sono stato vaccinato (vaccinata) contro il (la) _____.
SOH-noh STAH-toh vaht-chee-NAH-toh (vaht-chee-NAH-tah) KOHN-troh eel (lah) _____.

Vacuum

Please vacuum the rug.
Per favore, pulisca il tappeto con l'aspirapolvere.
pehr fah-VOH-reh poo-LEE-skah eel tahp-PEH-toh kohn lah-spee-rah-POHL-veh-reh.

Valid

For how long is the ticket valid?
Quanto a lungo è valido il biglietto?
KWAHN-toh ah LOONG-goh eh VAH-lee-doh eel bee-LYETT-toh?

Valuables

Please place my valuables in your safe.
Per favore, metta questi oggetti di valore nella cassaforte.
pehr fah-VOH-reh, METT-tah KWEH-stee ohd-JETT-tee dee vah-LOH-reh NELL-lah kahss-sah-FOHR-teh.

Vegetarian
I am a vegetarian.
Sono vegetariano.
SOH-*noh veh-jeh-tah*-RYAH-*noh*.

Vicinity
Are we in the vicinity of _____?
Siamo nelle vicinanze di _____?
see-AH-*moh* NELL-*leh vee-chee*-NAHN-*tseh dee* _____?

View
I want a room (a table) with a good view.
Vorrei una stanza (una tavola) con una bella vista.
vohr-RAY OON-*ah* STAHN-*tsah* (OON-*ah* TAH-*voh-lah*)
   kohn OON-*ah* BELL-*lah* VEE-*stah*.

Village
What village is this?
Che villaggio e questo?
keh veel-LAHD-*joh eh* KWEH-*stoh*?

How far is it to the next village?
Quant'è lontano il prossimo villaggio?
kwahn-TEH *lohn*-TAH-*noh eel* PROHSS-*see-moh veel*-
   LAHD-*joh*?

What is the next village?
Qual'è il prossimo villaggio?
kwah-LEH *eel* PROHSS-*see-moh veel*-LAHD-*joh*?

Visa
Do I need a visa for _____?
Mi occorre un visto per _____?
mee ohk-KOH-*reh oon* VEE-*stoh pehr* _____?

Here is my visa.
Ecco il mio visto.
EHK-*koh eel* MEE-*oh* VEE-*stoh*.

I don't have a visa.
Non ho il visto.
nohn oh eel VEE-*stoh*.

Visit

Come visit us when you are in the United States.
Ci venga a trovare quando visiterà gli Stati Uniti.
chee VEHN-*gah ah troh-*VAH-*reh* KWAHN-*doh vee-zee-teh-*
RAH *lyee* STAH-*tee* oo-NEE-*tee.*

This is our first visit.
È la nostra prima visita.
EH *lah* NOH-*stra* PREE-*mah* VEE-*zee-tah.*

We are visiting _____.
Stiamo visitando _____.
*stee-*AH-*moh vee-zee-*TAHN-*doh* _____.

Visitors

Can visitors come on board?
I visitatori possono salire a bordo?
*ee vee-zee-tah-*TOH-*ree* POHSS-*soh-noh sah-*LEE-*reh ah*
BOHR-*doh?*

Voltage

What is the voltage?
Qual'è il voltaggio?
*kwah-*LEH *eel vohl-*TAHD-*joh?*

Wait

Wait a moment!
Aspetti un momento!
*ah-*SPETT-*tee oon moh-*MENN-*toh!*

How long must I wait?
Quanto devo aspettare?
KWAHN-*toh* DEH-*voh ah-spett-*TAH-*reh?*

Please wait for me.
Per favore, mi aspetti.
*pehr fah-*VOH-*reh, mee ah-*SPETT-*tee.*

Waiter (Waitress)

Are you our waiter (our waitress)?
È lei il nostro cameriere (la nostra cameriera)?
EH *lay eel* NOH-*stroh kah-meh-*RYEH-*reh (lah noh-strah*
*kah-meh-*RYEH-*rah)?*

Waiting

Where is the waiting room?
Dov'è la sala d'aspetto?
doh-VEH *lah* SAH-*lah dah*-SPETT-*toh?*

Are you waiting for someone?
Aspetta qualcuno?
ah-SPETT-*tah kwahl*-KOO-*noh?*

Wake

Please wake me at _____.
Per favore, mi sveglia alle _____.
pehr fah-VOH-*reh,* mee ZVEH-*lyah* AHL-*leh* _____.

Walk

Let's walk to _____.
Passeggiamo fino a _____.
pahss-sedd-JAH-*moh* FEE-*noh ah* _____.

Is it an easy walk to _____.
È una passeggiata facile fino a _____.
eh oon-ah pahss-sedd-JAH-*tah* FAH-*chee-leh* FEE-*noh ah*

_____.

Want

I want _____.
Vorrei _____.
vohr-RAY _____.

Warm

It is not warm enough.
Non è abbastanza caldo (calda).
nohn EH *ahb-bah*-STAHN-*tsah* KAHL-*doh* (KAHL-*dah*).

I am warm.
Sto bene.
stoh BEH-*neh.*

Wash – see Laundry or Automobile

Watch

Watch this!
Guardi!
GWAR-*dee!*

Watch out!
Attenzione!
*aht-tenn-*TSYOH-*neh!*

Where can I find a watch repair shop?
Dove posso trovare un orologiaio?
DOH-*veh* POHSS-*soh troh-*VAH-*reh oon oh-roh-loh-*JAH-
yoh?

What do you charge to clean and regulate a watch?
Quanto costa far pulire e regolare un orologio?
KWAHN-*toh* KOH-*stah fahr poo-*LEE-*reh eh reh-goh-*
LAH-*reh oon oh-roh-*LOH-*joh?*

My watch is running fast (slow).
Il mio orologio va avanti (in ritardo).
eel MEE-*oh oh-roh-*LOH-*joh vah ah-*VAHN-*tee (een ree-*
TAHR-*doh).*

My watch is broken.
Il mio orologio e guasto.
eel MEE-*oh oh-roh-*LOH-*joh eh* GWAH-*stoh.*

Water
Please bring some water.
Per favore, mi porti dell'acqua.
*pehr fah-*VOH-*reh mee* POHR-*tee dell-*LAH-*kwah.*

There is no hot water.
Non c'è acqua calda.
nohn CHEH AH-*kwah* KAHL-*dah.*

Water-ski
I don't know how to water-ski.
Non so fare lo sci acquatico.
nohn soh FAH-*reh loh shee ah-*KWAH-*tee-koh.*

Where can I go water-skiing?
Dove posso fare dello sci acquatico?
DOH-*veh* POHSS-*soh* FAH-*reh* DELL-*loh shee ah-*KWAH-
tee-koh?

Way

Which way is _____?
Qual'è la via per _____?
*kwah-*LEH *lah* VEE-*ah pehr* _____?

Is this the way to _____?
È questa la via per _____?
eh KWEH-*stah lah* VEE-*ah pehr* _____?

Which is the best way to _____?
Qual'è la migliore via per _____?
*kwah-*LEH *lah mee-*LYOH-*reh* VEE-*ah pehr* _____?

Can I go by way of _____?
Posso andarci via _____?
POHSS-*soh ahn-*DAHR-*chee* VEE-*ah* _____?

Wear

What should I wear?
Che abito dovrei portare?
keh AH-*bee-toh doh-*VRAY *pohr-*TAH-*reh?*

Weather

What is the weather like in _____.
Che tempo fa in _____.
keh TEMM-*poh fah een* _____.

Week

I want it for one week (for two weeks).
Mi occorre per una settimana (per due settimane).
*mee ohk-*KOHR-*reh pehr* OON-*ah sett-tee-*MAH-*nah (pehr*
DOO-*eh sett-tee-*MAH-*neh).*

Weight

How much weight is allowed?
Che peso è permesso?
keh PEH-*soh eh pehr-*MESS-*soh?*

Is my baggage overweight?
Ho soprapeso?
*oh soh-prah-*PEH-*soh?*

What is the rate for excess weight?
Qual'è la tariffa per soprapeso?
*kwah-*LEH *lah tah-*REEF-*fah pehr soh-prah-*PEH-*soh?*

Well

I want my meat well done.
Vorrei la carne ben cotta.
*vohr-*RAY *lah* KAHR-*neh ben* KOHT-*tah.*

This is too well done; please take it back.
È troppo cotto; lo riporti, per favore.
eh TROHP-*poh* KOHT-*toh;* *loh ree-*POHR-*tee, pehr fah-*
  VOH-*reh.*

I don't feel well.
Non mi sento bene.
nohn mee SENN-*toh* BEH-*neh.*

What

What do you want?
Cosa desidera?
KOH-*sah deh-*SEE-*deh-rah.*

What is it?
Cos'è?
*koh-*SEH?

What did you say?
Cosa ha detto?
KOH-*sah ah* DETT-*toh?*

What is this (that) in _____?
Cos'è questo (quello) nel (nella, nell', nello) _____?
*koh-*SEH KWEH-*stoh (*KWELL-*loh) nell (*NELL-*lah, nell,*
  NELL-*loh)* _____?

When

When will we arrive?
Quando arriveremo?
KWAHN-*doh ahr-ree-veh-*REH-*moh?*

When do you open (close)?
A che ora si aprono (si chiudono)?
ah keh OH-*rah see* AH-*proh-noh (see* KYOO-*doh-noh)?*

When is breakfast (lunch) served?
A che ora è servita la prima colazione (la colazione)?
a keh OH-*rah eh sehr-*VEE-*tah lah* PREE-*mah koh-lah-*
  TSYOH-*neh (lah koh-lah-*TSYOH-*neh)?*

When is dinner served?
A che ora è servito il pranzo?
ah keh OH-*rah eh sehr-*VEE-*toh eel* PRAHN-*dzoh?*

Please tell me when to get off.
Per favore, mi dica quando devo scendere.
*pehr fah-*VOH-*reh, mee* DEE-*kah* KWAHN-*doh* DEH-*voh*
   SHENN-*deh-reh.*

Where

Where is _____?
Dov'è _____?
*doh-*VEH _____?

Where can I find (buy) _____?
Dove posso trovare (comprare) _____?
DOH-*veh* POHSS-*soh* troh-VAH-*reh (kohm-*PRAH-*reh)*
   _____?

Where are we?
Dove siamo?
DOH-*veh* see-AH-*moh?*

Please tell me where to get off.
Per favore, mi dica dove devo scendere.
*pehr fah-*VOH-*reh mee* DEE-*kah* DOH-*veh* DEH-*voh* SHENN-*deh-reh.*

Widow

I am a widow.
Sono vedova.
soh-noh VEH-*doh-vah.*

Widower

I am a widower.
Sono vedovo.
soh-noh VEH-*doh-voh.*

Window

Where is the ticket window?
Dov'è lo sportello?
*doh-*VEH *loh spohr-*TELL-*loh?*

A seat (a table) by the window, please.
Un posto (una tavola) vicino alla finestra, per favore.
oon POH-*stoh* (OON-*ah* TAH-*voh-lah) vee-*CHEE-*noh* AHL-*lah fee-*NEH-*strah, pehr fah-*VOH-*reh.*

Do you mind if I open (close) the window?
Le dispiace se apro (chiudo) la finestra?
*leh dee-*SPYAH*-cheh seh* AH*-proh (*KYOO*-doh) lah fee-*
NEH*-strah?*

Wine

May I have the wine list, please.
La lista dei vini, per favore.
lah LEE*-stah day* VEE*-nee, pehr fah-*VOH*-reh.*

Which wine do you recommend?
Quale vino mi raccomanda?
KWAH*-leh* VEE*-noh mee rahk-koh-*MAHN*-dah?*

A glass (a half-bottle, a bottle) of red (white) table
wine, please.
Un bicchiere (mezza bottiglia, una bottiglia) di vino
rosso (bianco) da tavola, per favore.
*oon beek-*KYEH*-reh (*MEDD*-zah boht-*TEE*-lyah,* OON*-ah
boht-*TEE*-lyah) dee* VEE*-noh* ROHSS*-soh (*BYAHNG*-koh)
dah* TAH*-voh-lah, pehr fah-*VOH*-reh.*

Woman

Who is that woman?
Chi è quella signora?
kee EH KWELL*-lah see-*NYOH*-rah.*

Wood

May I have some wood for the fireplace?
Potrei avere della legna per il camino?
*poh-*TRAY *ah-*VEH*-reh* DELL*-lah* LEH*-nyah pehr eel kah-*
MEE*-noh?*

Word

What is this word?
Cos'è questa parola?
*koh-*SEH KWEH*-stah pah-*ROH*-lah?*

Work

Where do you work?
Dove lavora?
DOH*-veh lah-*VOH*-rah?*

This does not work; can you fix it?
Questo non funziona; me lo può riparare?
KWEH-*stoh nohn foon*-TSYOH-*nah; meh loh* PWOH *ree-pah*-RAH-*reh?*

Worth
What is it worth?
Quanto vale?
KWAHN-*toh* VAH-*leh?*

It is worthless.
Non vale nulla.
nohn VAH-*leh* NOOL-*lah.*

Wrap
Please wrap this carefully.
Per favore, lo avvolga con cura.
pehr fah-VOH-*reh, loh ahv*-VOHL-*gah kohn* KOO-*rah.*

Write
Write it down, please.
Me lo scriva, per favore.
meh loh SKREE-*vah, pehr fah*-VOH-*reh.*

How do you write _____ in _____?
Come si scrive _____ in _____?
KOH-*meh see* SKREE-*veh* _____ *een* _____?

Let's write to each other.
Scriviamoci.
skree-VYAH-*moh-chee.*

Writing Paper
I need some writing paper.
Mi occorre della carta da lettere.
mee ohk-KOHR-*reh* DELL-*lah* KAHR-*tah dah* LETT-*teh-reh.*

Wrong

What is wrong?

Cosa c'è?

KOH-*sah* CHEH?

Is anything wrong?

C'è qualcosa che non va?

CHEH *kwahl*-KOH-*sah keh nohn* VAH?

Yours

Is that yours?

È suo (sua)?

eh SOO-*oh (*SOO-*ah)?*

That is yours

Quello è suo (sua),

KWELL-*loh* EH SOO-*oh (*SOO-*ah),*

Youth Hostel – see Hostel

Zoo

Can you direct me to the zoo?

Mi può indicare la strada per il giardino zoologico?

mee PWOH *een-dee-*KAH-*reh lah* STRAH-*dah pehr eel jahr-*DEE-*noh dzoh-oh-*LOH-*jee-koh?*

Can you take me to the zoo?

Mi può portare al giardino zoologico?

mee PWOH *pohr-*TAH-*reh ahl jahr-*DEE-*noh dzoh-oh-*LOH-*jee-koh?*

SIGNS AND NOTICES

ITALIAN	ENGLISH
ACCELERATO	LOCAL
ACCENDERE LA LUCE	TURN ON THE LIGHT
AL PIANO SUPERIORE	UPSTAIRS
ALT	STOP
APERTO	OPEN
ATTENZIONE	ATTENTION; CAUTION; DRIVE CAREFULLY
ATTENZIONE AI TRENI	RAILROAD CROSSING
ATTENZIONE AL CANE	BEWARE OF DOG
AVANTI	GO
CHIUSO	CLOSED
CUNETTA	DIP
CURVA	CURVE
CURVA E CONTRO-CURVA	DOUBLE CURVE
CURVA PERICOLOSA	DANGEROUS CURVE
CURVA STRETTA	SHARP TURN
DEVIAZIONE	DETOUR
DISCESA PERICO-LOSA	STEEP GRADE
DIVIETO DI SOR-PASSO	NO PASSING
DIVIETO DI SOSTA	NO PARKING
DIVIETO DI PAR-CHEGGIO	NO PARKING
DONNE	WOMEN
DOPPIA CURVA	DOUBLE CURVE
ENTRATA	ENTRANCE
È PROIBITO CALPES-TARE L'ERBA	KEEP OFF THE GRASS
È PROIBITO ENTRARE	DO NOT ENTER

ITALIAN	ENGLISH
FILI AD ALTA TENSIONE	HIGH TENSION LINES
GIÙ	DOWN
GUASTO	OUT OF ORDER
IL GABINETTO PER DONNE	LADIES' ROOM
IL GABINETTO PER UOMINI	MEN'S ROOM
INCROCIO	CROSSROADS
_____ KILOMETRI ALL'ORA	_____ KILOMETERS PER HOUR
LAVORI IN CORSO	ROAD REPAIRS
LAVATOIO	LAVATORY
L'UFFICIO DEGLI OGGETTI SMARRITI	LOST AND FOUND
PARCHEGGIO	PARKING
PASSAGGERI	PASSENGERS
PASSAGGIO A LIVELLO	GRADE CROSSING
PERICOLO	DANGER
PROPRIETÀ PRIVATA	PRIVATE PROPERTY
RALLENTARE	SLOW
RITARATA	LAVATORY
SALIRE	UP
SALITA RAPIDA	STEEP GRADE
SCUOLA	SCHOOL
SENSO OBBLIGATORIO A DESTRA	KEEP RIGHT
SENSO OBBLIGATORIO A SINISTRA	KEEP LEFT

ITALIAN	ENGLISH
SENSO OBBLIGATO-RIO DIRITTO	NO TURN; NO U-TURN
SENSO UNICO	ONE WAY
SIGNORE	WOMEN
SIGNORI	MEN
SPEGNERE LA LUCE	TURN OFF THE LIGHT
SPINGERE	PUSH
STRADA SERPEG-GIANTE	WINDING ROAD
STRADA STRETTA	NARROW ROAD
SU	UP
SUONARE IL CLACSON	SOUND HORN
TENERE LA DESTRA	KEEP RIGHT
TENERE LA SINISTRA	KEEP LEFT
TIRARE	PULL
TOELETTE	LAVATORY
TRENO RAPIDO	EXPRESS
USCITA	EXIT
VELOCITÀ MASSIMA	MAXIMUM SPEED
VELOCITÀ RIDOTTA	SLOW
VIAGGIATORI	PASSENGERS
VICOLO CIECO	DEAD END
VIETATO FUMARE	NO SMOKING
VIETATO IL TRANSITO	NO THOROUGHFARE
VIETATO L'ENTRATA	KEEP OUT
VIETATO SPUTARE	NO SPITTING
VIETATO VOLTARE A DESTRA	NO RIGHT TURN
VIETATO VOLTARE A SINISTRA	NO LEFT TURN

ENGLISH	ITALIAN	PRONUNCIATION
a (an)	un, uno, una, un'	OON, OO-*noh*, OO-*nah*, OON
able (capable)	capace	*kah*-PAH-*cheh*
aboard	a bordo	*ah* BOHR-*doh*
about (concerning)	circa	CHEER-*kah*
abroad (in foreign land)	all'estero	*ahl*-LEH-*steh-roh*
absence	assenza, f.	*ahss*-SENN-*tsah*
absent	assente	*ahss*-SENN-*teh*
accent (speech)	accento, m.	*aht*-CHENN-*toh*
accept, to	accettare	*aht*-*chett*-TAH-*reh*
accident (mishap)	accidente, m.	*aht*-*chee*-DENN-*teh*
accommodate (have room for), to	accomodare	*ahk*-*koh*-*moh*-DAH-*reh*
accompany (go along with), to	accompagnare	*ahk*-*kohm*-*pah*-NYAH-*reh*
accord (agreement)	accordo, m.	*ahk*-KOHR-*doh*
according to (in accordance with)	secondo	*seh* KOHN *doh*
account (bank account)	conto, m.	KOHN-*toh*
accountant	contabile, m.	*kohn*-TAH-*bee-leh*
accurate	accurato	*ahk*-*koo*-RAH-*toh*
accuse, to	accusare	*ahk*-*koo*-ZAH-*reh*
accustom oneself, to	abituarsi	*ah*-*bee*-TWAHR-*see*
ache	dolore, m.	*doh*-LOH-*reh*
ache, to	dolere	*doh*-LEH-*reh*
acknowledge (note receipt of), to	accusare ricevuta (di)	*ahk*-*koo*-ZAH-*reh* *ree*-*cheh*-VOO-*tah (dee)*
acquaintance (person known)	conoscenza, f.	*koh*-*noh*-SHENN-*tsah*
across (beyond)	al di là di	*ahl dee* LAH *dee*

ENGLISH	ITALIAN	PRONUNCIATION
across (to the other side)	attraverso	*aht-trah-*VEHR*-soh*
act (deed)	atto, m.	AHT*-toh*
act (dramatic unit)	atto, m.	AHT*-toh*
act (behave), to	comportarsi	*kohm-pohr-*TAHR*-see*
act (do), to	agire	*ah-*JEE*-reh*
action (deed)	azione, f.	*ah-*TSYOH*-neh*
actor (player)	attore, m.	*aht-*TOH*-reh*
actress	attrice, f.	*aht-*TREE*-cheh*
add (include), to	aggiungere	*ahd-*JOON*-jeh-reh*
address (speech)	discorso, m.	*dee-*SKOHR*-soh*
addressee	destinatario, m.	*deh-stee-nah-*TAH*-ryoh*
admire, to	ammirare	*ahm-mee-*RAH*-reh*
admission (right to enter)	ammissione, f.	*ahm-mees-*SYOH*-neh*
advance (go forward), to	avanzare	*ah-vahn-*TSAH*-reh*
adventure	avventura, f.	*ahv-venn-*TOO*-rah*
advertise (give notice of), to	annunziare	*ahn-noon-*TSYAH*-reh*
advertisement	annunzio, m.	*ahn-*NOON*-tsyoh*
advice	consiglio, m.	*kohn-*SEE*-lyoh*
aerial (antenna)	antenna, f.	*ahn-*TENN*-nah*
affect (influence), to	influenzare	*een-floo-enn-*TSAH*-reh*
afford (have the means), to	permettersi	*pehr-*METT*-tehr-see*
afraid	impaurito	*eem-pah-oo-*REE*-toh*
after (conj.)	dopo che	DOH*-poh keh*
after (prep.)	dopo	DOH*-poh*
afternoon	pomeriggio, m.	*poh-meh-*REED*-joh*
afterward (later)	dopo	DOH*-poh*

ENGLISH	ITALIAN	PRONUNCIATION
again	di nuovo	*dee* NWOH-*voh*
against	contro	KOHN-*troh*
age (accumulated years)	età f.	*eh*-TAH
agent (representative)	rappresentante, m., f.	*rahp-preh-zenn-*TAHN-*teh*
agree (assent), to	acconsentire	*ahk-kohn-senn-*TEE-*reh*
agreeable (pleasing)	gradevole	*grah*-DEH-*voh-leh*
agreement (mutual understanding)	accordo, m.	*ahk*-KOHR-*doh*
agree with, to	essere d'accordo	ESS-*seh-reh dah-*KOHR-*doh*
ahead (forward)	avanti	*ah*-VAHN-*tee*
ahead (in front)	davanti	*dah*-VAHN-*tee*
aim (purpose)	scopo, m.	SKOH-*poh*
air (atmosphere)	aria, f.	AH-*ryah*
air conditioning	aria condizionata, f.	*ah-ryah kohn-dee-tsyoh-*NAH-*tah*
air mail	Posta Aerea, f.	POH-*stah an-*EH-*rah ah*
airplane	aeroplano, m.	*ah-eh-roh-*PLAH-*noh*
airport	aeroporto, m.	*ah-eh-roh-*POHR-*toh*
aisle (passageway)	passaggio, m.	*pahss-*SAHD-*joh*
alcohol	alcool, m.	AHL-*kohl*
alive	vivo	VEE-*voh*
all (entirely, adv.)	tutto	TOOT-*toh*
all (every, adj.)	ogni	OH-*nyee*
all (everything, n.)	tutto, m.	TOOT-*toh*
all (hole of, adj.)	tutto	TOOT-*toh*

ENGLISH	ITALIAN	PRONUNCIATION
allergy	allergia, f.	*ahl-lehr-*JEE-*ah*
allow (permit), to	permettere	*pehr-*METT-*teh-reh*
almost	quasi	KWAH-*see*
alone	solo	SOH-*loh*
aloud	ad alta voce	*ahd* AHL-*tah* VOH-*cheh*
already	già	JAH
also	anche	AHNG-*keh*
although	benchè	*beng-*KEH
altogether (entirely)	interamente	*een-teh-rah-*MENN-*teh*
always	sempre	SEMM-*preh*
ambassador	ambasciatore, m.	*ahm-bah-shah-*TOH-*reh*
ambulance	ambulanza, f.	*ahm-boo-*LAHN-*tsah*
America	America, f.	*ah-*MEH-*ree-kah*
American (adj.)	americano	*ah-meh-ree-*KAH-*noh*
among	fra	FRAH
amount	somma, f.	SOHM-*mah*
amount to, to	ammontare a	*ahm-mohn-*TAH-*reh ah*
amuse, to	divertire	*dee-vehr-*TEE-*reh*
amusement	divertimento, m.	*dee-vehr-tee-*MENN-*toh*
ancestor	antenato, m.	*ahn-teh-*NAH-*toh*
anchor	ancora, f.	AHNG-*koh-rah*
ancient	antico	*ahn-*TEE-*koh*
angry	adirato	*ah-dee-*RAH-*toh*
animal	animale, m.	*ah-nee-*MAH-*leh*
ankle	caviglia, f.	*kah-*VEE-*lyah*
anniversary	anniversario, m.	*ahn-nee-vehr-*SAH-*ryoh*
announce, to	annunziare	*ahn-noon-*TSYAH-*reh*

ENGLISH	ITALIAN	PRONUNCIATION
announcement	annunzio, m.	*ahn*-NOON-*tsyoh*
annoy (irk), to	annoiare	*ahn-noh*-YAH-*reh*
annual	annuale	*ahn*-NWAH-*leh*
another (different one, pron.)	un altro	*oon* AHL-*troh*
another (one more, adj.)	un altro	*oon* AHL-*troh*
answer	risposta, f.	*ree*-SPOH-*stah*
answer (address reply to), to	rispondere a	*ree*-SPOHN-*deh-reh ah*
anticipate (expect), to	aspettarsi	*ah-spett*-TAHR-*see*
antiquity (ancientness)	antichità, f.	*ahn-tee-kee*-TAH
anxious (uneasy)	ansioso	*ahn*-SYOH-*soh*
any (any at all, adj.)	qualsiasi	*kwahl*-SEE-*ah-see*
any (any one, adj.)	qualsiasi	*kwahl*-SEE-*ah-see*
anybody (anybody whosoever)	chiunque	*kee*-OONG-*kweh*
anybody (not . . . anybody	nessuno	*ness*-SOO-*noh*
anyhow (in any case)	in ogni caso	*een* OH-*nyee* KAH-*soh*
anything (anything whatever)	qualunque cosa	*kwah*-LOONG-*kweh* KOH-*sah*
apartment	appartamento, m.	*ahp-pahr-tah*-MENN *toh*
apologize, to	scusarsi	*skoo*-ZAHR-*see*
apparent (obvious)	evidente	*eh-vee*-DENN-*teh*
appeal to (entreat), to	supplicare	*soop-plee*-KAH-*reh*
appear (seem), to	sembrare	*semm*-BRAH-*reh*
appearance (aspect)	apparenza, f.	*ahp-pah*-RENN-*tsah*
appendicitis	appendicite, f.	*ahp-penn-dee*-CHEE-*teh*

ENGLISH	ITALIAN	PRONUNCIATION
appetite	appetito, m.	*ahp-peh-*TEE-*toh*
apple	mela, f.	MEH-*lah*
application (request)	applicazione, f.	*ahp-plee-kah-*TSYOH-*neh*
appointment (meeting)	appuntamento, m.	*ahp-poon-tah-*MENN-*toh*
appraisal	valutazione, f.	*vah-loo-tah-*TSYOH-*neh*
appreciate (be grateful for), to	gradire	*grah-*DEE-*reh*
approach (come near to), to	avvicinarsi a	*ahv-vee-chee-*NAHR-*see ah*
apricot	albicocca, f.	*ahl-bee-*KOHK-*kah*
arch (curved structure)	arco, m.	AHR-*koh*
area (extent)	area, f.	AH-*reh-ah*
area (region)	regione, f.	*reh-*JOH-*neh*
argue (maintain), to	sostenere	*soh-steh-*NEH-*reh*
argument (dispute)	disputa, f.	DEE-*spoo-tah*
arm	braccio, m.	BRAHT-*choh*
arrange (plan), to	ordinare	*ohr-dee-*NAH-*reh*
arrangement (order)	disposizione, f.	*dee-spoh-zee-*TSYOH-*neh*
arrest (take into custody), to	arrestare	*ahr-reh-*STAH-*reh*
arrival	arrivo, m.	*ahr-*REE-*voh*
arrive, to	arrivare	*ahr-ree-*VAH-*reh*
art	arte, f.	AHR-*teh*
arthritis	artrite, f.	*ahr-*TREE-*teh*
article (literary composition)	articolo, m.	*ahr-*TEE-*koh-loh*
article (thing)	oggetto, m.	*ohd-*JETT-*toh*
artificial (synthetic)	artificiale	*ahr-tee-fee-*CHAH-*leh*
artist	artista, m., f.	*ahr-*TEE-*stah*
as (in the same way, conj.)	come	KOH-*meh*

ENGLISH	ITALIAN	PRONUNCIATION
ascend (go upward along), to	ascendere	*ah*-SHENN-*deh-reh*
ashamed (mortified)	vergognoso	*vehr-goh*-NYOH-*soh*
ash tray	portacenere, m.	*pohr-tah*-CHEH-*neh-reh*
ask (put question to), to	domandare	*doh-mahn-*DAH-*reh*
ask (request), to	chiedere	KYEH-*deh-reh*
ask about, to	interrogare circa	*een-teh-roh-*GAH-*reh* CHEER-*kah*
asleep (sleeping)	addormentato	*ahd-dohr-menn-*TAH-*toh*
asparagus	asparago, m.	*ah-*SPAH-*rah-goh*
aspirin	aspirina, f.	*ah-spee-*REE-*nah*
assent, to	assentire	*ahss-senn-*TEE-*reh*
assist, to	assistere	*ahss-*SEE-*steh-reh*
assistance	assistenza, f.	*ahss-see-*STENN-*tsah*
assistant	assistente, m., f.	*ahss-see-*STENN-*teh*
association (body of persons)	associazione, f.	*ahss-soh-chah-*TS-YOH-*neh*
assume (take for granted), to	assumere	*ahss-*SOO-*meh-reh*
astonish, to	stupire	*stoo-*PEE-*reh*
at (in)	in	EEN
at (near)	presso	PRESS-*soh*
at (on)	su	SOO
Athens	Atene, f.	*ah-*TEH-*neh*
athlete	atleta, m., f.	*aht-*LEH-*tah*
atmosphere (air)	atmosfera, f.	*aht-moh-*SFEH-*rah*
attach (join), to	attaccare	*aht-tahk-*KAH-*reh*
attack (assault physically), to	aggredire	*ahg-greh-*DEE-*reh*
attempt, to	tentare	*tenn-*TAH-*reh*
attendance (presence)	assistenza, f.	*ahss-see-*STENN-*tsah*

ENGLISH	ITALIAN	PRONUNCIATION
attention (heed)	attenzione, f.	*aht-tenn-*TSYOH-*neh*
attorney	avvocato, m.	*ahv-voh-*KAH-*toh*
attractive (pleasing)	attraente	*aht-trah-*ENN-*teh*
auction (sale)	vendita all'asta, f.	VENN-*dee-tah* *ahl-*LAH-*stah*
audience	uditorio, m.	*oo-dee-*TOH-*ryoh*
auditorium	auditorio, m.	*ow-dee-*TOH-*ryoh*
aunt	zia, f.	TSEE-*ah*
Austria	Austria, f.	OW-*stryah*
Austrian (adj.)	austriaco	*ow-*STREE-*ah-koh*
author	autore, m.	*ow-*TOH-*reh*
authority (power)	autorità, f.	*ow-toh-ree-*TAH
authorization	autorizzazione, f.	*ow-toh-reed-dzah-*TSYOH-*neh*
automobile	automobile, f.	*ow-toh-*MOH-*bee-leh*
autumn	autunno, m.	*ow-*TOON-*noh*
available	disponibile	*dee-spoh-*NEE-*bee-leh*
avenue (street)	corso, m.	KORH-*soh*
average (ordinary, adj.)	mediocre	*meh-*DYOH-*kreh*
avert (prevent), to	impedire	*eem-peh-*DEE-*reh*
aviator	aviatore, m.	*ah-vyah-*TOH-*reh*
avoid, to	evitare	*eh-vee-*TAH-*reh*
await, to	attendere	*aht-*TENN-*deh-reh*
awful	terribile	*tehr-*REE-*bee-leh*
awkward	goffo	GOHF-*foh*
baby	bambino, m.	*bahm-*BEE-*noh*
back (rearward, adv.)	indietro	*een-*DYEH-*troh*
back (reverse side)	dorso, m.	DOHR-*soh*
bacon	carnesecca, f.	*kahr-neh-*SEKK-*kah*

ENGLISH	ITALIAN	PRONUNCIATION
bad, worse, worst	cattivo, peggiore, (il) peggiore	*kaht-*TEE-*voh, pedd-*JOH-*reh, (eel) pedd-*JOH-*reh*
bag (purse)	borsa, f.	BOHR-*sah*
bag (sack)	sacco, m.	SAHK-*koh*
baggage (luggage)	bagaglio, m.	*bah-*GAH-*lyoh*
bake (be cooking), to	cuocere al forno	KWOH-*cheh-reh ahl* FOHR-*noh*
baker	panettiere, m.	*pah-nett-*TYEH-*reh*
bald (hairless)	calvo	KAHL-*voh*
ball-point pen	penna a sfera, f.	PENN-*neh ah* SFEH-*rah*
banana	banana, f.	*bah-*NAH-*nah*
band (ribbon)	nastro, m.	NAH-*stroh*
bandage	benda, f.	BENN-*dah*
bank (shore)	riva, f.	REE-*vah*
bank (treasury)	banca, f.	BAHN-*kah*
banker	banchiere, m.	*bahng-*KYEH-*reh*
bankruptcy	fallimento, m.	*fahl-lee-*MENN-*toh*
banner	bandiera, f.	*bahn-*DYEH-*rah*
bar (barroom)	bar, m.	*bahr*
barber	barbiere, m.	*bahr-*BYEH-*reh*
bare (nude)	nudo	NOO-*doh*
bargain (advantageous purchase)	occasione, f.	*ohk-kah-*ZYOH-*neh*
bargain (agreement)	patto, m.	PAHT-*toh*
bargain (negotiate), to	contrattare	*kohn-traht-*TAH-*reh*
barrier	barriera, f.	*bahr-*RYEH-*rah*
baseball	giuoco a palla, m.	JWOH-*koh ah* PAHL-*lah*
basement	sottosuolo	*soht-toh-*SWOH-*loh*
bashful	ritroso	*ree-*TROH-*soh*

ENGLISH	ITALIAN	PRONUNCIATION
basket	paniere, m.	*pah-*NYEH-*reh*
bathe (take a bath), to	prendere un bagno	PRENN-*deh-reh oon* BAH-*nyoh*
bathing suit	costume da bagno, m.	*koh-*STOO-*meh dah* BAH-*nyoh*
bathroom	stanza da bagno, f.	STAHN-*tsah dah* BAH-*nyoh*
bathtub	vasca da bagno, f.	VAH-*skah dah* BAH-*nyoh*
battery (primary cell)	pila elettrica, f.	PEE-*lah eh-*LETT-*tree-kah*
battle	battaglia, f.	*baht-*TAH-*lyah*
Bavaria	Baviera, f.	*bah-*VYEH-*rah*
bay (inlet)	baia, f.	BAH-*yah*
be, to	essere	ESS-*seh-reh*
beach (strand)	spiaggia, f.	SPYAHD-*jah*
bead (jewelry)	perla, f.	PEHR-*lah*
beam (ray)	raggio, m.	RAHD-*joh*
bean (string bean)	fagiolino, m.	*fah-joh-*LEE-*noh*
bear (carry), to	portare	*pohr-*TAH-*reh*
beard	barba, f.	BAHR-*bah*
beautiful	bello	BELL-*loh*
beauty	bellezza, f.	*bell-*LETT-*tsah*
because (conj.)	perchè	*pehr-*KEH
because of	a causa di	*ah* KOW-*zah dee*
become, to	diventare	*dee-venn-*TAH-*reh*
bed	letto, m.	LETT-*toh*
bedroom	camera, f.	KAH-*meh-rah*
bee	ape, f.	AH-*peh*
beef	manzo, m.	MAHN-*dzoh*
beer	birra, f.	BEER-*rah*
before (ahead, adv.)	davanti	*dah-*VAHN-*tee*
before (earlier, adv.)	prima	PREE-*mah*
beg (solicit alms), to	mendicare	*menn-dee-*KAH-*reh*

ENGLISH	ITALIAN	PRONUNCIATION
beggar	mendicante, m.	*menn-dee-*KAHN*-teh*
begin (start to do), to	cominciare	*koh-meen-*CHAH*-reh*
beginning	principio, m.	*preen-*CHEE*-pyoh*
behave (conduct oneself), to	comportarsi	*kohm-pohr-*TAHR*-see*
behavior	comportamento, m.	*kohm-pohr-tah-*MEN*-toh*
behind (in the rear, adv.)	di dietro	*dee-*DYEH*-troh*
behind (prep.)	dietro a	DYEH*-troh ah*
Belgium	Belgio, m.	BELL*-joh*
believe (accept), to	credere	KREH*-deh-reh*
belly (abdomen)	pancia, f.	PAHN*-chah*
belong to (be the property of), to	appartenere a	*ahp-pahr-teh-*NEH*-reh ah*
belt (article of clothing)	cintura, f.	*cheen-*TOO*-rah*
beneath (adv.)	di sotto	*dee* SOHT*-toh*
benefit (advantage)	profitto, m.	*proh-*FEET*-toh*
berry (fruit)	bacca, f.	BAHK*-kah*
berth (train bunk)	cucetta, f.	*koo-*CHETT*-tah*
beside (other than, prep.)	oltre a	OHL*-treh ah*
Bible	Bibbia, f.	BEEB*-byah*
bicycle	bicicletta, f.	*bee-chee-*KLETT*-tah*
bid (amount offered)	offerta, f.	*ohf-*FEHR*-tah*
big	grande	GRAHN*-deh*
bill (currency)	biglietto (di banca), m.	*bee-*LYETT*-toh*
bill (invoice)	fattura, f.	*faht-*TOO*-rah*
bill of sale	atto di vendita, m.	AHT*-toh dee* VENN*-dee-tah*

ENGLISH	ITALIAN	PRONUNCIATION
billiards	giuoco del bigliardo, m.	JWOH-*koh* dell *bee*-LYAHR-*doh*
bird	uccello, m.	*oot*-CHELL-*loh*
birthday	compleanno, m.	*kohm-pleh*-AHN-*noh*
bit (small part)	pezzetto, m.	*pett*-TSETT-*toh*
bite, to	mordere	MOHR-*deh-reh*
bitter	amaro	*ah*-MAH-*roh*
black	nero	NEH-*roh*
blackberry	mora di rovo, f.	MOH-*rah dee* ROH-*voh*
blackboard	lavagna, f.	*lah*-VAH-*nyah*
bladder	vescica, f.	*veh*-SHEE-*kah*
blame, to	biasimare	*byah-zee*-MAH-*reh*
blanket	coperta, f.	*koh*-PEHR-*tah*
bleach (make white), to	imbiancare	*eem-byahng*-KAH-*reh*
bleed (lose blood), to	sanguinare	*sahng-gwee*-NAH-*reh*
blind (lacking sight)	cieco	CHYEH-*koh*
blister	vescichetta, f.	*veh-shee*-KETT-*tah*
blond	biondo	BYOHN-*doh*
blood	sangue, m.	SAHNG-*gweh*
bloom, to	fiorire	*fyoh*-REE-*reh*
blouse (shirtwaist)	blusa, f.	BLOO-*zah*
blow (make move), to	fare volare	FAH-*reh voh*-LAH-*reh*
blue	azzurro	*ahd*-DZOOR-*roh*
blush, to	arrossire	*ahr-rohss*-SEE-*reh*
boarding house	pensione, f.	*penn*-SYOH-*neh*
boat	battello, m.	*baht*-TELL-*loh*
body	corpo, m.	KOHR-*poh*
boil (bubble up), to	bollire	*bohl*-LEE-*reh*
bolt (lock)	stanghetta, f.	*stahng*-GETT-*tah*
bone	osso, m.	OHSS-*soh*

ENGLISH	ITALIAN	PRONUNCIATION
book	libro, m.	LEE-*broh*
book (engage space), to	prenotare	*preh-noh-*TAH-*reh*
boot (footgear)	stivale, m.	*stee-*VAH-*leh*
boredom	noia, f.	NOH-*yah*
borrow, to	prendere a prestito	PRENN-*deh-reh ah* PREH-*stee-toh*
bosom	seno, m.	SEH-*noh*
boss (master)	padrone, m.	*pah-*DROH-*neh*
both (adj.)	tutti e due	TOOT-*tee eh* DOO-*eh*
both (pron.)	entrambi	*enn-*TRAHM-*bee*
bother (annoy), to	infastidire	*een-fah-stee-*DEE-*reh*
bottle	bottiglia, f.	*boht-*TEE-*lyah*
bottom	fondo, m.	FOHN-*doh*
boundary (limit line)	limite, m.	LEE-*mee-teh*
bow (nod)	inchino, m.	*een-*KEE-*noh*
bowels	viscere, f., pl.	VEE-*sheh-reh*
bowl (dish)	scodella, f.	*skoh-*DELL-*lah*
box (container)	scatola, f.	SKAH-*toh-lah*
boy (lad)	ragazzo, m.	*rah-*GAHT-*tsoh*
bracelet	braccialetto, m.	*braht-chah-*LETT-*toh*
brain	cervello, m.	*chehr-*VELL-*loh*
brake	freno, m.	FREH-*noh*
brand (trade mark)	marca, f.	MAHR-*kah*
brandy	acquavite, f.	*ahk-kwah-*VEE-*teh*
brass	ottone, m.	*oht-*TOH-*neh*
brassiere	reggipetto, m.	*red-jee-*PETT-*toh*
bread	pane, m.	PAH-*neh*
breadth (width)	larghezza, f.	*lahr-*GET-*tsah*
break (come apart), to	rompersi	ROHM-*pehr-see*
breakfast	prima colazione, f.	PREE-*mah koh-lah-*TSYOH-*neh*
breast	petto, m.	PETT-*toh*

ENGLISH	ITALIAN	PRONUNCIATION
breath	fiato, m.	FYAH-*toh*
breeze	brezza, f.	BREDD-*dzah*
bribe, to	corrompere	*koh-*ROHM-*peh-reh*
bridge (span)	ponte, m.	POHN-*teh*
briefcase	portafoglio, m.	*pohr-tah-*FOH-*lyoh*
bright (shining)	brillante	*breel-*LAHN-*teh*
bring, to	portare	*pohr-*TAH-*reh*
British (adj.)	britannico	*bree-*TAHN-*nee-koh*
broad (side)	largo	LAHR-*goh*
broadcasting	radio diffusione, f.	RAH-*dyoh* deef-*foo-*ZYOH-*neh*
bronchitis	bronchite, f.	*brohn-*KEE-*teh*
bronze	bronzo, m.	BROHN-*dzoh*
brooch	spillone, m.	*speel-*LOH-*neh*
broom	scopa, f.	SKOH-*pah*
brother	fratello, m.	*frah-*TELL-*loh*
brother-in-law	cognato, m.	*koh-*NYAH-*toh*
brown	marrone	*mahr-*ROH-*neh*
bruise	ammaccatura, f.	*ahm-mahk-kah-*TOO-*rah*
budget	bilancio, m.	*bee-*LAHN-*choh*
bug (insect)	insetto, m.	*een-*SETT-*toh*
building	fabbricato, m.	*fahb-bree-*KAH-*toh*
bulb (light bulb)	lampada (incandescente), f.	LAHM-*pah-dah (een-kahn-deh-*SHENN-*teh)*
bundle (parcel)	pacco, m.	PAHK-*koh*
bureau (chest)	cassettone, m.	*kahss-sett-*TOH-*neh*
bureau (office)	ufficio, m.	*oof-*FEE-*choh*
burglar	ladro, m.	LAH-*droh*
burial	sepoltura, f.	*seh-pohl-*TOO-*rah*
burn (be on fire), to	bruciare	*broo-*CHAH-*reh*
bury (entomb), to	seppellire	*sepp-pell-*LEE-*reh*
bus	autobus, m.	*ow-toh-*BOOSS

ENGLISH	ITALIAN	PRONUNCIATION
bush (plant)	cespuglio, m.	*cheh*-SPOO-*lyoh*
business (commerce)	affari, m., pl.	*ahf*-FAH-*ree*
businessman	uomo d'affari, m.	WOH-*moh dah*-FAH-*ree*
busy (occupied)	occupato	*ohk-koo*-PAH-*toh*
but (yet, conj.)	ma	MAH
butcher	macellaio, m.	*mah-chell*-LAH-*yoh*
butter	burro, m.	BOOR-*roh*
button	bottone, m.	*boht*-TOH-*neh*
buy, to	comprare	*kohm*-PRAH-*reh*
by (near, prep.)	presso	PRESS-*soh*
by (prior to, prep.)	prima di	PREE-*mah dee*
cab (taxi)	tassi, m.	*tahss*-SEE
cabbage	cavolo, m.	KAH-*voh-loh*
cabin (of ship)	cabina, f.	*kah*-BEE-*nah*
cablegram	cablogramma, m.	*kah-bloh*-GRAHM-*mah*
cake (dessert)	torta, f.	TOHR-*tah*
calendar	calendario, m.	*kah-lenn*-DAH-*ryoh*
call (shout), to	chiamare	*kyah*-MAH-*reh*
call (summon), to	chiamare	*kyah*-MAH-*reh*
camera	apparecchio fotografico, m.	*ahp-pah*-REKK-*kyoh foh-toh*-GRAH-*fee-koh*
can (tin)	latta, f.	LAHT-*tah*
canal	canale, m.	*kah*-NAH-*leh*
cancel (revoke), to	annullare	*ahn-nool*-LAH-*reh*
cancer	cancro, m.	KAHNG-*kroh*
candle	candela, f.	*kahn*-DEH-*lah*
candy	dolci, m., pl.	DOHL-*chee*
cane (walking stick)	bastone, m.	*bah*-STOH-*neh*
cap (hat)	berretto, m.	*behr*-RETT-*toh*
capital (city)	capitale, f.	*kah-pee*-TAH-*leh*

ENGLISH	ITALIAN	PRONUNCIATION
captain (officer)	capitano, m.	*kah-pee-*TAH*-noh*
car (auto)	auto, f.	OW*-toh*
car (railroad)	vagone, m.	*vah-*GOH*-neh*
carbon copy	copia (a carta carbone), f.	KOH*-pyah (ah* KAHR*-tah kahr-* BOH*-neh)*
card, calling	carta da visita, f.	KAHR*-tah dah* VEE*-zee tah*
card, playing	carta da giuoco, f.	KAHR*-tah dah* JWOH*-koh*
card, postal	cartolina, f.	*kahr-toh-*LEE*-nah*
cardboard	cartone, m.	*kahr-*TOH*-neh*
care (custody)	custodia, f.	*koo-*STOH*-dyah*
care (be concerned), to	preoccuparsi (di)	*preh-ohk-koo-* PAHR*-see (dee)*
careful (cautious)	cauto	KOW*-toh*
cargo	carico, m.	KAH*-ree-koh*
carpet	tappeto, m.	*tahp-*PEH*-toh*
carriage (horse-drawn vehicle	carrozza, f.	*kahr-*ROHT*-tsah*
carrot	carota, f.	*kah-*ROH*-tah*
carry (bear), to	portare	*pohr-*TAH*-reh*
cart	carretta, f.	*kahr-*RETT*-tah*
case (instance)	caso, m.	KAH*-zoh*
cash (money)	contanti, m., pl.	*kchn-*TAHN*-tee*
cash (receive cash for), to	incassare	*een-kahss-*SAH*-reh*
cashier	cassiere, m., f.	*kahss-*SYEH*-reh*
castle	castello, m.	*kah-*STELL*-loh*
cat	gatto, m.	GAHT*-toh*
cathedral	cattedrale, f.	*kaht-teh-*DRAH*-leh*
Catholic (adj.)	cattolico	*kaht-*TOH*-lee-koh*
cattle	bestiame, m.	*beh-*STYAH*-meh*
cauliflower	cavolfiore, m.	*kah-vohl-*FYOH*-reh*
cause	causa, f.	KOW*-zah*
caution (warn), to	avvertire	*ahv-vehr-*TEE*-reh*
ceiling (of room)	soffitto, m.	*sohf-*FEET*-toh*

ENGLISH	ITALIAN	PRONUNCIATION
celery	sedano, m.	SEH-*dah-noh*
cellar	cantina, f.	*kahn*-TEE-*nah*
cemetery	cimitero, m.	*chee-mee-*TEH-*roh*
center	centro, m.	CHENN-*troh*
century	secolo, m.	SEH-*koh-loh*
cereal (grain)	cereale, m.	*cheh-reh-*AH-*leh*
ceremony	cerimonia, f.	*cheh-ree-*MOH-*nyah*
certain (sure)	sicuro	*see-*KOO-*roh*
certainly (of course, interj.)	certamente	*chehr-tah-*MENN-*teh*
certify, to	certificare	*chehr-tee-fee-*KAH-*reh*
chair	sedia, f.	SEH-*dyah*
chance (opportunity)	occasione, f.	*ohk-kah-*ZYOH-*neh*
chance (possibility)	possibilità, f.	*pohss-see-bee-lee-*TAH
change (become different), to	cambiare	*kahm-*BYAH-*reh*
channel (strait)	stretto, m.	STRETT-*toh*
chapel	cappella, f.	*kah-*PELL-*lah*
character (person portrayed)	personaggio, m.	*pehr-soh-*NAHD-*joh*
charge (price)	prezzo, m.	PRETT-*tsoh*
charge account	conto corrente, m.	KOHN-*toh kohr-*RENN-*teh*
charming	incantevole	*een-kahn-*TEH-*voh-leh*
chat, to	conversare	*kohn-vehr-*SAH-*reh*
cheap (inexpensive)	a buon mercato	*ah* BWOHN *mehr-*KAH-*toh*
cheat (defraud), to	truffare	*troof-*FAH-*reh*
check (bank check)	assegno, m.	*ahss-*SEH-*nyoh*
check	guancia, f.	GWAHN-*chah*
cheer (applaud), to	acclamare	*ahk-klah-*MAH-*reh*

ENGLISH	ITALIAN	PRONUNCIATION
cheerful (joyful)	gaio	GAH-*yoh*
cheese	formaggio, m.	*fohr*-MAHD-*joh*
cherry (fruit)	ciliegia, f.	*chee*-LYEH-*jah*
chess	giuoco degli scacchi, m. pl.	JWOH-*koh deh-l yee* SKAHK-*kee*
chest	petto, m.	PETT-*toh*
chew, to	masticare	*mah-stee*-KAH-*reh*
chicken	pollo, m.	POHL-*loh*
chicken pox	varicella, f.	*vah-ree*-CHELL-*lah*
chief (leading)	primo	PREE-*moh*
child	bambino, m.	*bahm*-BEE-*noh*
chimney	camino, m.	*kah*-MEE-*noh*
chocolate	cioccolata, f.	*chohk-koh*-LAH-*tah*
choke, to	soffocare	*soh-foh*-KAH-*reh*
cholera	colera, f.	*koh*-LEH-*rah*
choose (select), to	scegliere	SHEH-*lyeh-reh*
Christmas	Natale, m.	*nah*-TAH-*leh*
church	chiesa, f.	KYEH-*zah*
cigar	sigaro, m.	SEE-*gah-roh*
cigarette	sigaretta, f.	*see-gah*-RETT-*tah*
citizen	cittadino, m.	*cheet-tah*-DEE-*noh*
city	città, f.	*cheet*-TAH
claim, to	reclamare	*reh-klah*-MAH-*reh*
clap (applaud), to	applaudire	*ahp-plow*-DEE-*reh*
class (kind)	genere, m.	JEH-*neh-reh*
classroom	aula, f.	OW-*lah*
clean	pulito	*poo*-LEE-*toh*
clear	chiaro	KYAH-*roh*
clearance (customs clearance)	sdoganamento, m.	*zdoh-gah-nah-*MENN-*toh*
clerk (salesperson)	commesso, m.	*kohm*-MESS-*soh*
clever	accorto	*ahk*-KOHR-*toh*
climate (weather)	clima, m.	KLEE-*mah*
climb (scale), to	salire	*sah*-LEE-*reh*
cloak (apparel)	mantello, m.	*mahn*-TELL-*loh*
clock	orologio, m.	*oh-roh*-LOH-*joh*

ENGLISH	ITALIAN	PRONUNCIATION
close (shut), to	chiudere	KYOO-*deh-reh*
cloth	stoffa, f.	STOHF-*fah*
clothing	vestiario, m.	*veh-*STYAH*-ryoh*
cloud	nuvola, f.	NOO-*voh-lah*
cloudy (overcast)	nuvoloso	*noo-voh-*LOH*-soh*
coach, railroad	carrozza, f.	*kahr-*ROHT*-tsah*
coal	carbone, n.	*kahr-*BOH*-neh*
coarse	grossolano	*grohss-soh-*LAH*-noh*
coast (seaboard)	costa, f.	KOH-*stah*
coat (man's overcoat)	soprabito, m.	*soh-*PRAH*-bee-toh*
coat (woman's overcoat)	paltò, m.	*pahl-*TOH
cocktail	cocktail, m.	KOHK-*tell*
cocoa	cacao, m.	*kah-*KAH*-oh*
coffee	caffè, m.	*kahf-*FEH
coffin	bara, f.	BAH-*rah*
coin	moneta, f.	*moh-*NEH*-tah*
cold (adj.)	freddo	FREDD-*doh*
cold (disease)	raffreddore, m.	*rahf-fredd-*DOH*-reh*
collar	colletto, m.	*kohl-*LETT*-toh*
color	colore, m.	*koh-*LOH*-reh*
column (pillar)	colonna, f.	*koh-*LOHN*-nah*
comb (for hair)	pettine, m.	PETT-*tee-neh*
combine (make join), to	combinare	*kohm-bee-*NAH*-reh*
come, to	venire	*vee-*NEE*-reh*
comedy (comic play)	commedia, f.	*kohm-*MEH*-dyah*
comfort (ease)	comodità, f.	*koh-mod-dee-*TAH
comfort (console), to	confortare	*kohn-fohr-*TAH*-reh*
comfortable	comodo	KOH-*moh-doh*
command (order), to	comandare	*koh-mahn-*DAH*-reh*
comment, to	commentare	*kohm-menn-*TAH*-reh*

ENGLISH	ITALIAN	PRONUNCIATION
commercial	commerciale	*kohm-mehr-*CHAH-*leh*
common (usual)	comune	*koh-*MOO-*neh*
communism	comunismo, m.	*koh-moo-*NEE-*zmoh*
community (neighborhood)	vicinanza, f.	*vee-chee-*NAHN-*tsah*
companion	compagno, m.	*kahm-*PAH-*nyoh*
company (business firm)	ditta, f.	DEET-*tah*
compare (consider relatively), to	confrontare	*kohn-frohn-*TAH-*reh*
comparison	confronto, m.	*kohn-*FROHN-*toh*
compartment (of train)	compartimento, m.	*kohm-pahr-tee-*MENN-*to*
complain, to	lagnarsi	*lah-*NYAHR-*see*
complaint	lagnanza, f.	*lah-*NYAHN-*tsah*
complete (entire)	completo	*kohm-*PLEH-*toh*
compliment	complimento, m.	*kohm-plee-*MEN-*toh*
comrade	compagno, m.	*kohm-*PAH-*nyoh*
conceal, to	celare	*cheh-*LAH-*reh*
concern (business firm)	ditta, f.	DEET-*tah*
concern (affect), to	riguardare	*ree-gwahr-*DAH-*reh*
concerning (regarding)	riguardo a	*ree-*GWAHR-*doh ah*
concert (musical performance)	concerto, m.	*kohn-*CHEHR-*toh*
condition (state)	condizione, f.	*kohn-dee-*TSYOH-*neh*
conductor	direttore, m.	*dee-rett-*TOH-*reh*
conductor (ticket collector)	controllore, m.	*kohn-trohl-*LOH-*reh*
confident (self-assured)	confidente	*kohn-fee-*DENN-*teh*
confidential (private)	confidenziale	*kohn-fee-den-*TSYAH-*leh*

ENGLISH	ITALIAN	PRONUNCIATION
confirm (corroborate), to	confermare	*kohn-fehr-*MAH*-reh*
confirmation (corroboration)	confermazione, f.	*kohn-fehr-mah-*TSYOH*-neh*
confusion (disorder)	confusione, f.	*kohn-foo-*ZYOH*-neh*
congregation (religious community)	parrocchiani, m., pl.	*pahr-rohk-*KYAH*-nee*
connection (relationship)	rapporto, m.	*rahp-*POHR*-toh*
conquer, to	vincere	VEEN-*cheh-reh*
conscious (aware)	conscio	KOHN-*shoh*
consequently	in conseguenza	*een kohn-seh-*GWENN*-tsah*
consider (reflect on), to	considerare	*kohn-see-deh-*RAH*-reh*
consideration (regard)	riguardo, m.	*ree-*GWAHR*-doh*
consist of (comprise), to	consistere in	*kohn-*SEE*-steh-reh een*
constitute (make up), to	costituire	*koh-stee-*TWEE*-reh*
construct, to	costruire	*koh-*STRWEE*-reh*
consul	console, m.	KOHN-*soh-leh*
consult (seek professional advice), to	consultare	*kohn-sool-*TAH*-reh*
contain, to	contenere	*kohn-teh-*NEH*-reh*
contemporary (modern)	contemporaneo	*kohm-temm-poh-*RAH*-neh-oh*
contempt (scorn)	disprezzo, m.	*dee-*SPRETT*-tsoh*
content (satisfied)	contento	*kohn-*TENN*-toh*
contents	contenuto, m.	*kohn-teh-*NOO*-toh*
continent	continente, m.	*kohn-tee-*NENN*-teh*
continual	continuo	*kohn-*TEE*-nwoh*
continuation	continuazione, f.	*kohn-tee-nwah-*TSYOH*-neh*

ENGLISH	ITALIAN	PRONUNCIATION
contraband	contrabbando, m.	*kohn-trahb-*BAHN-*doh*
contradict (deny), to	contraddire	*kohn-trahd-*DEE-*reh*
contrary (opposite)	contrario	*kohn-*TRAH-*ryoh*
contribute, to	contribuire	*kohn-tree-*BWEE-*re*
contribution	contribuzione, f.	*kohn-tree-boo-*TSYOH-*neh*
convenience	comodità, f.	*koh-moh-dee-*TAH
convenient	comodo	KOH-*moh-doh*
conversation	conversazione, f.	*kohn-vehr-sah-*TSYOH-*neh*
convince, to	convincere	*kohn-*VEEN-*cheh-r*
cook	cuoco, m.	KWOH-*koh*
cook (heat food), to	cuocere	KWOH-*cheh-reh*
cook (prepare meals), to	cucinare	*koo-chee-*NAH-*reh*
cool (having low temperature)	fresco	FREH-*skoh*
cool (make less hot), to	rinfrescare	*reen-freh-*SKAH-*reh*
cooperation	cooperazione, f.	*koh-oh-per-rah-*TSYOH-*neh*
copper	rame, m.	RAH-*meh*
copy (duplicate)	copia, f.	KOH-*pyah*
copy (of a publication)	esemplare, m.	*eh-zemm-*PLAH-*re*
copy (imitate), to	copiare	*koh-*PYAH-*reh*
cord (rope)	corda, f.	KOHR-*dah*
cork (stopper)	tappo, m.	TAHP-*poh*
corn (maize)	granturco, m.	*grahn-*TOOR-*koh*
corpse	cadavere, m.	*kah-*DAH-*veh-reh*
correspondence (letters)	corrispondenza, f.	*kohr-ree-spohn-*DENN-*tsah*
correspond with (write to), to	corrispondere con	*kohn-ree-*SPOHN-*deh-reh kohn*
cosmetics	cosmetici, m., pl.	*koh-*ZMEH-*tee-che*

ENGLISH	ITALIAN	PRONUNCIATION
cost (price)	costo, m.	KOH-*stoh*
cost, to	costare	*koh*-STAH-*reh*
cot (bed)	lettino, m.	*lett*-TEE-*noh*
cotton (fabric)	tela di cotone, f.	TEH-*lah dee koh*-TOH-*neh*
cough	tosse, f.	TOHSS-*seh*
counsel (advice)	consiglio, m.	*kohn*-SEE-*lyoh*
counsel (lawyer)	avvocato, m.	*ahv-voh*-KAH-*toh*
count (enumerate), to	contare	*kohn*-TAH-*reh*
counterfeit (adj.)	contraffatto	*kohn-trahf*-FAHT-*toh*
country (countryside)	campagna, f.	*kahm*-PAH-*nyah*
country (nation)	paese, m.	*pah*-EH-*zeh*
couple (pair, n.)	coppia, f.	KOHP-*pyah*
court (of law)	tribunale, m.	*tree-boo*-NAH-*leh*
courteous (polite)	cortese	*kohr*-TEH-*zeh*
cousin	cugino, m.	*koo-jee*-NOH
cover, to	coprire	*koh*-PREE-*reh*
cow	vacca, f.	VAHK-*kah*
crab (shellfish)	granchio, m.	GRAHNG-*kyoh*
cradle	culla, f.	KOOL-*lah*
cramp	crampo, m.	KRAHM-*poh*
crazy	pazzo	PAHT-*tsoh*
cream	panna, f.	PAHN-*nah*
create, to	creare	*kreh*-AH-*reh*
credit	credito, m.	KREH-*dee-toh*
crew	equipaggio, m.	*eh-kwee*-PAHD-*joh*
crime	delitto, m.	*deh*-LEET-*toh*
criminal	delinquente, m., f.	*deh-leeng*-KWENN-*teh*
crisp (brittle)	croccante	*krohk*-KAHN-*teh*
criticism	critica, f.	KREE-*tee-kah*
cross (crucifix)	croce, f.	KROH-*cheh*
cross (traverse), to	traversare	*trah-vehr*-SAH-*reh*

ENGLISH	ITALIAN	PRONUNCIATION
crossing (ocean voyage)	traversata, f.	*trah-vehr-*SAH-*tah*
crossroads	incrocio, m.	*een-*KROH-*choh*
crowd	folla, f.	FOHL-*lah*
cruel	crudele	*kroo-*DEH-*leh*
cruise (voyage)	crociera, f.	*kroh-*CHYEH-*rah*
crumb	bricioloa, f.	BREE-*choh-lah*
crutch	gruccia, f.	GROOT-*chah*
cry (weep), to	piangere	PYAHN-*jeh-reh*
cucumber	cetriolo, m.	*cheh-*TRYOH-*loh*
cuff (of sleeve)	polsino, m.	*pohl-*SEE-*noh*
cuff (of trouser)	orlo dei calzoni, m.	OHR-*loh day kahl-*TSOH-*nee*
cup	tazza, f.	TAHT-*tsah*
cupboard	credenza, f.	*kreh-*DENN-*tsah*
curb (edge of street)	cordone, m.	*kohr-*DOH-*neh*
cure (healing)	guarigione, f.	*gwah-ree-*JOH-*neh*
cure (heal), to	guarire	*gwah-*REE-*reh*
curious	curioso	*koo-*RYOH-*soh*
currency (money)	moneta, f.	*moh-*NEH-*tah*
current (contemporary, adj.)	attuale	*aht-*TWAH-*leh*
curse	maledizione, f.	*mah-leh-dee-*TSYOH-*neh*
curse (swear), to	bestemmiare	*beh-stemm-*MYAH-*reh*
curtain (drape)	tendina, f.	*tenn-*DEE-*nah*
custom (habit)	costume, m.	*koh-*STOO-*meh*
customer (buyer)	cliente, m., f.	*klee-*ENN-*teh*
customhouse	dogana, f.	*doh-*GAH-*nah*
customs (tax)	dogana, f.	*doh-*GAH-*nah*
cut (divide into parts), to	tagliare	*tah-*LYAH-*reh*
daily (adj.)	quotidiano	*kwoh-tee-*DYAH-*noh*
dairy	latteria, f.	*laht-teh-*REE-*ah*
damage (injury)	danno, m.	DAHN-*noh*
damage (injure), to	danneggiare	*dahn-nedd-*JAH-*reh*

ENGLISH	ITALIAN	PRONUNCIATION
damp (moist)	umido	oo-*mee-doh*
danger	pericolo, m.	*peh-*REE*-koh-loh*
dangerous	pericoloso	*peh-ree-koh-*LOH*-soh*
dark (in color, adj.)	oscuro	*oh-*SKOO*-roh*
dark (without light, adj.)	buio	BOO-*yoh*
darkness	oscurità, f.	*oh-skoo-ree-*TAH
darn, (mend), to	rammendare	*rahm-menn-*DAH*-reh*
date (appointment)	appuntamento, m.	*ahp-poon-tah-*MENN*-toh*
date (fruit)	dattero, m.	DAHT-*teh-roh*
daughter	figlia, f.	FEE-*lyah*
daughter-in-law	nuora, f.	NWOH-*rah*
dawn (daybreak)	alba, f.	AHL-*bah*
day (daytime)	giorno, m.	JOHR-*noh*
day (24-hour period)	giorno, m.	JOHR-*noh*
dead	morto	MOHR-*toh*
deaf	sordo	SOHR-*doh*
dealer (trader)	distributore, m.	*dee-stree-boo-*TOH*-reh*
dear (beloved, adj.)	caro	KAH-*roh*
death	morte, f.	MOHR-*teh*
debt	debito, m.	DEH-*bee-toh*
debtor	debitore, m.	*deh-bee-*TOH*-reh*
deceive (delude), to	deludere	*deh-*LOO*-deh-reh*
decent (respectable)	decente	*deh-*CHENN*-teh*
decide (make up one's mind), to	decidersi	*deh-*CHEE*-dehr-see*
decision (judgment)	decisione, f.	*deh-chee-*SYOH*-neh*
deck (of cards)	mazzo (di carte), m.	MAHT-*tsoh (dee* KAHR*-teh)*
deck (of ship)	ponte, m.	POHN-*teh*

ENGLISH	ITALIAN	PRONUNCIATION
declare (state), to	dichiarare	*dee-kyah-*RAH*-reh*
decorate (adorn), to	decorare	*deh-koh-*RAH*-reh*
decoration (decor)	decorazione, f.	*deh-koh-rah-*TSYOH*-neh*
deed (act)	atto, m.	AHT*-toh*
deep (in extent)	profondo	*proh-*FOHN*-doh*
defect (flaw)	difetto, m.	*dee-*FETT*-toh*
defend (protect), to	difendere	*dee-*FENN*-deh-reh*
definite	definito	*deh-fee-*NEE*-toh*
degree (unit of measurement)	grado, m.	GRAH*-doh*
delay	ritardo, m.	*ree-*TAHR*-doh*
delay (postpone), to	differire	*deef-feh-*REE*-reh*
deliberate (intentional)	deliberato	*deh-lee-beh-*RAH*-toh*
delicious	delizioso	*deh-lee-*TSYOH*-soh*
delightful	dilettevole	*dee-lett-*TEH*-voh-leh*
demand (ask for), to	richiedere	*ree-*KYEH*-deh-reh*
demonstrate (show), to	dimostrare	*dee-moh-*STRAH*-reh*
demonstration (proof)	dimostrazione, f.	*dee-moh-strah-*TSYOH*-neh*
dentist	dentista, m.	*denn-*TEE*-stah*
department store	grande magazzino, m.	GRAHN*-deh mah-gahd-*DZEE*-noh*
departure (setting out)	partenza, f.	*pahr-*TENN*-tsah*
depend (rely) on, to	contare su	*kohn-*TAH*-reh soo*
deposit, to	depositare	*deh-poh-zee-*TAH*-reh*
depot (station)	stazione, f.	*stah-*TSYOH*-neh*
depth (deepness)	profondità, f.	*proh-fohn-dee-*TAH

ENGLISH	ITALIAN	PRONUNCIATION
descent (move downward) to	discendere	*dee-*SHENN*-deh-reh*
descendant (offspring)	discendente, m., f.	*dee-shenn-*DENN*-teh*
describe (portray), to	descrivere	*deh-*SKREE*-veh-reh*
description (account)	descrizione, f.	*deh-skree-*TSYOH*-neh*
desert	deserto, m.	*deh-*ZEHR*-toh*
deserve, to	meritare	*meh-ree-*TAH*-reh*
design (intention)	proposito, m.	*proh-*POH*-zee-toh*
design (pattern)	disegno, m.	*dee-*SEH*-nyoh*
desire (long for), to	desiderare	*deh-see-deh-*RAH*-reh*
desk	scrivania, f.	*skree-vah-*NEE*-ah*
despite (prop.)	malgrado	*mahl-*GRAH*-doh*
dessert	dolce, m.	DOHL*-cheh*
destination	destinazione, f.	*deh-stee-nah-*TSYOH*-neh*
destiny	destino, m.	*deh-*STEE*-noh*
detail (minor item)	dettaglio, m.	*dett-*TAH*-lyoh*
determine (make up one's mind), to	determinarsi	*deh-tehr-mee-*NAHR*-see*
detour	deviazione, f.	*deh-vyah-*TSYOH*-neh*
dew	rugiada, f.	*roo-*JAH*-dah*
diabetes	diabete, m.	*dee-ah-*BEH*-teh*
dice (marked cubes)	dadi, m., pl.	DAH*-dee*
dictate (for transcription), to	dettare	*dett-*TAH*-reh*
dictionary	dizionario, m.	*dee-tsyoh-*NAH*-ryoh*
die, to	morire	*moh-*REE*-reh*
diet (restricted food allowance)	dieta, f.	DYEH*-tah*
difference (dissimilarity)	differenza, f.	*deef-feh-*RENN*-tsah*
different (unlike)	differente	*deef-feh-*RENN*-teh*

ENGLISH	ITALIAN	PRONUNCIATION
difficult	difficile	*deef*-FEE-*chee-leh*
difficulty (hardness)	difficoltà, f.	*deef-fee-kohl*-TAH
dig (excavate), to	scavare	*skah*-VAH-*reh*
digest, to	digerire	*dee-jeh*-REE-*reh*
dim	oscuro	*oh*-SKOO-*roh*
dine, to	pranzare	*prahn*-DZAH-*reh*
diner (railway dining car)	vagone ristorante, m.	*vah*-GOH-*neh ree-stoh*-RAHN-*teh*
dining room	sala da pranzo, f.	SAH-*lah dah* PRAHN-*dzoh*
dinner	pranzo, m.	PRAHN-*dzoh*
direct (immediate)	immediato	*eem-meh*-DYAH-*toh*
direction (course)	direzione, f.	*dee-reh*-TSYOH-*neh*
director	direttore, m.	*dee-rett*-TOH-*reh*
dirt (unclean matter)	sporcizia f.	*spohr*-CHEE-*tsyah*
dirty (spoiled)	sporco	SPOHR-*koh*
disagree (differ), to	non essere d'accordo	*nohn* ESS-*seh-reh dah*-KOHR-*doh*
disagreeable	sgradevole	*zgrah*-DEH-*voh-leh*
disappear, to	sparire	*spah*-REE-*reh*
disappoint, to	deludere	*deh*-LOO-*deh-reh*
disappointment	delusione, f.	*deh-loo*-ZYOH-*neh*
discover, to	scoprire	*skoh*-PREE-*reh*
discuss, to	discutere	*dee*-SKOO-*teh-reh*
discussion	discussione, f.	*dee-skooss*-SYOH-*neh*
disease	malattia, f.	*mah-laht*-TEE-*ah*
dish (food)	piatto, m.	PYAHT-*toh*
dishes (tableware)	stoviglie, f., pl.	*stoh*-VEE-*lyeh*
dislike, to	non piacere	*nohn pyah*-CHEH-*reh*
display (exhibit), to	esibire	*eh-zee*-BEE-*reh*
dispute	disputa, f.	DEE-*spoo-tah*
distance	distanza, f.	*dee*-STAHN-*tsah*

ENGLISH	ITALIAN	PRONUNCIATION
distant (far off)	distante	*dee*-STAHN-*teh*
distinct (different)	distinto	*dee*-STEEN-*toh*
distinction (difference)	distinzione, f.	*dee*-steen-TSYOH-*neh*
distinguish (differentiate), to	distinguere	*dee*-STEENG-*gweh-reh*
distinguished (notable)	distinto	*dee*-STEEN-*toh*
distress	afflizione, f.	*ahf-flee*-TSYOH-*neh*
distribute (allot), to	distribuire	*dee-stree*-BWEE-*reh*
district (locality)	distretto, m.	*dee*-STRETT-*toh*
disturb, to	disturbare	*dee-stoor*-BAH-*reh*
dive, to	precipitarsi	*preh-chee-pee*-TAHR-*see*
divine, (adj.)	divino	*dee*-VEE-*noh*
division (portion)	divisione, f.	*dee-vee*-ZYOH-*neh*
divorce (law)	divorzio, m.	*dee*-VOHR-*tsyoh*
dizzy, to be	avere le vertigini	*ah*-VEH-*reh* LEH *vehr*-TEE-*jee-nee*
do, to	fare	FAH-*reh*
dock	calata, f.	*kah*-LAH-*tah*
doctor	dottore, m.	*doht*-TOH-*reh*
doctrine	dottrina, f.	*doht*-TREE-*nah*
dog	cane, m.	KAH-*neh*
domestic (not foreign)	indigeno	*een*-DEE-*jeh-noh*
donkey	asino, m.	AH-*see-noh*
door	porta, f.	POHR-*tah*
doubt	dubbio, m.	DOOB-*byoh*
doubt (be uncertain about), to	dubitare	*doo-bee*-TAH-*reh*
doubtful	dubbioso	*doob*-BYOH-*soh*
doubtless	senza dubbio	SENN-*tsah* DOOB-*byoh*

ENGLISH	ITALIAN	PRONUNCIATION
down (downward, adv.)	giù	JOO
down payment	acconto, m.	*ahk*-KOHN-*toh*
downstairs (on a lower floor)	in basso	*een* BAHSS-*soh*
dozen	dozzina, f.	*dohd*-DZEE-*nah*
draft (air current)	corrente d'aria, f.	*kohr*-RENN-*teh* DAH-*ryah*
draft (check)	tratta, f.	TRAHT-*tah*
draw (pull along), to	trarre	TRAHR-*reh*
draw (sketch), to	disegnare	*dee-seh*-NYAH-*reh*
drawing (sketch)	disegno, m.	*dee*-SEH-*nyoh*
dreadful	terribile	*tehr*-REE-*bee-leh*
dream	sogno, m.	SOH-*nyoh*
dream, to	sognare	*soh*-NYAH-*reh*
dress (frock)	veste, f.	VEH-*steh*
dress (clothe), to	vestire	*veh*-STEE-*reh*
dress (get dressed), to	vestirsi	*veh*-STEER-*see*
dresser (bureau)	comò, m.	*koh*-MOH
dressing (sauce)	condimento, m.	*kohn-dee*-MENN-*toh*
drink (beverage)	bibita, f.	BEE-*bee-tah*
drink, to	bere	BEH-*reh*
drive (a vehicle), to	condurre	*kohn*-DOOR-*reh*
driver (of automobile)	autista, m.,f.	*ow*-TEE-*stah*
drop (droplet)	goccia, f.	GOHT-*chah*
drown (die by drowning), to	affogare	*ahf-fog*-GAH-*reh*
drug (medicine)	medicamento, m.	*meh-dee-kah*-MENN-*toh*
drunk (intoxicated)	ubriaco	*oo*-BRYAH-*koh*
dry	secco	SEKK-*koh*
dry (make dry), to	asciugare	*ah-shoo*-GAH-*reh*

ENGLISH	ITALIAN	PRONUNCIATION
duck	anitra, f.	AH-*nee-trah*
duplicate (copy)	duplicato, m.	*doo-plee-*KAH-*toh*
during	durante	*doo-*RAHN-*teh*
dust	polvere, f.	POHL-*veh-reh*
dusty	polveroso	*pohl-veh-*ROH-*soh*
duty (obligation)	dovere, m.	*doh-*VEH-*reh*
duty (tax)	dazio, m.	DAH-*tsyoh*
duty-free	esente da dazio	*eh-*SENN-*teh dah* DAH-*tsyoh*
dwell (reside), to	dimorare	*dee-moh-*RAH-*reh*
dwelling	abitazione, f.	*ah-bee-tah-*TSYOH-*neh*
dye, to	tingere	TEEN-*jeh-reh*
dysentery	dissenteria, f.	*dees-senn-teh-*REE-*ah*
each (every, adj.)	ogni	OH-*nyee*
each one (pron.)	ognuno	*oh-*NYOO-*noh*
ear (external ear)	orecchio, m.	*oh-*REKK-*kyoh*
earache	mal d'orecchi, m.	*mahl doh-*REKK-*kee*
earn (be paid), to	guadagnare	*gwad-dah-*NYAH-*reh*
earnest	zeloso	*dzeh-*LOH-*soh*
earring	orecchino, m.	*oh-rekk-*KEE-*noh*
earth (land)	terra, f.	TEHR-*rah*
earthquake	terremoto, m.	*tehr-reh-*MOH-*toh*
east	est, m.	EST
Easter	Pasqua, f.	PAH-*skwah*
easy (not difficult)	facile	FAH-*chee-leh*
eat, to	mangiare	*mahn-*JAH-*reh*
economical (thrifty)	economico	*eh-koh-*NOH-*mee-koh*
economy (thrift)	economia, f.	*eh-koh-noh-*MEE-*ah*
edge (border)	orlo, m.	OHR-*loh*
edge (sharp side)	filo, m.	FEE-*loh*

ENGLISH	ITALIAN	PRONUNCIATION
edition	edizione, f.	*eh-dee-*TSYOH*-neh*
educate, to	educare	*eh-doo-*KAH*-reh*
education (schooling process)	educazione, f.	*eh-doo-kah-*TSYOH*-neh*
effort	sforzo, m.	SFOHR*-tsoh*
egg	uovo, m.	WOH*-voh*
either (one or the other, adj.)	l'uno o l'atro	LOO*-noh oh* LAHL*-troh*
either . . . or (conj.)	o . . . o	OH . . . OH
elbow	gomito, m.	GOH*-mee-toh*
elect, to	eleggere	*eh-*LEDD*-jeh-reh*
electric	elettrico	*eh-*LETT*-tree-koh*
electricity	elettricità, f.	*eh-lett-tree-chee-*TAH
element	elemento, m.	*eh-leh-*MENN*-toh*
elevator (passenger lift)	ascensore, m.	*ah-shenn-*SOH*-reh*
else (different, adj.)	altro	AHL*-troh*
else (instead, adv.)	altro	AHL*-troh*
elsewhere	altrove	*ahl-*TROH*-veh*
embarrassment	imbarazzo, m.	*eem-bah-*RAHT*-tsoh*
emergency	emergenza, f.	*eh-mehr-*JENN*-tsah*
emotion	emozione, f.	*eh-moh-*TSYOH*-neh*
employ (hire), to	impiegare	*eem-pyeh-*GAH*-reh*
employ (use), to	impiegare	*eem-pyeh-*GAH*-reh*
employee	impiegato, m.	*eem-pyeh-*GAH*-toh*
employer (boss)	padrone, m.	*pah-*DROH*-neh*
employment (work)	impiego, m.	*eem-*PYEH*-goh*
empty	vuoto	VWOH*-toh*
empty (remove contents of), to	vuotare	*vwoh-*TAH*-reh*
enclose (include in envelope), to	accludere	*ahk-*KLOO*-deh-reh*

ENGLISH	ITALIAN	PRONUNCIATION
encourage, to	incoraggiare	*een-koh-rahd-*JAH-*reh*
end (conclusion)	fine, f.	FEE-*neh*
endeavor, to	sforzarsi di	*sfohr-*TSAHR-*see dee*
endure (bear), to	sopportare	*soph-pohr-*TAH-*reh*
enema	clistere, m.	*klee-*STEH-*reh*
energy	energia, f.	*eh-nehr-*JEE-*ah*
engagement (appointment)	appuntamento, m.	*ahp-poon-tah-*MENN-*toh*
engagement (betrothal)	fidanzamento, m.	*fee-dahn-tsah-*MENN-*toh*
engine (locomotive)	locomotiva, f.	*loh-koh-moh-*TEE-*vah*
engine (motor)	motore, m.	*moh-*TOH-*reh*
English (adj.)	inglese	*een-*GLEH-*seh*
enjoy (derive joy from), to	godere	*goh-*DEH-*reh*
enough (adv.)	bastantemente	*bah-stahn-teh-*MENN-*teh*
enter (come or go into), to	entrare in	*enn-*TRAH-*reh een*
entertain (amuse), to	divertire	*dee-vehr-*TEE-*reh*
entertain (be host to), to	ricevere	*ree-*CHEH-*veh-reh*
entertainment	trattenimento, m.	*traht-teh-nee-*MENN-*toh*
entrance	entrata, f.	*enn-*TRAH-*tah*
epidemic	epidemia, f.	*eh-pee-deh-*MEE-*ah*
equal (adj.)	eguale	*eh-*GWAH-*leh*
errand (commission)	commissione, f.	*kohm-meess-*SYOH-*neh*
escape, to	scappare	*skahp-*PAH-*reh*

ENGLISH	ITALIAN	PRONUNCIATION
escort (social companion)	cavaliere, m.	*kah-vah-*LYEH*-reh*
especially	specialmente	*speh-chahl-*MENN*-teh*
establishment (firm)	stabilimento, m.	*stah-bee-lee-*MENN*-toh*
evening	sera, f.	SEH*-rah*
ever (at all times)	sempre	SEMM*-preh*
ever (at any time)	sempre	SEMM*-preh*
every	ogni	OH*-nyee*
everybody	ognuno	*oh-*NYOO*-noh*
everyone	ciascuno	*chah-*SKOO*-noh*
everything	tutto	TOOT*-toh*
everywhere	dappertutto	*dahp-pehr-*TOOT*-toh*
evident	evidente	*eh-vee-*DENN*-teh*
exact (precise)	esatto	*eh-*ZAHT*-toh*
examination	esame, m.	*eh-*ZAH*-meh*
example	esempio, m.	*eh-*ZEMM*-pyoh*
excellent	eccellente	*ett-chell-*LENN*-teh*
except (prep.)	salvo	SAHL*-voh*
exception (unusual case)	eccezione, f.	*ett-cheh-*TSYOH*-neh*
exchange (barter)	scambio, m.	SKAHM*-byoh*
exclude, to	escludere	*eh-*SKLOO*-deh-reh*
exclusive (not including	esclusivo	*eh-skloo-*SEE*-voh*
excuse (pardon), to	scusare	*shoo-*ZAH*-reh*
exempt (adj.)	esente	*eh-*SENN*-teh*
exercise (physical exertion)	esercizio fisico, m.	*eh-zehr-*CHEE*-tsyoh* FEE*-zee-koh*
exist, to	esistere	*eh-*ZEE*-steh-reh*
existence	esistenza, f.	*eh-zee-*STENN*-tsah*
exit	uscita, f.	*oo-*SHEE*-tah*

ENGLISH	ITALIAN	PRONUNCIATION
expedition (journey)	spedizione, f.	*speh-dee-*TSYOH-*neh*
expense (cost)	spesa, f.	SPEH-*sah*
expensive	costoso	*koh-*STOH-*soh*
experience (conscious event)	esperienza, f.	*eh-speh-*RYENN-*tsah*
expire (become void), to	scadere	*skah-*DEH-*reh*
explain (account for), to	spiegare	*spyeh-*GAH-*reh*
explanation	spiegazione, f.	*spyeh-gah-*TSYOH-*neh*
export, to	esportare	*eh-spohr-*TAH-*reh*
express (state), to	esprimere	*eh-*SPREE-*meh-reh*
expression (sign of feeling; word or phrase)	espressione, f.	*eh-spress-*SYOH-*neh*
extend (stretch out), to	allungare	*ahl-loong-*GAH-*reh*
extensive	esteso	*eh-*STEH-*soh*
extent (magnitude)	estensione, f.	*eh-stenn-*SYOH-*neh*
exterior (adj.)	esterno	*eh-*STEHR-*noh*
extra (additional)	addizionale	*ahd-dee-tsyoh-*NAH-*leh*
extraordinary	straordinario	*strah-ohr-dee-*NAH-*ryoh*
eye	occhio, m.	OHK-*kyoh*
eyebrow	sopracciglio, m.	*soh-praht-*CHEE-*lyoh*
eyelash	ciglio, m.	CHEE-*lyoh*
eyelid	palpebra, f.	*pahl-*PEH-*brah*
fabric (cloth)	tessuto, m.	*tess-*SOO-*toh*
face	faccia, f.	FAHT-*chah*
fact	fatto, m.	FAHT-*toh*
factor (element)	fattore, m.	*faht-*TOH-*reh*

ENGLISH	ITALIAN	PRONUNCIATION
factory	fabbrica, f.	FAHB-*bree-kah*
fade (lose color), to	sbiadire	*zbyah-*DEE-*reh*
fail (be unsuccessful), to	non riuscire	*nohn ree-oo-*SHEE-*reh*
fail (neglect) to, to	mancare di	*mahn-*KAH-*reh dee*
failure (lack of success)	insuccesso, m.	*een-soot-*CHESS-*soh*
faint, to	svenire	*zveh-*NEE-*reh*
fair (impartial)	giusto	JOO-*stoh*
fair (not cloudy)	chiaro	KYAH-*roh*
faith (creed)	fede, f.	FEH-*deh*
faith (trust)	fiducia, f.	*fee-*DOO-*chah*
fall (autumn)	autunno, m.	*ow-*TOON-*noh*
fall, to	cadere	*kah-*DEH-*reh*
false (erroneous)	erroneo	*ehr-*ROH-*neh-oh*
falsehood (lie)	menzogna, f.	*menn-*TSOH-*nyah*
familiar (well-known)	conosciuto	*koh-noh-*SHOO-*toh*
family	famiglia, f.	*fah-*MEE-*lyah*
famous	famoso	*fah-*MOH-*soh*
fan, electric	ventilatore, m.	*venn-tee-lah-*TOH-*reh*
fancy (imagine), to	immaginare	*eem-mah-jee-*NAH-*reh*
far (afar, adv.)	lontano	*lohn-*TAH-*noh*
far (distant, adj.)	lontano	*lohn-*TAH-*noh*
fare	prezzo del viaggio, m.	PRETT-*tsoh dell* VYAHD-*joh*
farewell (leave-taking)	addio, m.	*ahd-*DEE-*oh*
farm	podere, m.	*poh-*DEH-*reh*
farmer	coltivatore, m.	*kohl-tee-vah-*TOH-*reh*
fashion (current style)	moda, f.	MOH-*dah*

ENGLISH	ITALIAN	PRONUNCIATION
fast (quick, adj.)	rapido	RAH-*pee-doh*
fast (quickly, adv.)	rapidamente	*rah-pee-dah-*MENN-*teh*
fat (obese, adj.)	grasso	GRAHSS-*soh*
fate	destino, m.	*deh-*STEE-*noh*
father	padre, m.	PAH-*dreh*
father-in-law	suocero, m.	SWOH-*cheh-roh*
faucet	rubinetto, m.	*roo-bee-*NETT-*toh*
favorite (adj.)	favorito	*fah-voh-*REE-*toh*
fear	paura, f.	*pah-oo-rah*
fear (be afraid of), to	temere	*teh-*MEH-*reh*
feather	piuma, f.	PYOO-*mah*
feature (part of face)	fattezza, f.	*faht-*TETT-*tsah*
fee	onorario, m.	*oh-noh-*RAH-*ryoh*
feed (give food to), to	nutrire	*noo-*TREE-*reh*
feel (experience), to	sentire	*senn-*TEE-*reh*
feel (touch), to	toccare	*tohk-*KAH-*reh*
feeling (emotion)	sentimento, m.	*senn-tee-*MENN-*toh*
feeling (sensation)	sensazione, f.	*senn-sah-*TSYOH-*neh*
female (adj.)	femminile	*femm-mee-*NEE-*leh*
feminine	femminile	*femm-mee-*NEE-*leh*
fence (barrier)	barriera, f.	*bahr-*RYEH-*rah*
ferry (boat)	barca di passaggio, f.	BAHR-*kah dee pahss-*SAHD-*joh*
festival	festa pubblica, f.	FEH-*stah* POOB-*blee-kah*
fever	febbre, f.	FEBB-*breh*
few (not many, adj.)	pochi, poche	POH-*kee,* POH-*keh*
few, a	alcuni, m., alcune, f.	*ahl-*KOO-*nee, ahl-*KOO-*neh*
fig	fico, m.	FEE-*koh*

ENGLISH	ITALIAN	PRONUNCIATION
fight	lotta, f.	LOHT-*tah*
figure (human form)	persona, f.	*pehr*-SOH-*nah*
figure (numeral)	cifra, f.	CHEE-*frah*
fill (make full), to	empire	emm-PEE-*reh*
film	pellicola, f.	*pell*-LEE-*koh-lah*
fine (good)	buono	BWOH-*noh*
fine (penalty)	ammenda, f.	*ahm*-MENN-*dah*
finger	dito, m.	DEE-*toh*
finish (complete), to	finire	*fee*-NEE-*reh*
fire	fuoco, m.	FWOH-*koh*
fireplace	camino, m.	*kah*-MEE-*noh*
firm (business company)	ditta, f.	DEET-*tah*
first (adj.)	primo	PREE-*moh*
fish	pesce, m.	PEH-*skeh*
fish, to	pescare	*peh*-SKAH-*reh*
fix (repair), to	riparare	*ree-pah*-RAH-*reh*
flag	bandiera, f.	*bahn*-DYEH-*rah*
flashlight	lampadina tascabile, f.	*lahm-pah*-DEE-*nah tah-SKAH-bee-leh*
flat (level, adj.)	piano	PYAH-*noh*
flavor (savor)	sapore, m.	*sah*-POH-*reh*
flesh	carne, f.	KAHR-*neh*
flight (journey by air)	volo, m.	VOH-*loh*
flood	inondazione, f.	*ee-nohn-dah*-TSYOH-*neh*
floor (bottom surface)	pavimento, m.	*pah-vee*-MENN-*toh*
floor (story)	piano, m.	PYAH-*noh*
flour	farina, f.	*fah*-REE-*nah*
flow (circulate), to	scorrere	SKOHR-*reh-reh*
flower (blossom)	fiore, m.	FYOH-*reh*

ENGLISH	ITALIAN	PRONUNCIATION
fly (housefly)	mosca, f.	MOH-*skah*
fly, to	volare	*voh*-LAH-*reh*
fog (mist)	nebbia, f.	NEBB-*byah*
food	cibo, m.	CHEE-*boh*
foolish	imprudente	*eem-proo*-DENN-*teh*
foot	piede, m.	PYEH-*deh*
forbidden	proibito	*proh-ee* BEE-*toh*
force (coercion)	forza, f.	FOHR-*tsah*
force, to	forzare	*fohr*-TSAH-*reh*
forehead	fronte, f.	FROHN-*teh*
foreign	straniero	*strah*-NYEH-*roh*
foreigner	straniero, m.	*strah*-NYEH-*roh*
forest	foresta, f.	*for*-REH-*stah*
forever	sempre	SEMM-*preh*
forget, to	dimenticare	*dee-menn-tee*-KAH-*reh*
forgive, to	perdonare	*pehr-doh*-NAH-*reh*
forgotten	dimenticato	*dee-menn-tee*-KAH-*toh*
fork (eating utensil)	forchetta, f.	*fohr*-KETT-*tah*
form (shape)	forma, f.	FOHR-*mah*
form (shape), to	formare	*fohr*-MAH-*reh*
fort	forte, m.	FOHR-*teh*
fortunate	fortunato	*fohr-too*-NAH-*toh*
foul (filthy)	sudicio	SOO-*dee-choh*
fountain	fontana, f.	*fohn*-TAH-*nah*
fowl (poultry)	pollo, m.	POHL-*loh*
fracture	frattura, f.	*fraht*-TOO-*rah*
free (gratuitous)	gratis	GRAH-*teess*
free (independent)	libero	LEE-*behr-roh*
freeze (turn to ice), to	gelare	*jeh*-LAH-*reh*
freight	merci, f., pl.	MEHR-*chee*
French (adj.)	francese	*frahn*-CHEH-*zeh*
fresh (not stale)	fresco	FREH-*skoh*
friend	amico, m.	*ah*-MEE-*koh*

ENGLISH	ITALIAN	PRONUNCIATION
friendly	amichevole	*ah-mee-*KEH-*voh-leh*
friendship	amicizia, f.	*ah-mee-*CHEE-*tsyah*
from	da	DAH
front (forward part)	davanti, m.	*dah-*VAHN-*tee*
frontier	frontiera, f.	*frohn-*TYEH-*rah*
frost	brina, f.	BREE-*nah*
frown, to	aggrottare le ciglia	*ahg-groht-*TAH-*reh leh* CHEE-*lyah*
frozen	gelato	*jeh-*LAH-*toh*
fruit	frutto, m.	FROOT-*toh*
fuel	combustibile, m.	*kohm-boo-*STEE-*bee-leh*
full (complete)	completo	*kohm-*PLEH-*toh*
full (filled)	pieno	PYEH-*noh*
fun	spasso, m.	SPAHSS-*soh*
fund	fondo, m.	FOHN-*doh*
funds	fondi, m., pl.	FOHN-*dee*
funeral	esequie, f., pl.	*eh-*ZEH-*kwyeh*
funny (comical)	comico	KOH-*mee-koh*
fur	pelliccia, f.	*pell-*LEET-*chah*
furnace (home heater)	calorifero, m.	*kah-loh-*REE-*feh-roh*
furniture	mobilia, f.	*moh-*BEE-*lyah*
fuse (elec.)	valvola (elettrica), f.	VAHL-*voh-lah (eh-*LETT-*tree-kah)*
fuss (ado)	storie, f., pl.	STOH-*ryeh*
future (adj.)	futuro	*foo-*TOO-*roh*
future (n.)	futuro, m.	*foo-*TOO-*roh*
gain (increase)	aumento, m.	*ow-*MENN-*toh*
gain (get), to	ottenere	*oht-teh-*NEH-*reh*
galoshes	galosce, f., pl.	*gah-*LOH-*sheh*

ENGLISH	ITALIAN	PRONUNCIATION
game (contest)	giuoco, m.	JWOH-*koh*
garage	autorimessa, f.	*ow-toh-ree-*MESS-*sah*
garbage	rifiuti, m., pl.	*ree-*FYOO-*tee*
garden	giardino, m.	*jahr-*DEE-*noh*
garlic	aglio, m.	AH-*lyoh*
garment	abito, m.	AH-*bee-toh*
garter	giarrettiera, f.	*jahr-rett-*TYEH-*rah*
gas	gas, m.	GAHZ
gasoline	benzina, f.	*benn-*DZEE-*nah*
gate	cancello, m.	*kahn-*CHELL-*loh*
gather (bring together), to	raccogliere	*rahk-*KOH-*lyeh-reh*
gather (congregate), to	riunirsi	*ree-oo-*NEER-*see*
gear	ingranaggio, m.	*een-grah-*NAHD-*joh*
general (adj.)	generale	*jeh-neh-*RAH-*leh*
generous	generoso	*jeh-neh-*ROH-*soh*
gentle (soothing)	soave	*soh-*AH-*veh*
gentleman	galantuomo, m.	*gah-lahn-*TWOH-*moh*
genuine	genuino	*jeh-*NWEE-*noh*
German (adj.)	tedesco	*teh-*DEH-*skoh*
get (obtain), to	ottenere	*oht-teh-*NEH-*reh*
gift (present)	dono, m.	DOH-*noh*
girl	ragazza, f.	*rah-*GAHT-*tsah*
give (bestow), to	dare	DAH-*reh*
glad	allegro	*ahl-*LEH-*groh*
glass (material)	vetro, m.	VEH-*troh*
glass (vessel)	bicchiere, m.	*beek-*KYEH-*reh*
glasses (spectacles)	occhiali, m., pl.	*ohk-*KYAH-*lee*
glide, to	scivolare	*shee-voh-*LAH-*reh*
gloomy (melancholy)	malinconico	*mah-leen-*KOH-*nee-koh*

ENGLISH	ITALIAN	PRONUNCIATION
glorious (resplendent)	glorioso	*gloh-*RYOH*-soh*
glove	guanto, m.	GWAHN*-toh*
go (ride), to	andare	*ahn-*DAH*-reh*
go (walk), to	andare	*ahn-*DAH*-reh*
God	Dio, m.	DEE*-oh*
gold	oro, m.	OH*-reh*
good, better, best	buono, migliore, (il) migliore	BWOH*-noh,* mee-LYOH*-reh, (eel)* mee-LYOH*-reh*
good-by	addio	*ahd-*DEE*-oh*
goods	merci, f., pl.	MEHR*-chee*
government	governo, m.	*goh-*VEHR*-noh*
governor	governatore, m.	*goh-vehr-nah-* H*-reh*
grade (school division)	classe, f.	KLAHSS*-seh*
grain (cereal)	cereale, m.	*cheh-reh-*AH*-leh*
grammar	grammatica, f.	*grahm-*MAH*-tee-kah*
grand (imposing)	grandioso	*grahn-*DYOH*-soh*
granddaughter	nipote, f.	*nee-*POH*-teh*
grandfather	nonno, m.	NOHN*-noh*
grandmother	nonna, f.	NOHN*-nah*
grandson	nipote, m.	*nee-*POH*-teh*
grape	uva, f.	OO*-vah*
grass	erba, f.	EHR*-bah*
grateful	riconoscente	*ree-koh-noh-*SHENN*-teh*
gratitude	gratitudine, f.	*grah-tee-*TOO*-dee-neh*
grave (serious)	grave	GRAH*-veh*
gray	grigio	GREE*-joh*
grease (cooking fat)	grasso, m.	GRAHSS*-soh*
great	grande	GRAHN*-deh*
greatness (eminence)	grandezza, f.	*grahn-*DETT*-tsah*

ENGLISH	ITALIAN	PRONUNCIATION
greedy	avido	AH-*vee-doh*
Greek (adj.)	greco	GREH-*koh*
green	verde	VEHR-*deh*
greet (salute), to	salutare	*sah-loo-*TAH-*reh*
greeting	accoglienza, f.	*ahk-koh-*LYENN-*tsah*
grief	afflizione, f.	*ahf-flee-*TSYOH-*neh*
grin, to	ghignare	*ghee-*NYAH-*reh*
grocery	generi alimen-tari, m., pl.	JEH-*neh-ree* *ah-lee-menn-*TAH-*ree*
ground (earth)	terra, f.	TEHR-*rah*
group	gruppo, m.	GROOP-*poh*
grow (expand), to	crescere	KREH-*sheh-reh*
growth (development)	crescita, f.	KREH-*shee-tah*
guard (watcher)	guardiano, m.	*gwahr-*DYAH-*noh*
guardian	tutore, m.	*too-*TOH-*reh*
guess (suppose), to	supporre	*soop-*POHR-*reh*
guest (visitor)	ospite, m., f.	OH-*spee tch*
guide (one who guides)	guida, f.	GWEE-*dah*
gulf (large bay)	golfo, m.	GOHL-*foh*
gum	gengiva, f.	*jenn-*JEE-*vah*
gum (chewing gum)	gomma da masticare, f.	GOHM-*mah dah mah-stee-*KAH-*reh*
gun	fucile, m.	*foo-*CHEE-*leh*
gutter (of street)	cunetta, f.	*koo-*NETT-*tah*
gymnasium	palestra, f.	*pah-*LEH-*strah*
habit (custom)	abitudine, f.	*ah-bee-*TOO-*dee-neh*
hail (ice)	grandine, f.	GRAHN-*dee-neh*
hail (precipitate hail), to	grandinare	*grahn-dee-*NAH-*reh*
hair	capelli, m., pl.	*kah-*PELL-*lee*
half (adj.)	mezzo	MEDD-*dzoh*
half (n.)	metà, f.	*meh-*TAH

ENGLISH	ITALIAN	PRONUNCIATION
hall (corridor)	corridoio, m.	*kohr-ree-*DOH*-yoh*
hall (meeting room)	sala, f.	SAH*-lah*
halt (come to a stop), to	fermarsi	*fehr-*MAHR*-see*
handkerchief	fazzoletto, m.	*faht-tsoh-*LETT*-toh*
handle	manico, m.	MAH*-nee-koh*
happen (occur), to	accadere	*ahk-kah-*DEH*-reh*
happiness	felicità, f.	*feh-lee-chee-*TAH
happy (glad)	felice	*feh-*LEE*-cheh*
harbor	porto, m.	POHR*-toh*
hard (difficult)	difficile	*deef-*FEE*-chee-leh*
hard (not soft)	duro	DOO*-roh*
hardly (barely)	appena	*ahp-*PEH*-nah*
hardship (privation)	privazione, f.	*pree-vah-*TSYOH*-neh*
hardware	chincaglieria, f.	*keeng-kah-lyeh-*REE*-ah*
harm (damage), to	nuocere a	NWOH*-cheh-reh ah*
haste	fretta, f.	FRETT*-tah*
hat	cappello, m.	*kahp-*PELL*-loh*
hate, to	odiare	*oh-*DYAH*-reh*
have, to	avere	*ah-*VEH*-reh*
he	egli	EH*-lyee*
head	testa, f.	TEH*-stah*
head (leader)	capo, m.	KAH*-poh*
headache	mal di capo, m.	MAHL *dee* KAH*-poh*
headquarters	quartiere generale, m.	*kwahr-*TYEH*-reh jeh-neh-*RAH*-leh*
heal (cure), to	guarire	*gwah-*REE*-reh*
health	salute, f.	*sah-*LOO*-teh*
healthy	sano	SAH*-noh*
hear, to	udire	*oo-*DEE*-reh*
heart	cuore, m.	KWOH*-reh*
hearty (cordial)	cordiale	*kohr-*DYAH*-leh*

ENGLISH	ITALIAN	PRONUNCIATION
heat	calore, m.	*kah-*LOH-*reh*
heat, to	riscaldare	*ree-skahl-*DAH-*reh*
heaven	cielo, m.	CHYEH-*loh*
heavy	pesante	*peh-*SAHN-*teh*
heel	calcagno, m.	*kahl-*KAH-*nyoh*
height (highness)	altezza, f.	*ahl-*TETT-*tsah*
helicopter	elicottero, m.	*eh-lee-*KOHT-*teh-roh*
help (assistance)	aiuto, m.	*ah-*YOO-*toh*
help, to	aiutare	*ah-yoo-*TAH-*reh*
helper	aiutante, m., f.	*ah-yoo-*TAHN-*teh*
helpful (useful)	utile	OO-*tee-leh*
helpless	impotente	*eem-poh-*TENN-*teh*
hem	orlo, m.	OHR-*loh*
hemisphere	emisfero, m.	*eh-mee-*SFEH-*roh*
herb	erba, f.	EHR-*bah*
herring	aringa, f.	*ah-*REENG-*gah*
hide (conceal), to	nascondere	*nah-*SKOHN-*deh-reh*
high	alto	AHL-*toh*
highway	autostrada, f.	*oh-toh-*STRAH-*dah*
hill	collina, f.	*kohl-*LEE-*nah*
hinder, to	impedire	*eem-peh-*DEE-*reh*
hip	anca, f.	AHNG-*kah*
hire (employ), to	impiegare	*eem-pyeh-*GAH-*reh*
history	storia, f.	STOH-*ryah*
hit (strike), to	colpire	*kohl-*PEE-*reh*
hog (animal)	maiale, m.	*mah-*YAH-*leh*
hold, to	tenere	*teh-*NEH-*reh*
holiday	giorno festivo, m.	JOHR-*noh feh-*STEE-*voh*
hollow (adj.)	cavo	KAH-*voh*
holy	santo	SAHN-*toh*
home	casa, f.	KAH-*sah*
homesick	nostalgico	*noh-*STAHL-*jee-koh*
honest	onesto	*oh-*NEH-*stoh*
honesty	onestà, f.	*oh-neh-*STAH

ENGLISH	ITALIAN	PRONUNCIATION
honey	miele, m.	MYEH-*leh*
honor	onore, m.	*oh*-NOH-*reh*
honor (respect), to	onorare	*oh-noh*-RAH-*reh*
hood (automobile)	cofano, m.	KOH-*fah-noh*
hook	gancio, m.	GAHN-*choh*
hope	speranza, f.	*speh*-RAHN-*tsah*
hope, to	sperare	*speh*-RAH-*reh*
horn (automobile)	tromba, f.	TROHM-*bah*
horn (musical instrument)	corno, m.	KOHR-*noh*
horse	cavallo, m.	*kah*-VAHL-*loh*
hospital	ospedale, m.	*oh-speh*-DAH-*leh*
host	ospite, m., f.	OH-*spee-teh*
hot	caldo	KAHL-*doh*
hotel	albergo, m.	*ahl*-BEHR-*goh*
hour	ora, f.	OH-*rah*
house	casa, f.	KAH-*sah*
how (interrog. adv.)	come	KOH-*meh*
however (nevertheless)	però	*peh*-ROH
human (adj.)	umano	*oo*-MAH-*noh*
hunger	fame, f.	FAH-*meh*
hungry	affamato	*ahf-fah*-MAH-*toh*
hungry, to be	aver fame	*ah-vehr* FAH-*meh*
hunting (sport)	caccia, f.	KAHT-*chah*
hurry (haste)	fretta, f.	FRETT-*tah*
hurry (hasten), to	affrettarsi	*ahf-frett*-TAHR-*see*
hurt (be painful), to	dolere	*doh*-LEH-*reh*
husband	marito, m.	*mah*-REE-*toh*
I	io	EE-*oh*
ice (frozen water)	ghiaccio, m.	GYAHT-*choh*
icebox	ghiacciaia, f.	*gyaht*-CHAH-*yah*
ice-cream	gelato, m.	*jeh*-LAH-*toh*
idea	idea, f.	*ee*-DEH-*ah*

ENGLISH	ITALIAN	PRONUNCIATION
idle (not busy)	ozioso	*oh*-TSYOH-*soh*
if (supposing that)	se	SEH
if (whether)	se	SEH
ignorant	ignorante	*ee-nyoh*-RAHN-*teh*
ill (sick)	ammalato	*ahm-mah*-LAH-*toh*
illegal	illegale	*eel-leh*-GAH-*leh*
illness	malattia, f.	*mahl-aht*-TEE-*ah*
illuminate (light up), to	illuminare	*eel-loo-mee*-NAH-*reh*
imagination	immaginazione, f.	*eem-mah-jee-nah*-TSYOH-*neh*
imagine (picture mentally), to	figurarsi	*fee-goo*-RAHR-*see*
immediately (instantly)	subito	SOO-*bee-toh*
impatient	impaziente	*eem-pah*-TSYENN-*teh*
importance	importanza, f.	*eem-pohr*-TAHN-*tsah*
important	importante	*eem-pohr*-TAHN-*teh*
impossibility	impossibilità, f.	*eem-pohss-see-bee-lee*-TAH
impossible	impossibile	*eem-pohss*-SEE-*bee-leh*
impress (affect deeply), to	commuovere	*kohm*-MWOH-*veh-reh*
improve (make better), to	migliorare	*mee-lyoh*-RAH-*reh*
improvement (betterment)	miglioramento, m.	*mee-lyoh-rah*-MENN-*toh*
in (during, prep.)	durante	*doo*-RAHN-*teh*
in (inside, prep.)	dentro	DENN-*troh*
in (into, prep.)	in	EEN
include (contain), to	includere	*een*-KLOO-*deh-reh*
income	entrata, f.	*enn*-TRAH-*tah*

ENGLISH	ITALIAN	PRONUNCIATION
income tax	imposta sul reddito, f.	*eem-*POH*-stah sool* REDD*-dee-toh*
inconvenience	inconvenienza, f.	*een-kohn-veh-*NYENN*-tsah*
indeed (adv.)	veramente	*veh-rah-*MENN*-teh*
independence	independenza, f.	*eén-deh-penn-*DENN*-tsah*
independent	independente	*een-deh-penn-*DENN*-teh*
indicate (point out), to	indicare	*een-dee-*KAH*-reh*
indifferent (unconcerned)	indifferente	*een-deef-feh-*RENN*-teh*
indigestion	indigestione, f.	*een-dee-jeh-*STYOH*-neh*
individual (person, n.)	individuo, m.	*een-dee-*VEE*-dwoh*
indoors (adv.)	dentro	DENN*-troh*
infant (n.)	bambino, m.	*bahm-*BEE*-noh*
infection	infezione, f.	*een-feh-*TSYOH*-neh*
inferior (mediocre)	inferiore	*een-feh-*RYOH*-reh*
inflammation	infiammazione, f.	*een-fyahm-mah-*TSYOH*-neh*
inform (apprise), to	informare	*een-fohr-*MAH*-reh*
information (knowledge)	informazioni, f., pl.	*een-fohr-mah-*TSYOH*-nee*
inhabit, to	abitare	*ah-bee-*TAH*-reh*
inhabitant	abitante, m., f.	*ah-bee-*TAHN*-teh*
initial (letter)	iniziale, f.	*ee-nee-*TSYAH*-leh*
injection	iniezione, f.	*ee-nyeh-*TSYOH*-neh*
injury	ferita, f.	*feh-*REE*-tah*
ink	inchiostro, m.	*een-*KYOH*-stroh*
inn	albergo, m.	*ahl-*BEHR*-goh*

ENGLISH	ITALIAN	PRONUNCIATION
innocent (guiltless)	innocente	*een-noh-*CHENN*-teh*
inquire (ask), to	domandare	*doh-mahn-*DAH*-reh*
inquiry (question)	domanda, f.	*doh-*MAHN*-dah*
insect	insetto, m.	*een-*SETT*-toh*
inspection (scrutiny)	ispezionare	*ee-speh-*TSYOH*-neh*
install (set up for use), to	installare	*een-stahl-*LAH*-reh*
installment (payment)	rata, f.	RAH*-tah*
instance (example)	esempio, m.	*eh-*ZEMM*-pyoh*
instead of	invece di	*een-*VEH*-cheh dee*
instruct (teach), to	istruire	*ee-*STRWEE*-reh*
instruction (teaching)	istruzione, f.	*ee-stroo-*TSYOH*-neh*
instrument (implement)	strumento, m.	*stroo-*MENN*-toh*
insurance	assicurazione, f.	*ahss-see-koo-rah-*TSYOH*-neh*
intelligence (understanding)	intelligenza, f.	*een-tell-lee-*JENN*-tsah*
intelligent	intelligente	*een-tell-lee-*JENN*-teh*
intend (propose), to	avere l'intenzione di	*ah-*VEH*-reh leen-tenn-*TSYOH*-neh dee*
intention	intenzione, f.	*een-tenn-*TSYOH*-neh*
interest (attention)	attenzione, f.	*aht-tenn-*TSYOH*-neh*
interest (money rate)	interesse, m.	*een-teh-*RESS*-seh*
interest, to	interessare	*een-teh-ress-*SAH*-reh*

ENGLISH	ITALIAN	PRONUNCIATION
interesting	interessante	*een-teh-ress-*SAHN-*teh*
interfere (meddle), to	immischiarsi	*eem-mee-*SKYAHR-*see*
interior (inside, n.)	interno, m.	*een-*TEHR-*noh*
interpret (explain), to	interpretare	*een-tehr-preh-*TAH-*reh*
interrupt, to	interrompere	*een-tehr-*ROHM-*peh-reh*
intimate (personal)	intimo	EEN-*tee-moh*
into (to the inside)	in	EEN
introduce (make acquainted), to	presentare	*preh-zenn-*TAH-*reh*
invest, to	investire	*een-veh-*STEE-*reh*
invitation	invito, m.	*een-*VEE-*toh*
invite, to	invitare	*een-vee-*TAH-*reh*
involve (entail), to	richiedere	*ree-*KYEH-*deh-reh*
iodine (antiseptic)	tintura d'iodio, f.	*teen-*TOO-*rah* DYOH-*dyoh*
Irish (adj.)	irlandese	*eer-lahn-*DEH-*seh*
iron (metal)	ferro, m.	FEHR-*roh*
iron (electric)	ferro elettrico (per stirare), m.	FEHR-*roh eh-*LETT-*tree-koh (pehr stee-*RAH-*reh)*
island	isola, f.	EE-*zoh-lah*
isthmus	istmo, m.	EE-*stmoh*
Italian (adj.)	italiano	*ee-tah-*LYAH-*noh*
jacket (short coat)	giacca, f.	JAHK-*kah*
jail	carcere, m.	KAHR-*cheh-reh*
Japanese (adj.)	giapponese	*jahp-poh-*NEH-*seh*
jar (vessel)	barattolo, m.	*bah-*RAHT-*toh-loh*
jaw	mascella, f.	*mah-*SHELL-*lah*
jelly	gelatina, f.	*jeh-lah-*TEE-*nah*
Jew (n.)	ebreo, m.	*eh-*BREH-*oh*

ENGLISH	ITALIAN	PRONUNCIATION
jewel	gioiello, m.	*joh-*YELL*-loh*
jewelry	gioielli, m., pl.	*joh-*YELL*-lee*
Jewish (adj.)	ebreo	*eh-*BREH*-oh*
job (employment)	impiego, m.	*eem-*PYEH*-goh*
job (task)	compito, m.	KOHM*-pee-toh*
joke (jest)	scherzo, m.	SKEHR*-tsoh*
joke (jest), to	scherzare	*skehr-*TSAH*-reh*
journey	viaggio, m.	VYAHD*-joh*
joy	gioia, f.	JOH*-yah*
judge	giudice, m.	JOO*-dee-cheh*
judge, to	giudicare	*joo-dee-*KAH*-reh*
juice	succo, m.	SOOK*-koh*
jump (bound), to	saltare	*sahl-*TAH*-reh*
jury	giurati, m., pl.	*joo-*RAH*-tee*
just (merely)	semplicemente	*semm-plee-cheh-*MENN*-teh*
keep (retain), to	ritenere	*ree-teh-*NEH*-reh*
kettle	caldaia, f.	*kahl-*DAH*-yah*
key	chiave, f.	KYAH*-veh*
kidney	rene, m.	REH*-neh*
kill, to	uccidere	*oot-*CHEE*-deh-reh*
kind (adj.)	gentile	*jenn-*TEE*-leh*
kind (n.)	specie, f.	SPEH*-cheh*
kindness (goodness)	gentilezza, f.	*jenn-tee-*LETT*-tsah*
king	re, m.	REH
kiss	bacio, m.	BAH*-choh*
kiss, to	baciare	*bah-*CHAH*-reh*
kitchen	cucina, f.	*koo-*CHEE*-nah*
knee	ginocchio, m.	*jee-*NOHK*-kyoh*
knife	coltello, m.	*kohl-*TELL*-loh*
knock (hit), to	picchiare	*peek-*KYAH*-reh*
knot	nodo, m.	NOH*-doh*
know (be acquainted with), to	conoscere	*koh-*NOH*-sheh-reh*
knowledge (information)	conoscenza, f.	*koh-noh-*SHENN*-tsah*

ENGLISH	ITALIAN	PRONUNCIATION
known (familiar)	conosciuto	*koh-noh-*SHOO-*toh*
label	etichetta, f.	*eh-tee-*KETT-*tah*
lace (fabric)	merletto, m.	*mehr-*LETT-*toh*
lace (shoelace)	laccio, m.	LAHT-*choh*
lack (be without), to	mancare di	*mahn-*KAH-*reh dee*
lady	signora, f.	*see-*NYOH-*rah*
lake	lago, m.	LAH-*goh*
lamb	agnello, m.	*ah-*NYELL-*loh*
lamb chop	costoletta d'agnello, f.	*koh-stoh-*LETT-*tah dah-*NYELL-*loh*
lamp	lampada, f.	LAHM-*pah-dah*
land (ground)	terra, f.	TEHR-*rah*
land (property)	terreno, m.	*tehr-*REH-*noh*
land (region)	terra, f.	TEHR-*rah*
land (from a ship), to	sbarcare	*zbahr-*KAH-*reh*
landscape (scenery)	paesaggio, m.	*pah-eh-*ZAHD-*joh*
language	lingua, f.	LEENG-*gwah*
large	largo	LAHR-*goh*
last (final, adj.)	ultimo	OOL-*tee-moh*
last (most recent, adj.)	ultimo	OOL-*tee-moh*
late (tardily, adv.)	in ritardo	*een ree-*TAHR-*doh*
laugh, to	ridere	REE-*deh-reh*
laughter	risa, f., pl.	REE-*sah*
laundry (articles laundered)	bucato, m.	*boo-*KAH-*toh*
law (statute)	legge, f.	LEDD-*jeh*
lawful	legittimo	*leh-*JEET-*tee-moh*
lawyer	avvocato, m.	*ahv-voh-*KAH-*toh*
lay (put down), to	collocare	*kohl-loh-*KAH-*reh*
lead (guide), to	condurre	*kohn-*DOOR-*reh*
learn (acquire knowledge), to	imparare	*eem-pah-*RAH-*reh*
least (adv.)	(il) meno	*(eel)* MEH-*noh*

ENGLISH	ITALIAN	PRONUNCIATION
leather (n.)	cuoio, m.	KWOH-*yoh*
leave (depart), to	partire	*pahr*-TEE-*reh*
leave (let remain), to	lasciare	*lah*-SHAH-*reh*
left (adj.)	sinistro	*see*-NEE-*stroh*
left (adv.)	a sinistra	*ah see*-NEE-*strah*
leg	gamba, f.	GAHM-*bah*
legal	legale	*leh*-GAH-*leh*
leisure	agio, m.	AH-*joh*
lemon	limone, m.	*lee*-MOH-*neh*
lend, to	prestare	*preh*-STAH-*reh*
length	lunghezza, f.	*loong*-GETT-*tsah*
less (adv.)	meno	MEH-*noh*
less (minus, prep.)	meno	MEH-*noh*
lesson (assignment)	lezione, f.	*leh*-TSYOH-*neh*
let (permit), to	permettere	*pehr*-METT-*teh-reh*
letter (character)	lettera, f.	LETT-*teh-rah*
letter (epistle)	lettera, f.	LETT-*teh-rah*
level (plane, n.)	livello, m.	*lee*-VELL-*loh*
liability (responsibility)	responsabilità, f.	*reh-spohn-sah-bee-lee-*TAH
liable (responsible)	responsabile	*ree-spohn-*SAH-*bee-leh*
liberty (freedom)	libertà, f.	*lee behr* TAH
library	biblioteca, f.	*bee-blyoh-*TEH-*kah*
license (permit)	patente, f.	*pah-*TENN-*teh*
lid (cover)	coperchio, m.	*koh-*PEHR-*kyoh*
lie (be located), to	trovarsi	*troh-*VAHR-*see*
lie (be prone), to	giacere	*jah-*CHEH-*reh*
lie (prevaricate), to	mentire	*menn-*TEE-*reh*
lie down, to	coricarsi	*koh-ree-*KAHR-*see*
life	vita, f.	VEE-*tah*
lift (raise), to	sollevare	*sohl-leh-*VAH-*reh*
light (illumination)	luce, f.	LOO-*cheh*

ENGLISH	ITALIAN	PRONUNCIATION
light (of little weight)	leggero	LEDD-*jeh-roh*
light (set fire to), to	accendere	*aht*-CHENN-*deh-reh*
lightning	fulmine, m.	FOOL-*mee-neh*
like, (adj.)	simile	SEE-*mee-leh*
like (adv.)	come	KOH-*meh*
like (be fond of), to	piacere (a)	*pyah*-CHEH-*reh (ah)*
likely (probable, adj.)	probabile	*proh*-BAH-*bee-leh*
limb	membro, m.	MEMM-*broh*
limit	limite, m.	LEE-*mee-teh*
limit, to	limitare	*lee-mee*-TAH-*reh*
line (row)	fila, f.	FEE-*lah*
linen (fabric)	tela di lino, f.	TEH-*lah dee* LEE-*noh*
liner, ocean	piroscafo, m.	*pee*-ROH-*skah-foh*
lip	labbro, m.	LAHB-*broh*
lipstick	matita per labbra, f.	*mah*-TEE-*tah pehr* LAHB-*brah*
listen, to	ascoltare	*ah-skohl*-TAH-*reh*
litter (stretcher)	barella, f.	*bah*-RELL-*lah*
little (not much, adj.)	poco	POH-*koh*
little (small, adj.)	piccolo	PEEK-*koh-loh*
little (small amount, n.)	poco, m.	POH-*koh*
live (adj.)	vivo	VEE-*voh*
live (be alive), to	vivere	VEE-*veh-reh*
liver	fegato, m.	FEH-*gah-toh*
living (livelihood)	vita, f.	VEE-*tah*
load (burden)	carico, m.	KAH-*ree-koh*
loaf	pane, m.	PAH-*neh*
lobster	aragosta, f.	*ah-rah*-GOH-*stah*

ENGLISH	ITALIAN	PRONUNCIATION
local (regional)	locale	*loh-*KAH*-leh*
locality (place)	località, f.	*loh-kah-lee-*TAH
locate (find), to	trovare	*troh-*VAH*-reh*
lock (fastening)	serratura, f.	*sehr-rah-*TOO*-rah*
lock (fasten with key), to	chiudere a chiave	KYOO*-deh-reh ah* KYAH*-veh*
lodging (temporary quarters)	alloggio, m.	*ahl-*LOHD*-joh*
lone (solitary)	solo	SOH*-loh*
lonely (unfrequented)	solitario	*soh-lee-*TAH*-ryoh*
lonesome	solitario	*soh-lee-*TAH*-ryoh*
long (not short)	lungo	LOONG*-goh*
long for, to	desiderare	*deh-see-deh-*RAH*-reh*
look (gaze), to	guardare	*gwahr-*DAH*-reh*
look (seem), to	sembrare	*semm-*BRAH*-reh*
look for, to	cercare	*chehr-*KAH*-reh*
lose, to	perdere	PEHR*-deh-reh*
loss	perdita, f.	PEHR*-dee-tah*
loud (resounding)	forte	FOHR*-teh*
love	amore, m.	*uh-*MOH*-reh*
love, to	amare	*ah-*MAH*-reh*
low	basso	BAHSS*-soh*
luck	fortuna, f.	*fohr-*TOO*-nah*
lucky (fortunate)	fortunato	*fohr-too-*NAH*-toh*
luggage	bagaglio, m.	*bah-*GAH*-lyoh*
lunch (midday meal)	(seconda) cola-zione, f.	*(seh-*KOHN*-dah) koh-lah-*TSYOH*-neh*
lung	polmone, m.	*pohl-*MOH*-neh*
machine	macchina, f.	MAHK*-kee-nah*
mad (insane)	pazzo	PAHT*-tsoh*
magazine (periodical)	rivista, f.	*ree-*VEE*-stah*
maid (servant)	cameriera, f.	*kah-meh-*RYEH*-rah*

ENGLISH	ITALIAN	PRONUNCIATION
maiden name	nome di fan-ciulla, m.	NOH-*meh dee fahn*-CHOOL-*lah*
mail (letters exchanged)	corriere, m.	*koh*-RYEH-*reh*
mail (postal system)	posta, f.	POH-*stah*
mail (post), to	impostare	*eem-poh*-STAH-*reh*
main (principal)	principale	*preen-chee*-PAH-*leh*
make, to	fare	FAH-*reh*
malaria	malaria, f.	*mah*-LAH-*ryah*
male (adj.)	maschio	MAH-*skyoh*
man	uomo, m.	WOH-*moh*
manage (administer), to	gestire	*jeh*-STEE-*reh*
management (administration)	direzione, f.	*dee-reh*-TSYOH-*neh*
manager (administrator)	direttore, m.	*dee-rett*-TOH-*reh*
manual (small book)	manuale, m.	*mah*-NWAH-*leh*
many, more, most	molti, più, (il) più di	MOHL-*tee,* PYOO, *(eel)* PYOO *(dee)*
map	carta, f.	KAHR-*tah*
mark (designate), to	marcare	*mahr*-KAH-*reh*
market (trading center)	mercato, m.	*mehr*-KAH-*toh*
marriage	matrimonio, m.	*mah-tree*-MOH-*nyoh*
married	sposato	*spoh*-ZAH-*toh*
marry, to	sposare	*spoh*-ZAH-*reh*
marvelous	maraviglioso	*mah-rah-vee*-LYOH-*soh*
master (great artist)	maestro, m.	*mah*-EH-*stroh*
match (lucifer)	fiammifero, m.	*fyahm*-MEE-*feh-roh*

ENGLISH	ITALIAN	PRONUNCIATION
material (substance)	materia, f.	*mah-*TEH*-ryah*
matinee (theater performance)	recita diurna, f.	REH*-chee-tah* DYOOR*-nah*
matter (affair)	affare, m.	*ahf-*FAH*-reh*
mattress	materasso, m.	*mah-teh-*RAHSS*-soh*
maybe	forse	FOHR*-seh*
mayor	sindaco, m.	SEEN*-dah-koh*
meal (repast)	pasto, m.	PAH*-stoh*
mean (have in mind), to	voler dire	*voh-*LEHR *DEE-reh*
mean (intend), to	avere l'intenzione	*ah-*VEH*-reh leen-tenn-*TSYOH*-neh*
meaning (sense)	significato, m.	*see-nyee-fee-*KAH*-toh*
meantime (n.)	frattempo, m.	*fraht-*TEMM*-poh*
meanwhile (adv.)	intanto	*een-*TAHN*-toh*
measles	rosolia, f.	*roh-zoh-*LEE*-ah*
meat	carne, f.	KAHR*-neh*
mechanic	meccanico, m.	*mekk-*KAH*-nee-koh*
medical	medico	MEH*-dee-koh*
medicine (medicament)	medicina, f.	*meh-dee-*CHEE*-nah*
meet (be introduced to), to	essere presentato a	ESS*-seh-reh preh-zenn-*TAH*-toh ah*
meet (come together), to	incontrarsi (con)	*een-kohn-*TRAHR*-see (kohn)*
meet (encounter), to	incontrare	*een-kohn-*TRAH*-reh*
memory	ricordo, m.	*ree-*KOHR*-doh*
mend (repair), to	accomodare	*ahk-koh-moh-*DAH*-reh*
mention, to	menzionare	*menn-tsyoh-*NAH*-reh*

ENGLISH	ITALIAN	PRONUNCIATION
menu	lista (delle vivande), f.	LEE-*stah (dell-leh vee-*VAHN*-deh)*
merchant	mercante, m.	*mehr-*KAHN*-teh*
merciful	clemente	*kleh-*MENN*-teh*
mercy	misericordia, f.	*mee-zeh-ree-*KOHR*-dyah*
merely	semplicemente	*semm-plee-cheh-*MENN*-teh*
merit, to	meritare	*meh-ree-*TAH*-reh*
messenger (courier)	messaggero, m.	*mess-sahd-*JEH*-roh*
metal (n.)	metallo, m.	*meh-*TAHL*-loh*
middle (center)	mezzo, m.	MEDD-*dzoh*
midnight	mezzanotte, f.	*medd-dzah-*NOHT*-teh*
milk	latte, m.	LAHT-*teh*
mind (opinion)	avviso, m.	*ahv-*VEE*-zoh*
mineral	minerale, m.	*mee-neh-*RAH*-leh*
minister (clergyman)	ministro, m.	*mee-*NEE*-stroh*
minute (unit of time)	minuto, m.	*mee-*NOO*-toh*
mirror	specchio, m.	SPEKK-*kyoh*
miscellaneous	miscellaneo	*mee-shell-*LAH*-neh-oh*
mischief (harm)	danno, m.	DAHN-*noh*
miserable (unhappy)	infelice	*een-feh-*LEE*-cheh*
misfortune	sfortuna, f.	*sfohr-*TOO*-nah*
mislay, to	smarrire	*zmahr-*REE*-reh*
Miss	(la) signorina, f.	*(lah) see-nyoh-*REE*-nah*
miss (fail to do), to	non riuscire a	*nohn-ree-oo-*SHEE*-reh ah*
miss (feel the loss of), to	sentire la mancanza di	*senn-*TEE*-reh lah mahng-*KAHN*-tsah dee*
mist	nebbia, f.	NEBB-*byah*
mistake	sbaglio, m.	ZBAH-*lyoh*

ENGLISH	ITALIAN	PRONUNCIATION
mitten	mezzo-guanto, m.	MEDD-*dzoh-*GWAHN-*toh*
mix, to	mischiare	mee-SKYAH-*reh*
mixture	mistura, f.	mee-STOO-*rah*
mob (disorderly crowd)	turba, f.	TOOR-*bah*
model (exemplar)	modello, m.	moh-DELL-*loh*
model (small copy)	modello, m.	moh-DELL-*loh*
modest	modesto	moh-DEH-*stoh*
moist	umido	oo-*mee-doh*
moldy	ammuffito	ahm-moof-FEE-*toh*
moment (instant)	momento, m.	moh-MENN-*toh*
monastery	monastero, m.	moh-nah-STEH-*roh*
money	denaro, m.	deh-NAH-*roh*
money order	vaglia, m.	VAH-*lyah*
monk	monaco, m.	MOH-*nah-koh*
monkey	scimmia, f.	SHEEM-*myah*
month	mese, m.	MEH-*seh*
monthly (every month, adj.)	mensile	menn-SEE-*leh*
monument	monumento, m.	moh-noo-MENN-*toh*
mood (humor)	umore, m.	oo-MOH-*reh*
moon	luna, f.	LOO-*nah*
more (adj.)	più	PYOO
moreover	inoltre	ee-NOHL-*treh*
morning	mattino, m.	maht-TEE-*noh*
morrow	giorno dopo, m.	JOHR-*noh* DOH-*poh*
mosquito	zanzara, f.	dzahn-DZAH-*rah*
most (adv.)	(il) più	(*eel*) PYOO
most (n.)	(la) massima parte, f.	(*lah*) MAHSS-*see-mah*-PAHR-*teh*
mostly	per la massima parte	pehr lah MAHSS-*see-mah* PAHR-*teh*

ENGLISH	ITALIAN	PRONUNCIATION
moth	tarma, f.	TAHR-*mah*
mother	madre, f.	MAH-*dreh*
mother-in-law	suocera, f.	SWOH-*cheh-rah*
motor (engine)	motore, m.	*moh*-TOH-*reh*
mountain	montagna, f.	*mohn*-TAH-*nyah*
mountainous	montagnoso	*mohn-tah*-NYOH-*soh*
mouse	topo, m.	TOH-*poh*
mouth	bocca, f.	BOHK-*kah*
move (change residence), to	sgomberare	*zgohm-beh*-RAH-*reh*
move (shift the position of) to	muovere	MWOH-*veh-reh*
movement (motion)	movimento, m.	*moh-vee*-MENN-*toh*
movies	cinema, m.	CHEE-*neh-mah*
Mr. (Mister)	(il) signore, m.	*(eel)* see-NYOH-*reh*
Mrs. (Mistress)	(la) signora, f.	*(lah)* see-NYOH-*rah*
much, more, most	molto, più, (il) più di	MOHL-*toh, (eel)* PYOO *dee*
mud	fango, m.	FAHNG-*goh*
muscle	muscolo, m.	MOO-*skoh-loh*
museum	museo, m.	*moo*-ZEH-*oh*
mushroom	fungo, m.	FOONG-*goh*
music	musica, f.	MOO-*zee-kah*
musician	musicista, m.	*moo-zee*-CHEE-*stah*
mustache	baffi, m., pl.	BAHF-*fee*
mustard	senape, m.	SEH-*nah-peh*
mutton	carne di montone, f.	KAHR-*neh dee mohn*-TOH-*neh*
mutual	mutuo	MOO-*twoh*
nail	unghia, f.	OONG-*gyah*
name	nome, m.	NOH-*meh*
namely	cioè	*choh*-EH
nap	pisolino, m.	*pee-soh*-LEE-*noh*

ENGLISH	ITALIAN	PRONUNCIATION
napkin	tovagliolo, m.	*toh-vah-*LYOH*-loh*
narrow	stretto	STRETT*-toh*
national	nazionale	*nah-tsyoh-*NAH*-leh*
natural	naturale	*nah-too-*RAH*-leh*
near (not far, adv.)	vicino	*vee-*CHEE*-noh*
near (prep.)	vicino a	*vee-*CHEE*-noh ah*
nearly (almost)	quasi	KWAH*-zee*
necessary	necessario	*neh-chess-*SAH*-ryoh*
necessity	necessità, f.	*neh-chess-see-*TAH
neck	collo, m.	KOHL*-loh*
necklace	collana, f.	*kohl-*LAH*-nah*
need	bisogno, m.	*bee-*ZOH*-nyoh*
need (require), to	avere bisogno di	*ah-*VEH*-reh bee-*ZOH*-nyoh dee*
needle	ago, m.	AH*-goh*
neglect (slight), to	trascurare	*trah-skoo-*RAH*-reh*
Negro	negro, m.	NEH*-groh*
neighbor	vicino, m.	*vee-*CHEE*-noh*
neighborhood	vicinato, m.	*vee-chee-*NAH*-toh*
neither (adj.)	nè l'uno . . .	*neh* LOO*-noh* . . .
neither (pron.)	nè l'uno . . .	*neh* LOO*-noh* . . .
neither . . . nor (conj.)	(non) . . . ne . . . ne	(NOHN) . . . NEH . . . NEH
nephew	nipote, m.	*nee-*POH*-teh*
nervous	nervoso	*nehr-*VOH*-soh*
never	mai	MY
new	nuovo	NWOH*-voh*
newspaper	giornale, m.	*johr-*NAH*-leh*
newsstand	edicola, f.	*eh-*DEE*-koh-lah*
New Year's Day	Capo d'Anno, m.	*kah-poh-*DAHN*-noh*
next (adv.)	in seguito	*een* SEH*-gwee-toh*
next (following, adj.)	seguente	*seh-*GWENN*-teh*

ENGLISH	ITALIAN	PRONUNCIATION
next to (alongside of, prep.)	accanto a	*ahk*-KAHN-*toh ah*
nice (agreeable	gentile	*jenn*-TEE-*leh*
nickname	soprannome, m.	*soh-prahn*-NOH-*meh*
niece	nipote, f.	*nee*-POH-*teh*
night	notte, f.	NOHT-*teh*
nightgown	camicia da notte, f.	*kah*-MEE-*chah dah* NOHT-*teh*
no	no	NOH
no (not any, adj.)	nessuno	*ness*-SOO-*noh*
nobody (pron.)	nessuno	*ness*-SOO-*noh*
noise (din)	rumore, m.	*roo*-MOH-*reh*
noisy	rumoroso	*roo-moh*-ROH-*soh*
none (pron.)	nessuno	*ness*-SOO-*noh*
nonsense	sciochezza, f.	*shoh*-KETT-*tsah*
noon	mezzogiorno, m.	*medd-dzoh*-JOHR-*noh*
nor	ne	NEH
normal (adj.)	normale	*nohr*-MAH-*leh*
north (adv.)	a nord	*ah* NOHRD
north (n.)	settentrione, m.	*sett-tenn*-TRYOH-*neh*
nose	naso, m.	NAH-*soh*
nostril	narice, f.	*nah*-REE-*cheh*
not	non	NOHN
notary	notaio, m.	*no*-TAH-*yoh*
nothing	niente	NYENN-*teh*
notice (notification)	avviso, m.	*ahv*-VEE-*zoh*
notice (see), to	osservare	*ohss-sehr*-VAH-*reh*
notify, to	notificare	*noh-tee-fee*-KAH-*reh*
nourish, to	nutrire	*noo*-TREE-*reh*
nourishment	nutrimento, m.	*noo-tree*-MENN-*toh*
novel (book)	romanzo, m.	*roh*-MAHN-*dzoh*

ENGLISH	ITALIAN	PRONUNCIATION
now (adv.)	ora	OH-*rah*
nowhere	in nessuna parte	*een ness*-SOO-*nah* PAHR-*teh*
number (numeral)	numero, m.	NOO-*meh-roh*
number (quantity)	quantità, f.	*kwahn-tee*-TAH
nut (food)	noce, f	NOH-*cheh*
oath (vow)	giuramento, m.	*joo-rah*-MENN-*toh*
obedience (compliance)	obbedienza, f.	*ohb-beh*-DYENN-*tsah*
obedient	obbediente	*ohb-beh*-DYENN-*teh*
obey, to	obbedire a	*ohb-beh*-DEE-*reh ah*
object (aim)	oggetto, m.	*ohd*-JETT-*toh*
object (thing)	oggetto, m.	*ohd*-JETT-*toh*
obligation (duty)	obbligazione, f.	*ohb-blee-gah*-TSYOH-*neh*
oblige (compel), to	obbligare	*ohb-blee*-GAH-*reh*
observe (remark), to	osservare	*ohss-sehr*-VAH-*reh*
observe (watch), to	osservare	*ohss-sehr*-VAH-*reh*
obstacle	ostacolo, m.	*oh*-STAH-*koh-loh*
obtain (get), to	ottenere	*oht-teh*-NEH-*reh*
obvious	ovvio	OHV-*vyoh*
occasion	occasione, f.	*ohk-kah*-ZYOH-*neh*
occupation (calling)	occupazione, f.	*ohk-koo-pah*-TSYOH-*neh*
occupy (make busy), to	occupare	*ohk-koo*-PAH-*reh*
occur (happen), to	accadere	*ahk-kah*-DEH-*reh*
ocean	oceano, m.	*oh*-CHEH-*ah-noh*
odor (scent)	odore, m.	*oh*-DOH-*reh*
of	di	DEE
office (place of business)	ufficio, m.	*oof*-FEE-*choh*
often	spesso	SPESS-*soh*
oil	olio, m.	OH-*lyoh*

ENGLISH	ITALIAN	PRONUNCIATION
old (elderly)	anziano	*ahn*-TSYAH-*noh*
omit (leave out), to	omettere	*oh*-METT-*teh-reh*
on (prep.)	su	SOO
once (one time, adv.)	una volta	*oo-nah* VOHL-*tah*
once (formerly, adv.)	un tempo	*oon* TEMM-*poh*
onion	cipolla, f.	*chee*-POHL-*lah*
only (merely)	soltanto	*sohl*-TAHN-*toh*
only (sole)	unico	OO-*nee-koh*
open (adj.)	aperto	*ah*-PEHR-*toh*
open (make open), to	aprire	*ah*-PREE-*reh*
operate (perform surgery), to	operare	*oh-peh*-RAH-*reh*
operation (med.)	operazione, f.	*oh-peh-rah*-TSYOH-*neh*
opinion	opinione, f.	*oh-pee*-NYOH-*neh*
opportunity	occasione, f.	*ohk-kah*-ZYOH-*neh*
opposite (n.)	opposto, m.	*ohp*-POH-*stoh*
opposite (prep.)	in faccia a	*een* FAHT-*chah ah*
or	o	OH
orange (fruit)	arancia, f.	*ah*-RAHN-*chah*
order (command)	ordine, m.	OHR-*dee-neh*
order (purchase)	ordinazione, f.	*ohr-dee-nah*-TSYOH-*neh*
order (sequence)	ordine, m.	OHR-*dee-neh*
order (command), to	comandare	*koh-mahn*-DAH-*reh*
order (purchase), to	comandare	*koh-mahn*-DAH-*reh*
ordinary (usual)	usuale	*oo*-ZWAH-*leh*
original (first)	originale	*oh-ree-jee*-NAH-*leh*
ornament	ornamento, m.	*ohr-nah*-MENN-*toh*
orphan	orfano, m.	OHR-*fah-noh*

ENGLISH	ITALIAN	PRONUNCIATION
other (adj.)	altro	AHL-*troh*
other (pron.)	altro	AHL-*troh*
otherwise (under other conditions)	altrimenti	*ahl-tree-* MENN-*tee*
out (forth, adv.)	fuori	FWOH *ree*
out (not in, adv.)	fuori	FWOH-*ree*
outdoors (adv.)	all'aria libera	*ahl-*LAH-*ryah* LEE-*beh-rah*
outfit (equipment)	equipaggia-mento, m.	*eh-kwee-pahd-jah* MENN-*toh*
outside (adj.)	esterno	*eh-*STEHR-*noh*
outside (adv.)	fuori	FWOH-*ree*
outside (n.)	di fuori, m.	*dee* FWOH-*ree*
oven	forno, m.	FOHR-*noh*
over (above, prep.)	sopra	SOH-*prah*
overcoat	soprabito, m.	*soh-*PRAH-*bee-toh*
overlook (disregard), to	passare sopra	*pahss-*SAH-*reh* SOH-*prah*
oversea(s) (adj.)	d'oltremare	*dohl-treh-*MAH-*reh*
owe, to	dovere	*doh-*VEH-*reh*
own (adj.)	proprio	PROH-*pryoh*
own (possess), to	possedere	*pohss-seh-*DEH-*reh*
owner	proprietario, m.	*proh-pryeh-*TAH-*ryoh*
oyster	ostrica, f.	OH-*stree-kah*
pack (wrap), to	impaccare	*eem-pahk-*KAH-*reh*
package	pacco, m.	PAHK-*koh*
page (leaf)	pagina, f.	PAH-*jee-nah*
pail	secchia, f.	SEKK-*kyah*
pain (ache)	dolore, m.	*doh-*LOH-*reh*
painful	doloroso	*doh-loh-*ROH-*soh*
painter (artist)	pittore, m.	*peet-*TOH-*reh*
painting (picture)	pittura, f.	*peet-*TOO-*rah*
pair	paio, m.	PAH-*yoh*
pajamas	pigiama, m.	*pee-*JAH-*mah*
pal	amico, m.	*ah-*MEE-*koh*

ENGLISH	ITALIAN	PRONUNCIATION
palace	palazzo, m.	*pah-*LAHT*-tsoh*
pale (wan)	pallido	PAHL*-lee-doh*
pane, window	vetro, m.	VEH*-troh*
paper	carta, f.	KAHR*-tah*
parade (procession)	sfilata, f.	*sfee-*LAH*-tah*
paragraph	paragrafo, m.	*pah-*RAH*-grah-foh*
parcel (package)	pacco, m.	PAHK*-koh*
parcel post	pacco postale, m.	PAHK*-koh pohss-*TAH*-leh*
parents	genitori, m. pl.	*jeh-nee-*TOH*-ree*
park	parco, m.	PAHR*-koh*
park (put in place), to	parcare	*pahr-*KAH*-reh*
parlor (living room)	salotto, m.	*sah-*LOHT*-toh*
part (portion)	parte, f.	PAHR*-teh*
participate, to	partecipare	*pahr-teh-chee-*PAH*-reh*
particular (detail, n.)	dettagglio, m.	*dett-*TAH*-lyoh*
particular (specific, adj.)	particolare	*pahr-tee-koh-*LAH*-reh*
partly	parzialmente	*pahr-tsyahl-*MENN*-teh*
partner	socio, m.	SOH*-choh*
party (political)	partito, m.	*pahr-*TEE*-toh*
party (social gathering)	ricevimento, m.	*ree-cheh-vee-*MENN*-toh*
pass (go by), to	passare	*pahss-*SAH*-reh*
passage (passageway)	passaggio, m.	*pahss-*SAHD*-joh*
passenger	passeggiero, m.	*pahss-sedd-*JEH*-roh*
passport	passaporto, m.	*pahss-sah-*POHR*-toh*
past (beyond, prep)	al di là di	*ahl dee* LAH *dee*

ENGLISH	ITALIAN	PRONUNCIATION
past (bygone, adj.)	passato	*pahss*-SAH-*toh*
past (n.)	passato, m.	*pahss*-SAH-*toh*
pastor	pastore, m.	*pah*-STOH-*reh*
patch (repair)	pezza, f.	PETT-*tsah*
patience	pazienza, f.	*pah*-TSYENN-*tsah*
patient (forbearing)	paziente	*pah*-TSYENN-*teh*
patient (invalid)	paziente, m., f.	*pah*-TSYENN-*teh*
patron (customer)	cliente, m., f.	*klee*-ENN-*teh*
pattern (design)	disegno, m.	*dee*-SEH-*nyoh*
pavement	pavimento, m.	*pah*-vee-MENN-*toh*
pawn, to	dare in pegno	DAH-*reh een* PEH-*nyoh*
pawnshop	Monte di Pietà, m.	MOHN-*teh dee pyeh*-TAH
pay, to	pagare	*pah*-GAH-*reh*
payable (due)	pagabile	*pah*-GAII-*bee lch*
payment	pagamento, m.	*pah*-gah-MENN-*toh*
peace	pace, f.	PAH-*cheh*
peach	pesca, f.	PEH-*skah*
pear	pera, f.	PEH-*rah*
pearl (gem)	perla, f.	PEIIR-*lah*
peculiar (odd)	strano	STRAH-*noh*
peel (take skin from), to	sbucciare	*zbool*-CHAH-*reh*
pen, fountain	penna stilografica, f.	PENN-*nah stee-loh*-GRAH-*fee-kah*
pencil	matita, f.	*mah*-TEE-*tah*
peninsula	penisola, f.	*peh*-NEE-*zoh-lah*
people (persons)	gente, f.	JENN-*teh*
pepper (seasoning)	pepe, m.	PEH-*peh*
perfect (flawless)	perfetto	*pehr*-FETT-*toh*
perform (do), to	compiere	KOHM-*pyeh-reh*
performance (stage presentation)	rappresentazione f.	*rahp-preh-zenn-tah*-TSYOH-*neh*
perfume (fragrance)	profumo, m.	*proh*-FOO-*moh*

ENGLISH	ITALIAN	PRONUNCIATION
perhaps	forse	FOHR-*seh*
period (of time)	periodo, m.	*peh*-REE-*oh-doh*
permanent (adj.)	permanente	*pehr-mah*-NENN-*teh*
permission	permesso, m.	*pehr*-MESS-*soh*
permit (allow), to	permettere	*pehr*-METT-*teh-reh*
person	persona, f.	*pehr*-SOH-*nah*
personal	personale	*pehr-soh*-NAH-*leh*
persuade, to	persuadere	*pehr-swah*-DEH-*reh*
pet (animal)	animale favorito, m.	*ah-nee*-MAH-*leh fah-voh*-REE-*toh*
petticoat	sottana, f.	*soht*-TAH-*nah*
pharmacist	farmacista, m.	*fahr-mah*-CHEE-*stah*
pharmacy (drug store)	farmacia, f.	*fahr-mah*-CHEE-*ah*
phone, to	telefonare	*teh-leh-foh*-NAH-*reh*
phonograph	fonografo, m.	*foh*-NOH-*grah-foh*
photograph	fotografia, f.	*foh-toh-grah*-FEE-*ah*
physician	medico, m.	MEH-*dee-koh*
piano	pianoforte, m.	*pyah-noh*-FOHR-*teh*
pick (choose), to	scegliere	SHEH-*lyeh-reh*
picture (depiction)	quadro, m.	KWAH-*droh*
pie	torta, f.	TOHR-*tah*
piece (bit)	pezzo, m.	PETT-*tsoh*
pig (animal)	porco, m.	POHR-*koh*
pigeon	piccione, m.	*peet*-CHOH-*neh*
pill	pillola, f.	PEEL-*loh-lah*
pillow	guanciale, m.	*gwahn*-CHAH-*leh*
pin (sewing accessory)	spillo, m.	SPEEL-*loh*
pipe (tobacco pipe)	pipa, f.	PEE-*pah*
pitcher (container)	brocca, f.	BROHK-*kah*
pity (compassion)	compassione, f.	*kohm-pahss*-SYOH-*neh*

ENGLISH	ITALIAN	PRONUNCIATION
pity, to	compatire	*kohm-pah-*TEE-*reh*
place (locality)	luogo, m.	LWOH-*goh*
place (lay), to	collocare	*kohl-loh-*KAH-*reh*
plain (clear)	chiaro	KYAH-*roh*
plane	aeroplano, m.	*ah-eh-roh-*PLAH-*noh*
plant (flora)	pianta, f.	PYAHN-*tah*
plate (shallow dish)	piatto, m.	PYAHT-*toh*
platform, railroad	marciapiede, m.	*mahr-chah-*PYEH-*deh*
play (stage presentation)	spettacolo, m.	*spett-*TAH-*koh-loh*
play (engage in recreation), to	giocare	*joh-*KAH-*reh*
play (perform music upon), to	suonare	*swoh-*NAH-*reh*
playmate	compagno di guoco, m.	*kohm-*PAH-*nyoh dee* JWOH-*koh*
pleasant	piacevole	*pyah-*CHEH-*voh-leh*
please (satisfy), to	accontentare	*ahk kohn tenn* TAH-*reh*
pleasure	piacere, m.	*pyah-*CHEH-*reh*
plenty (n.)	abbondanza, f.	*ahb-bohn-*DAHN-*tsah*
plug (elec.)	spina, f.	SPEE-*nah*
plum (fruit)	prugna, f.	PROO-*nyah*
pneumonia	polmonite, f.	*pohl-moh-*NEE-*teh*
pocket	tasca, f.	TAH-*skah*
poem	poesia, f.	*poh-eh-*ZEE-*ah*
poet	poeta, m.	*poh-*EH-*tah*
poetry	poesia, f.	*poh-eh-*ZEE-*ah*
point (indicate), to	indicare	*een-dee-*KAH-*reh*
poison	veleno, m.	*veh-*LEH-*noh*
poison, to	velenare	*veh-leh-*NAH-*reh*
police	polizia, f.	*poh-lee-*TSEE-*ah*

ENGLISH	ITALIAN	PRONUNCIATION
policeman	vigile, m.	VEE-*jee-leh*
polish, to	lucidare	*loo-chee-*DAH-*reh*
polite	garbato	*gahr-*BAH-*toh*
political	politico	*poh-*LEE-*tee-koh*
politician	uomo politico, m.	WOH-*moh poh-*LEE-*tee-koh*
politics	politica, f.	*poh-*LEE-*tee-kah*
pool (standing water)	pozzo, m.	POHT-*tsoh*
poor (needy)	povero	POH-*veh-roh*
poor (unfortunate)	povero	POH-*veh-roh*
pope	papa, m.	PAH-*pah*
popular (prevalent)	popolare	POH-*poh-lah-reh*
population (number of people)	popolazione, f.	*poh-poh-lah-*TSYOH-*neh*
porcelain (n.)	porcellana, f.	*pohr-chell-*LAH-*nah*
pork	carne di maiale, f.	KAHR-*neh dee mah-*YAH-*leh*
pork chop	costoletta di maiale, f.	*koh-stoh-*LETT-*tah dee mah-*YAH-*leh*
port (harbor)	porto, m.	POHR-*toh*
porter (baggage carrier)	portabagagli, m.	*pohr-tah-bah-*GAH-*lyee*
possess, to	possedere	*pohss-seh-*DEH-*reh*
possession (ownership)	possessione, f.	*pohss-sess-*SYOH-*neh*
possibility	possibilità, f.	*pohss-see-bee-lee-*TAH
possible	possibile	*pohss-*SEE-*bee-leh*
postage (postal charge)	porto, m.	POHR-*toh*
post office	ufficio postale, m.	*oof-*FEE-*choh poh-*STAH-*leh*
postpone, to	posporre	*poh-*SPOHR-*reh*
potato (white)	patata, f.	*pah-*TAH-*tah*

ENGLISH	ITALIAN	PRONUNCIATION
poverty	povertà, f.	*poh-vehr-*TAH
powder (cosmetic)	cipria, f.	CHEE-*pryah*
power (authority)	potere, m.	*poh-*TEH-*reh*
powerful	potente	*poh-*TENN-*teh*
practice (custom)	uso, m.	OO-*zoh*
praise, to	lodare	*loh-*DAH-*reh*
pray, to	pregare	*preh-*GAH-*reh*
prayer (petition)	preghiera, f.	*preh-*GYEH-*rah*
prefer (like better), to	preferire	*preh-feh-*REE-*reh*
prejudice	pregiudizio, m	*pre-joo-*DEE-*tsyoh*
prescription	ricetta, f.	*ree-*CHETT-*tah*
present (give), to	presentare	*preh-zenn-*TAH-*reh*
present (introduce), to	presentare	*preh-zenn-*TAH-*reh*
press (newspapers and periodicals)	stampa, f.	STAHM-*pah*
press (iron), to	stirare	*stee-*RAH-*reh*
pretend (feign), to	fingere	FEEN-*jeh-reh*
pretty	grazioso	*grah-*TSYOH-*soh*
prevent (stop), to	prevenire	*preh-veh-*NEE-*reh*
previous	anteriore	*ahn-teh-*RYOH-*reh*
price	prezzo, m.	PRETT-*tsoh*
priest	prete, m.	PREH-*teh*
principal (adj.)	principale	*preen-chee-*PAH-*leh*
principle (basic truth)	principio, m.	*preen-*CHEE-*pyoh*
print (printed reproduction)	incisione, f.	*een-chee-*ZYOH-*neh*
print, to	stampare	*stahm-*PAH-*reh*
prison	prigione, f.	*pree-*JOH-*neh*
prisoner	prigioniero, m.	*pree-joh-*NYEH-*roh*
private (personal)	particolare	*pahr-tee-koh-*LAH-*reh*
privilege	privilegio, m.	*pree-vee-*LEH-*joh*

ENGLISH	ITALIAN	PRONUNCIATION
prize (trophy)	premio, m.	PREH-*myoh*
probable (likely)	probabile	proh-BAH-*bee-leh*
product	prodotto, m.	proh-DOHT-*toh*
profession (occupation)	professione, f.	proh-fess-SYOH-*neh*
professor (teacher)	professore, m.	proh-fess-SOH-*reh*
profit	profitto, m.	proh-FEET-*toh*
prohibition	proibizione, f.	proh-ee-bee-TSYOH-*neh*
prominent (eminent)	eminente	eh-mee-NENN-*teh*
promise (pledge)	promessa, f.	proh-MESS-*sah*
promise (pledge), to	promettere	proh-METT-*teh-reh*
prompt (quick)	pronto	PROHN -*toh*
proper (acceptable)	corretto	kohr-RETT-*toh*
property (possession)	avere, m.	ah-VEH-*reh*
propose (suggest), to	proporre	proh-POHR-*reh*
prosperity	prosperità, f.	proh-speh-ree-TAH
prosperous	prospero	PROH-*speh-roh*
protect, to	proteggere	proh-TEDD-*jeh-reh*
proud (taking pride in)	orgoglioso	ohr-goh-LYOH-*soh*
prove (verify), to	provare	proh-VAH-*reh*
prune	prugna secca, f.	PROO-*nyah* SEKK-*kah*
public (common, adj.)	pubblico	POOB-*blee-koh*
publication (published work)	pubblicazione, f.	poob-blee-kah-TSYOH-*neh*
publish, to	pubblicare	poob-blee-KAH-*reh*
publisher	editore, m.	eh-dee-TOH-*reh*
pudding (dessert)	bodino, m.	boh-DEE-*noh*
pull (draw), to	tirare	tee-RAH-*reh*
punctual	puntuale	poon-TWAH-*leh*
punish, to	punire	poo-NEE-*reh*

ENGLISH	ITALIAN	PRONUNCIATION
punishment	punizione, f.	*poo-nee-*TSYOH-*neh*
pupil (student)	pupilla, f.	*poo-*PEEL-*lah*
purchase (act of buying)	compra, f.	KOHM-*prah*
pure (unadulterated)	puro	POO-*roh*
purpose (aim)	scopo, m.	SKOH-*poh*
purse (coin pouch)	borsa, f.	BOHR-*sah*
pursue (chase), to	inseguire	*een-seh-*GWEE-*reh*
push (shove), to	spingere	SPEEN-*jeh-reh*
put (place), to	mettere	METT *teh-reh*
quaint (unusual)	originale	*oh-ree-jee-*NAH-*leh*
quantity	quantità, f.	*kwahn-tee-*TAH
quarrel (dispute)	alterco, m.	*ahl-*TEHR-*koh*
quarrel (dispute), to	litigare	*lee-tee-*GAH-*reh*
quarter (one-fourth)	quarto, m.	KWAHR-*toh*
queen	regina, f.	*reh-*JEE-*nah*
queer	bizzaro	*beed-*DZAHR-*roh*
question (query)	domanda, f.	*doh-*MAHN *dah*
question (doubt), to	mettere in dubbio	METT-*teh-reh een* DOOB-*byoh*
question (query), to	interrogare	*een-tehr-roh-*GAH-*reh*
quick (rapid)	rapido	RAH-*pee-doh*
quiet (silent, adj.)	silenzioso	*see-lenn-*TSYOH-*soh*
quiet (stillness)	quiete, f.	KWYEH-*teh*
quite (considerably)	abbastanza	*ahb-bah-*STAHN-*tsah*
rabbi	rabino, m.	*rah-*BEE-*noh*
rabbit	coniglio, m.	*koh-*NEE-*lyoh*
race (contest)	corsa, f.	KOHR-*sah*
radiator (heater)	termosifone, m.	*tehr-moh-see-*FOH-*neh*

ENGLISH	ITALIAN	PRONUNCIATION
radio (receiving set)	radio, f.	RAH-*dyoh*
rag (piece of cloth)	straccio, m.	STRAHT-*choh*
rail (bar on track)	rotaia, f.	*roh*-TAH-*yah*
railroad	ferrovia, f.	*fehr-roh*-VEE-*ah*
rain	pioggia, f.	PYOHD-*jah*
rain, to	piovere	PYOH-*veh-reh*
rainbow	arcobaleno, m.	*ahr-koh-bah*-LEH-*noh*
raincoat	impermeabile, m.	*eem-pehr-meh*-AH-*bee-leh*
rainy	piovigginoso	*pyoh-veed-jee*-NOH-*soh*
raisin	uva secca, f.	OO-*vah* SEKK-*kah*
range (of mountains)	catena, f.	*kah*-TEH-*nah*
rapid (adj.)	rapido	RAH-*pee-doh*
rare (uncommon)	raro	RAH-*roh*
raspberry	lampone, m.	*lahm*-POH-*neh*
rat	topo, m.	TOH-*poh*
rate (degree of speed)	posso, m.	PAHSS-*soh*
rate (exchange)	corso, m.	KOHR-*soh*
rather (somewhat)	assai	*ahss*-SYE
raw	grezzo	GREDD-*dzoh*
ray (beam)	raggio, m.	RAHD-*joh*
rayon	seta artificiale, f.	SEH-*tah ahr-tee-fee*-CHAH-*leh*
razor	rasoio, m.	*rah*-ZOH-*yoh*
razor blade	lama di rasoio, f.	LAH-*mah dee rah*-SOH-*yoh*
reach (arrive at), to	giungere	JOON-*jeh-reh*
read, to	leggere	LEDD-*jeh-reh*
ready (prepared)	pronto	PROHN-*toh*
real (actual)	vero	VEH-*roh*

ENGLISH	ITALIAN	PRONUNCIATION
really (actually)	in realtà	*een reh-ahl-*TAH
reason (ground)	ragione, f.	*rah-*JOH*-neh*
reason (intellect)	ragione, f.	*rah-*JOH*-neh*
reasonable (rational)	ragionevole	*rah-joh-*NEH*-voh-leh*
recall (remember), to	ricordarsi	*ree-kohr-*DAHR*-see*
receipt (voucher)	ricevuta, f.	*ree-cheh-*VOO*-tah*
recent	recente	*reh-*CHENN*-teh*
reception	accoglienza, f.	*ahk-koh-*LYENN*-tsah*
recipe	ricetta, f.	*ree-*CHETT*-tah*
reckon (compute), to	computare	*kohm-poo-*TAH*-reh*
recognition (acknowledgment)	riconoscimento m.	*ree-koh-noh-shee-*MENN*-toh*
recognize (identify), to	riconoscere	*ree-koh-*NOH*-sheh reh*
recommend (advise), to	raccomandare	*rahk-koh-mahn-*DAH*-reh*
recommendation	raccomanda-zione, f.	*rahk-koh-mahn-dah-*TSYOH *neh*
recover (get well), to	guarire	*gwah-*REE*-reh*
red	rosso	ROHSS*-soh*
refer (allude), to	riferire	*ree-feh-*REE*-reh*
reference (allusion)	riferimento, m.	*ree-feh-ree-*MENN*-toh*
reflection (meditation)	riflessione, f.	*ree-fless-*SYOH*-neh*
refresh, to	ristorare	*ree-stoh-*RAH*-reh*
refreshments	rinfreschi, m., pl.	*reen-*FREH*-skee*
refrigerator	frigorifero, m.	*free-goh-*REE*-feh-roh*
regard (consider), to	considerare	*kohn-see-deh-*RAH*-reh*

ENGLISH	ITALIAN	PRONUNCIATION
regarding (concerning)	(con) riguardo a	*(kohn)* ree-GWAHR-*doh ah*
region (area)	regione, f.	*reh-*JOH*-neh*
register, to	registrare	*reh-jee-*STRAH*-reh*
registered (postal designation)	raccommandato	*rahk-koh-mahn-*DAH*-toh*
regret, to	rincrescere	*reeng-*KREH*-sheh-reh*
regular (normal)	ordinario	*ohr-dee-*NAH*-ryoh*
reimburse, to	rimborsare	*reem-bohr-*SAH*-reh*
related (connected)	connesso	*kohn-*NESS*-soh*
relation (connection)	rapporto, m.	*rahp-*POHR*-toh*
relative (kinsman)	parente, m.	*pah-*RENN*-teh*
reliable	sicuro	*see-*KOO*-roh*
relieve (ease), to	sollevare	*sohl-leh-*VAH*-reh*
religion	religione, f.	*reh-lee-*JOH*-neh*
religious (adj.)	religioso	*reh-lee-*JOH*-soh*
remain (be left), to	rimanere	*ree-mah-*NEH*-reh*
remain (stay behind), to	rimanere	*ree-mah-*NEH*-reh*
remainder	resto, m.	REH*-stoh*
remark (comment)	osservazione, f.	*ohss-sehr-vah-*TSYOH*-neh*
remark (say), to	osservare	*ohss-sehr-*VAH*-reh*
remedy	rimedio, m.	*ree-*MEH*-dyoh*
remember (recollect), to	ricordarsi (di)	*ree-kohr-*DAHR*-see (dee)*
remind, to	ricordare a	*ree-kohr-*DAH*-reh ah*
remit (send payment), to	rimettere	*ree-*METT*-teh-reh*
remittance	rimessa, f.	*ree-*MESS*-sah*
remote (far-off)	remoto	*reh-*MOH*-toh*
remove (take away), to	togliere	TOH*-lyeh-reh*

ENGLISH	ITALIAN	PRONUNCIATION
renew, to	rinnovare	*renn-noh-*VAH*-reh*
rent (payment)	affitto, m.	*ahf-*FEET*-toh*
rent (charge rent for), to	affittare	*ahf-feet-*TAH*-reh*
rent (pay rent for), to	affittare	*ahf-feet-*TAH*-reh*
repair (fix), to	riparare	*ree-pah-*RAH*-reh*
repay (reimburse), to	rimborsare	*reem-bohr-*SAH*-reh*
repeat (reiterate), to	ripetere	*ree-*PEH*-teh-reh*
repent, to	pentirsi	*penn-*TEER*-see*
reply	risposta, f.	*ree-*SPOH*-stah*
reply, to	rispondere	*ree-*SPOHN*-deh-reh*
represent (act for), to	rappresentare	*rahp-preh-zenn-*TAH*-reh*
representation	rappresentazione, f.	*rahp-preh-zenn-tah-*TSYOH*-neh*
representative (deputy)	deputato, m.	*deh-poo-*TAH*-toh*
reproach	rimprovero, m.	*reem-*PROH*-veh-roh*
reproach, to	rimproverare	*reem-proh-veh-*RAH*-reh*
reputation	riputazione, f.	*ree-poo-tah-*TSYOH*-neh*
request	richiesta, f.	*ree-*KYEH*-stah*
request, to	richiedere	*ree-*KYEH*-deh-reh*
resemble, to	assomigliare a	*ahss-soh-mee-*LYAH*-reh ah*
reserve (order in advance), to	prenotare	*preh-noh-*TAH*-reh*
residence (abode)	residenza, f.	*reh-see-*DENN*-tsah*
resident (n.)	abitante, m., f.	*ah-bee-*TAHN*-teh*
resist, to	resistere a	*reh-*SEE*-steh-reh ah*
resistance	resistenza, f.	*reh-see-*STENN*-tsah*

ENGLISH	ITALIAN	PRONUNCIATION
resort (spa)	stazione climatica, f.	*stah*-TSYOH-*neh klee*-MAH-*tee-kah*
respect (esteem)	rispetto, m.	*ree*-SPETT-*toh*
respect (esteem), to	rispettare	*ree-spett*-TAH-*reh*
respectable	rispettabile	*ree-spett*-TAH-*bee-leh*
respective (adj.)	rispettivo	*ree-spett*-TEE-*voh*
respond (reply), to	rispondere	*ree*-SPOHN-*deh-reh*
respond (reply)	risposta, f.	*ree*-SPOH-*stah*
responsibility (accountability)	responsabilità, f.	*reh-spohn-sah-bee-lee*-TAH
responsible (answerable)	responsabile	*reh-spohn*-SAH-*bee-leh*
rest (remainder)	resto, m.	REH-*stoh*
rest (repose)	riposo, m.	*ree*-POH-*soh*
rest (repose), to	riposarsi	*ree-poh*-SAHR-*see*
restaurant	ristorante, m.	*ree-stoh*-RAHN-*teh*
result (consequence)	conseguenza, f.	*kohn-seh*-GWENN-*tsah*
retire (stop working), to	ritirarsi	*ree-tee*-RAHR-*see*
return (coming or going back)	ritorno, m.	*ree*-TOHR-*noh*
return (give back), to	restituire	*reh-stee*-TWEE-*reh*
return (go back), to	ritornare	*ree-tohr*-NAH-*reh*
reverence (respect)	reverenza, f.	*reh-veh*-RENN-*tsah*
revolution	rivoluzione, f.	*ree-voh-loo*-TSYOH-*neh*
reward (recompense)	ricompensa, f.	*ree-kohm*-PENN-*sah*
reward, to	ricompensare	*ree-kohm-penn*-SAH-*reh*
rheumatism	reumatismo, m.	*reh-oo-mah*-TEE-*zmoh*

ENGLISH	ITALIAN	PRONUNCIATION
rib	costola, f.	KOH-*stoh-lah*
ribbon	nastro, m.	NAH-*stroh*
rice	riso, m.	REE-*soh*
rich	ricco	REEK-*koh*
ride (in a car)	passeggiata (in automobile), f.	*pahss-sedd-*JAH-*tah (een ow-toh-*MOH-*bee-leh)*
ride (in a car), to	andare (in automobile)	*ahn-*DAH-*reh (een-ow-toh-*MOH-*bee-leh)*
ridiculous	ridicolo	*ree-*DEE-*koh-loh*
right (correct)	esatto	*eh-*ZAHT-*toh*
right (on the right, adj.)	destro	DEH-*stroh*
right (right-hand side)	destra, f.	DEH-*strah*
right (to the right, adv.)	a destra	*uh* DEH-*strah*
ring (jewelry)	anello, m.	*ah-*NELL-*loh*
ring (resound), to	risuonare	*ree-swoh-*NAH-*reh*
ripe	maturo	*mah-*TOO-*roh*
rise (ascend), to	salire	*sah-*LEE-*rch*
rise (stand up), to	levarsi	*leh-*VAHR-*see*
risk (danger)	rischio, m.	REE-*skyoh*
river	fiume, m.	FYOO-*meh*
road	strada, f.	STRAH-*dah*
roast	arrosto, m.	*ahr-*ROH-*stoh*
roast (be roasted), to	arrostirsi	*ah roh-*STEER-*see*
rob (steal from), to	rubare	*roo-*BAH-*reh*
robber	ladro, m.	LAH-*droh*
robe (dressing gown)	vestaglia, f.	*veh-*STAH-*lyah*
rock (large stone)	roccia, f.	ROHT-*chah*
rocky (rock-covered)	roccioso	*roht-*CHOH-*soh*

ENGLISH	ITALIAN	PRONUNCIATION
role	ruolo, m.	RWOH-*loh*
roll (bread)	panino, m.	pah-NEE-*noh*
romantic	romantico	roh-MAHN-*tee-koh*
roof	tetto, m.	TETT-*toh*
room (of house)	stanza, f.	STAHN-*tsah*
room (space)	spazio, m.	SPAH-*tsyoh*
rope	fune, f.	FOO-*neh*
rotten (decayed)	marcio	MAHR-*choh*
rouge	rossetto, m.	rohss-SETT-*toh*
rough (harsh)	aspro	AH-*sproh*
rough (uneven)	scabro	SKAH-*broh*
round (adj.)	rotondo	roh-TOHN-*doh*
rouse (awaken), to	destare	deh-STAH-*reh*
royal	reale	reh-AH-*leh*
rubber	gomma, f.	GOHM-*mah*
rubbers (overshoes)	soprascarpe, f., pl.	soh-prah-SKAHR-*peh*
rubbish (litter)	rifiuti, m., pl.	ree-FYOO-*tee*
rude (impolite)	sgarbato	zgahr-BAH-*toh*
rug	tappeto, m.	tahp-PEH-*toh*
ruins (remains)	rovina, f.	roh-VEE-*nah*
rule (regulation)	regola, f.	REH-*goh-lah*
rule (govern), to	governare	goh-vehr-NAH-*reh*
ruler (measuring instrument)	riga, f.	REE-*gah*
run (extend), to	estendersi	eh-STENN-*dehr-see*
run (flow), to	correre	KOHR-*reh-reh*
run (sprint), to	correre	KOHR-*reh-reh*
rural	rurale	roo-RAH-*leh*
rush (dash), to	slanciarsi	zlahn-CHAHR-*see*
Russian (adj.)	russo	ROOSS-*soh*
rust	ruggine, f.	ROOD-*jee-neh*
rusty	arrugginito	ahr-rood-jee-NEE-*toh*
sack (bag)	sacco, m.	SAHK-*koh*
sacred	sacro	SAH-*kroh*
sad (sorrowful)	triste	TREE-*steh*

ENGLISH	ITALIAN	PRONUNCIATION
sadness	tristezza, f.	*tree*-STETT-*tsah*
safe (unharmed)	salvo	SAHL-*voh*
safe (without risk)	sicuro	*see*-KOO-*roh*
safety (n.)	sicurezza, f.	*see*-koo-RETT-*tsah*
safety pin	spillo di sicu-rezza, m.	SPEEL-*loh dee see*-koo-RETT-*tsah*
saint	santo, m.	SAHN-*toh*
salad	insalata, f.	*een*-sah-LAH-*tah*
sale (exchange)	vendita, f.	VENN-*dee-tah*
salesman	venditore, m.	*venn*-dee-TOH-*reh*
salmon	salmone, m.	*sahl*-MOH-*neh*
salt	sale, m.	SAH-*leh*
same (adj.)	stesso	STESS-*soh*
sample	campione, m.	*kahm*-PYOH-*neh*
sandwich	sandwich, m.	SEND-*weech*
sane	sano di mente	SAH-*noh dee* MENN-*teh*
satin	raso, m.	RAH-*soh*
satisfactory	soddisfacente	*sohd*-dee-sfah-CHENN-*teh*
satisfied (contented)	soddisfatto	*sohd*-dee-SFAHT-*toh*
satisfy, to	soddisfare	*sohd*-dee-SFAH-*reh*
saucer	sottotazza, f.	*soht*-toh-TAHT-*tsah*
sausage	salsiccia, f.	*sahl*-SEET-*chah*
save (rescue), to	salvare	*sahl*-VAH-*reh*
save (store up), to	economizzare	*eh*-koh-noh-meed-DZAH-*reh*
savings (money)	risparmio, m.	*ree*-SPAHR-*myoh*
saw (tool)	sega, f.	SEH-*gah*
say, to	dire	DEE-*reh*
scarce	scarso	SKAHR-*soh*
scare (frighten), to	spaventare	*spah*-venn-TAH-*reh*
scarf (neck cloth)	sciarpa, f.	SHAHR-*pah*

ENGLISH	ITALIAN	PRONUNCIATION
scarlet (adj.)	scarlatto	*skahr*-LAHT-*toh*
scarlet fever	scarlattina, f.	*skahr-laht*-TEE-*nah*
scene (dramatic unit)	scena, f.	SHEH-*nah*
scent (odor)	odore, m.	*oh*-DOH-*reh*
schedule (timetable)	orario, m.	*oh*-RAH-*ryoh*
school	scuola, f.	SKWOH-*lah*
schooling (instruction)	istruzione, f.	*ee-stroo*-TSYOH-*neh*
science	scienza, f.	SHYENN-*tsah*
scientific	scientifico	*shyenn*-TEE-*fee-koh*
scissors	forbici, f., pl.	FOHR-*bee-chee*
Scotch (adj.)	scozzese	*skoht*-TSEH-*seh*
scrambled eggs	uova strapazzate, f., pl.	WOH-*vah strah-paht*-TSAH-*teh*
scrap (fragment)	pezzetto, m.	*pett*-TSETT-*toh*
scratch, to	grattare	*graht*-TAH-*reh*
screen (partition)	paravento, m.	*pah-rah*-VENN-*toh*
screw (threaded nail)	vite, f.	VEE-*teh*
screw driver	cacciavite, f.	*kaht-chah*-VEE-*teh*
scrub, to	strofinare	*stroh-fee*-NAH-*reh*
sculptor	scultore, m.	*skool*-TOH-*reh*
sea	mare, m.	MAH-*reh*
search (hunt)	ricerca, f.	*ree*-CHEHR-*kah*
season (of year)	stagione, f.	*stah*-JOH-*neh*
second (adj.)	secondo	*seh*-KOHN-*doh*
second (time unit)	secondo, m.	*seh*-KOHN-*doh*
secret (n.)	segreto, m.	*seh*-GREH-*toh*
secretary (stenographer)	segretaria, f.	*seh-greh*-TAH-*ryah*
secure (safe)	sicuro	*see*-KOO-*roh*
security (safety)	sicurezza, f.	*see-koo*-RETT-*tsah*
seldom	raramente	*rah-rah*-MENN-*teh*

ENGLISH	ITALIAN	PRONUNCIATION
select, to	scegliere	SHEH-*lyeh-reh*
selection (things chosen)	selezione, f.	*seh-leh-*TSYOH-*neh*
sell, to	vendere	VENN-*deh-reh*
send, to	mandare	*mah-*DAH-*reh*
sense (intelligence)	giudizio, m.	*joo-*DEE-*tsyoh*
sense (signification)	senso, m.	SENN-*soh*
sensible (reasonable)	ragionevole	*rah-joh-*NEH-*voh-loh*
sensitive (susceptible)	sensibile	*senn-*SEE-*bee-leh*
sentence	frase, f.	FRAH-*zeh*
separate	separato	*seh-pah-*RAH-*toh*
separate (disconnect), to	separare	*seh-pah-*RAH-*reh*
series	serie, f.	SEH-*ryeh*
serious	serio	SEH-*ryoh*
servant (in a household)	domestico, m.	*doh-*MEH-*stee-koh*
serve, to	servire	*sehr-*VEE-*reh*
service	servizio, m.	*sehr-*VEE-*tsyoh*
set (put), to	collocare	*kohl-loh-*KAH-*reh*
settle (agree on), to	fissare	*feess-*SAH-*reh*
several (a few, adj.)	parecchi	*pah-*REKK-*kee*
severe (strict)	severo	*seh-*VEH-*roh*
sew, to	cucire	*koo-*CHEE-*reh*
sewing machine	macchina da cucire, f.	MAHK-*kee-nah dah koo-*CHEE-*reh*
sex	sesso, m.	SESS-*soh*
shade (window blind)	tendina, f.	*tenn-*DEE-*nah*
shadow	ombra, f.	OHM-*brah*

ENGLISH	ITALIAN	PRONUNCIATION
shake, to	scuotere	SKWOH-*teh-reh*
shallow	poco profondo	POH-*koh* proh-FOHN-*doh*
shame	vergogna, f.	*vehr-*GOH-*nyah*
shape (contour)	forma, f.	FOHR-*mah*
share (part)	parte, f.	PAHR-*teh*
share, to	condividere	*kohn-dee-*VEE-*deh-reh*
sharp	affilato	*ahf-fee-*LAH-*toh*
shave (oneself), to	farsi la barba	FAHR-*see lah* BAHR-*bah*
shaver, electric	rasoio elettrico, m.	*rah-*ZOH-*yoh eh-*LETT-*tree-koh*
shaving cream	sapone per la barba, m.	*sah-*POH-*neh pehr lah* BAHR-*bah*
she	ella	ELL-*lah*
sheet (bedding)	lenzuolo, m.	*lenn-*TSWOH-*loh*
sheet (of paper)	foglio, m.	FOH-*lyoh*
shelf	palchetto, m.	*pahl-*KETT-*toh*
shell (covering)	guscio, m.	GOO-*shoh*
shine (gleam), to	luccicare	*loot-chee-*KAH-*reh*
shine (polish), to	lucidare	*loo-chee-*DAH-*reh*
ship	nave, f.	NAH-*veh*
ship (send goods), to	spedire	*speh-*DEE-*reh*
shipping agent	spedizioniere, m.	*speh-dee-tsyoh-*NYEH-*reh*
shirt	camicia, f.	*kah-*MEE-*chah*
shoe (footwear)	scarpa, f.	SKAHR-*pah*
shoemaker	calzolaio, m.	*kahl-tsoh-*LAH-*yoh*
shop (store)	negozio, m.	*neh-*GOH-*tsyoh*
shop, to	fare compere	FAH-*reh* KOHM-*peh-reh*
shore	riva, f.	REE-*vah*
short (brief)	breve	BREH-*veh*
shoulder	spalla, f.	SPAHL-*lah*
show (exhibit)	mostra, f.	MOH-*strah*

ENGLISH	ITALIAN	PRONUNCIATION
show (make visible), to	mostrare	*moh-*STRAH*-reh*
shower (bath)	doccia, f.	DOHT*-chah*
shower (rainfall)	acquazzone, m.	*ahk-kwaht-*TSOH*-neh*
shrill	acuto	*ah-*KOO*-toh*
shrimp	gamberetto, m.	*gahm-beh-*RETT*-toh*
shudder, to	rabbrividire	*rahb-bree-vee-*DEE*-reh*
shut (make close), to	chiudere	KYOO*-deh-reh*
shy (bashful)	timido	TEE*-mee-doh*
sick (ailing)	malato	*mah-*LAH*-toh*
sickness	malattia, f.	*mah-laht-*TEE*-ah*
side	lato, m.	LAH*-toh*
sidewalk	marciapiede, m.	*mahr-chah-*PYEH*-deh*
sigh, to	sospirare	*soh-spee-*RAH*-reh*
sight (eyesight)	vista, f.	VEE*-stah*
sight (spectacle)	spettacolo, m.	*spett-*TAH*-kol-loh*
sign (indication)	segno, m.	SEH*-nyoh*
sign (endorse), to	firmare	*feer-*MAH*-reh*
signature (name)	firma, f.	FEER*-mah*
silk (n.)	seta, f.	SEH*-tah*
silly	sciocco	SHOHK*-koh*
silver (metal, n.)	argento, m.	*ahr-*JENN*-toh*
similar	simile	SEE*-mee-leh*
similarity	similarità, f.	*see-mee-lah-ree-*TAH
simple (uninvolved)	semplice	SEMM*-plee-cheh*
since (after, prep.)	da	DAH
since (because, conj.)	siccome	*seek-*KOH*-meh*
since (from then to now, adv.)	da allora	*dah ahl-*LOH*-rah*

ENGLISH	ITALIAN	PRONUNCIATION
sing, to	cantare	*kahn-*TAH*-reh*
single (unmarried)	celibe	CHEH*-lee-beh*
singular (peculiar)	originale	*oh-ree-jee-*NAH*-leh*
sink (n.)	acquaio, m.	*ahk-*KWAH*-yoh*
sir	signore, m.	*see-*NYOH*-reh*
sister	sorella, f.	*soh-*RELL*-lah*
sister-in-law	cognata, f.	*koh-*NYAH*-tah*
sit (be sitting), to	sedere	*seh-*DEH*-reh*
sit down, to	sedersi	*seh-*DEHR*-see*
size (of hats)	misura, f.	*mee-*ZOO*-rah*
size (of shoes, gloves)	numero, m.	NOO*-meh-roh*
size (of suits, dresses, coats)	misura, f.	*mee-*ZOO*-rah*
skate, ice	pattino, m.	PAHT*-tee-noh*
ski, to	sciare	*shee-*AH*-reh*
skin (animal hide)	pelle, f.	PELL*-leh*
skin (human skin)	pelle, f.	PELL*-leh*
skirt (garment)	gonnella, f.	*gohn-*NELL*-lah*
sky	cielo, m.	CHYEH*-loh*
sled	slitta, f.	ZLEET*-tah*
sleep	sonno, m.	SOHN*-noh*
sleep, to	dormire	*dohr-*MEE*-reh*
sleeve	manica, f.	MAH*-nee-kah*
slide, to	scivolare	*shee-voh-*LAH*-reh*
slipper	pantofola, f.	*pahn-*TOH*-foh-lah*
slippery	sdrucciolevole	*zdroot-choh-*LEH*-voh-leh*
slow (not fast)	lento	LENN*-toh*
smallpox	vaiolo, m.	*vah-*YOH*-loh*
smell (odor)	odore, m.	*oh-*DOH*-reh*
smell (perceive odor), to	odorare	*oh-doh-*RAH*-reh*
smile	sorriso, m.	*sohr-*REE*-soh*
smile, to	sorridere	*sohr-*REE*-deh-reh*

ENGLISH	ITALIAN	PRONUNCIATION
smoke	fumo, m.	FOO-*moh*
smoke, to	fumare	foo-MAH-*reh*
smooth (adj.)	liscio	LEE-*shoh*
snail	lumaca, f.	loo-MAH-*kah*
sneeze, to	starnutare	stahr-noo-TAH-*reh*
snow	neve, f.	NEH-*veh*
so (in order that, conj.)	acciocchè	aht-chohk-KEH
so (therefore, adv.)	dunque	DOONG-*kweh*
soap	sapone, m.	sah-POH-*neh*
social (societal)	sociale	soh-CHAH-*leh*
society (association)	società, f.	soh-chyeh-TAH
sock (garment)	calzino, m.	kahl-TSEE-*noh*
soft (not hard)	soffice	SOHF-*fee-cheh*
soil, to	sporcare	spohr-KAH-*reh*
sole (of shoe)	suola, f.	SWOH-*lah*
solemn (grave)	grave	GRAH-*veh*
solution (solving)	soluzione, f.	soh-loo-TSYOH-*neh*
solve, to	risolvere	ree-SOHL-*veh-reh*
some (a few, adj.)	alcuni	ahl-KOO-*nee*
some (unspecified, adj.)	qualche	KWAHL-*keh*
some (a quantity, pron.)	ne	NEH
somebody	qualcuno	kwahl-KOO-*noh*
somehow	in qualche modo	een KWAHL-*keh* MOH-*doh*
someone	qualcuno	kwahl-KOO-*noh*
something	qualche cosa	KWAHL-*keh* KOH-*sah*
sometimes	qualche volta	KWAHL-*keh* VOHL-*tah*
son	figlio, m.	FEE-*lyoh*
song	canzone, f.	kahn-TSOH-*neh*
son-in-law	genero, m.	JEH-*neh-roh*

ENGLISH	ITALIAN	PRONUNCIATION
soon (shortly)	tra poco	*trah* POH-*koh*
sore throat	mal di gola, m.	MAHL *dee* GOH-*lah*
sorrow (sadness)	dolore, m.	*doh*-LOH-*reh*
sorry, (to be)	dispiacere a	*dee-spyah*-CHEH-*reh ah*
sort	sorta, f.	SOHR-*tah*
sound (healthy)	sano	SAH-*noh*
sound (noise)	suono, m.	SWOH-*noh*
soup	minestra, f.	*mee*-NEH-*strah*
sour (tart)	agro	AH-*groh*
south	sud, m.	SOOD
southern	meridionale	*meh-ree-dyoh*-NAH-*leh*
space (area)	spazio, m.	SPAH-*tsyoh*
Spanish (adj.)	spagnuolo	*spah*-NYWOH-*loh*
spark	scintilla, f.	*sheen*-TEEL-*lah*
speak (talk), to	parlare	*pahr*-LAH-*reh*
special	speciale	*speh*-CHAH-*leh*
spectacles (glasses)	oochiali, m. pl.	*ohk*-KYAH-*lee*
speed (rapidity)	velocità, f.	*veh-loh-chee*-TAH
spell, to	scrivere	SKREE-*veh-reh*
spirit	spirito, m.	SPEE-*ree-toh*
spit, to	sputare	*spoo*-TAH-*reh*
spoon (tablespoon)	cucchiaio, m.	*kook*-KYAH-*yoh*
spoon (teaspoon)	cucchiaino, m.	*kook-kyah*-EE-*noh*
sport (game)	giuoco, m.	JWOH-*koh*
spot (place)	luogo, m.	LWOH-*goh*
spot (stain)	macchia, f.	MAHK-*kyah*
sprain, to	storcersi	STOHR-*chehr-see*
square (adj.)	quadrato	*kwah*-DRAH-*toh*
square (plaza)	piazza, f.	PYAHT-*tsah*
squirrel	scoiattolo, m.	*skoh*-YAHT-*toh-loh*
staff (personnel)	personale, m.	*pehr-soh*-NAH-*leh*
stage (dais)	palcoscenico, m.	*pahl-koh*-SHEH-*nee-koh*

ENGLISH	ITALIAN	PRONUNCIATION
stain	macchia, f.	MAHK-*kyah*
stairway	scala, f.	SKAH-*lah*
stale	stantio	STAHN-*tyoh*
stall (stop going), to	indugiare	een-doo-JAH-*reh*
stamp, postage	francobollo, m.	*frahng-koh-*BOHL-*loh*
stand (bear), to	resistere a	reh-SEE-*steh-reh ah*
stand (be upright), to	tenersi in piedi	teh-NEHR-*see een* PYEH-*dee*
stand up, to	levarsi	leh-VAHR-*see*
star	stella, f.	STELL-*lah*
start (beginning)	inizio, m.	ee-NEE-*tsyoh*
start (initiate), to	iniziare	ee-nee-TSYAH-*reh*
state (condition)	stato, m.	STAH-*toh*
station, railroad	stazione, f.	stah-TSYOH-*neh*
statue	statua, f.	STAH-*twah*
stay (sojourn)	soggiorno, m.	sohd-JOHR-*noh*
stay (remain), to	restare	reh-STAH-*reh*
steal, to	rubare	roo-BAH-*reh*
steam	vapore, m.	vah-POH-*reh*
steep (adj.)	erto	EHR-*toh*
step (stair)	gradino, m.	grah-DEE-*noh*
step (stride)	passo, m.	PAHSS-*soh*
steward (attendant on ship)	cameriere (di bordo), m.	kah-meh-RYEH-*reh (dee* BOHR-*doh)*
stick (small branch)	rametto, m.	rah-METT-*toh*
stick (adhere), to	aderire	ah-deh-REE-*reh*
still (adv.)	ancora	ahng-KOH-*rah*
still (motionless, adj.)	immobile	eem-MOH-*bee-leh*
still (nevertheless, conj.)	tuttavia	toot-tah-VEE-*ah*
Stockholm	Stoccolma, f.	stohk-KOHL-*mah*

ENGLISH	ITALIAN	PRONUNCIATION
stocking	calza, f.	KAHL-*tsah*
stomach	stomaco, m.	STOH-*mah-koh*
stone	pietra, f.	PYEH-*trah*
stop (halt)	fermata, f.	fehr-MAH-*tah*
stop (cease), to	cessare	chess-SAH-*reh*
stop (come to a standstill), to	fermarsi	fehr-MAHR-*see*
store (shop)	negozio, m.	neh-GOH-*tsyoh*
stormy	tempestoso	temm-peh-STOH-*soh*
story (account)	racconto, m.	rahk-KOHN-*toh*
story (floor)	piano, m.	PYAH-*noh*
stove (for cooking)	fornello, m.	fohr-NELL-*loh*
strange (peculiar)	strano	STRAH-*noh*
strawberry	fragola, f.	FRAH-*goh-lah*
stream (rivulet)	corrente, f.	kohr-RENN-*teh*
street	strada, f.	STRAH-*dah*
strength	forza, f.	FOHR-*tsah*
stretch (draw out), to	stendere	STENN-*deh-reh*
string (cord)	spago, m.	SPAH-*goh*
strip (band)	lista, f.	LEE-*stah*
stroll, to	passeggiare	pahss-sedd-JAH-*reh*
strong	forte	FOHR-*teh*
structure (thing built)	costruzione, f.	koh-stroo-TSYOH-*neh*
stubborn	testardo	teh-STAHR-*doh*
student	studente, m.	stoo-DENN-*teh*
study (active learning)	studio, m.	STOO-*dyoh*
study, to	studiare	stoo-DYAH-*reh*
stupid	stupido	STOO-*pee-doh*
style (manner)	maniera, f.	man-NYEH-*rah*
subject (topic)	argomento, m.	ahr-goh-MENN-*toh*
subscription (for periodicals, etc.)	abbonamento, m.	ahb-boh-nah-MENN-*toh*

ENGLISH	ITALIAN	PRONUNCIATION
subsequent	susseguente	*sooss-seh-*GWENN-*teh*
substitute (thing replacing another)	surrogato, m.	*soor-rah-*GAH-*toh*
substitute (put in place of), to	sostituire	*soh-stee-*TWEE-*reh*
subtract, to	sottrarre	*soht-*TRAHR-*reh*
subway (underground railway)	metropolitana, f.	*meh-troh-poh-lee-*TAH-*nah*
succeed (attain goal), to	riuscire (a)	*ree-oo-*SHEE-*reh (ah)*
success (attainment)	successo, m.	*soot-*CHESS-*soh*
successful	felice	*feh-*LEE-*cheh*
such (of that kind, adj.)	tale	TAH-*leh*
sudden (unexpected)	improvviso	*eem-prohv-*VEE-*zoh*
sue (bring action against), to	citare in giudizio	*chee-*TAH-*reh een joo-*DEE-*tsyoh*
suede	pelle camosciata, f.	PELL-*leh kah-moh-*SHAH-*tah*
suffer (undergo), to	soffrire	*sohf-*FREE-*reh*
sugar	zucchero, m.	TSOOK-*keh-roh*
suggestion (proposal)	suggerimento, m.	*sood-jeh-ree-*MENN-*toh*
suit (lawsuit)	causa, f.	KOW-*zah*
suit, man's	abito, m.	AH-*bee-toh*
suit, woman's	vestito, m.	*veh-*STEE-*toh*
summer	estate, f.	*eh-*STAH-*teh*
summit	sommità, f.	*sohm-mee-*TAH
sun	sole, m.	SOH-*leh*
sunburn	bruciatura di sole, f.	*broo-chah-*TOO-*rah dee* SOH-*leh*
sunglasses	occhiali da sole, m., pl.	*ohk-*KYAH-*lee dah* SOH-*leh*

ENGLISH	ITALIAN	PRONUNCIATION
sunlight	luce del sole, f.	LOO-*cheh dell* SOH-*leh*
sunny	soleggiato	*soh-ledd-*JAH-*toh*
sunrise	levata del sole, f.	*leh-*VAH-*tah dell* SOH-*leh*
sunset	tramonto, m.	*trah-*MOHN-*toh*
sunshine	sole, m.	SOH-*leh*
superstition	superstizione, f.	*soo-pehr-stee-*TSYOH-*neh*
supply (provide), to	provvedere	*prohv-veh-*DEH-*reh*
surgeon	chirurgo, m.	*kee-*ROOR-*goh*
surname	cognome, n.	*koh-*NYOH-*meh*
surprise	sorpresa, f.	*sohr-*PREH-*sah*
surprise (astonish), to	sorprendere	*sohr-*PRENN-*deh-reh*
surroundings	dintorni, m., pl.	*deen-*TOHR-*nee*
suspect (distrust), to	sospettare	*soh-spett-*TAH-*reh*
suspenders	bretelle, f., pl.	*breh-*TELL-*leh*
suspicion	sospetto, m.	*soh-*SPETT-*toh*
swallow, to	inghiottire	*een-gyoht-*TEE-*reh*
swear (curse), to	bestemmiare	*beh-stemm-*MYAH-*reh*
sweat	sudore, m.	*soo-*DOH-*reh*
sweater	maglia, f.	MAH-*lyah*
Swedish (adj.)	svedese	*zveh-*DEH-*seh*
sweep (clean), to	spazzare	*spaht-*TSAH-*reh*
sweet (pleasant tasting)	dolce	DOHL-*cheh*
sweetheart	innamorato, m.	*een-nah-mah-*RAH-*toh*
swim, to	nuotare	*nwoh-*TAH-*reh*
Swiss (adj.)	svizzero	ZVEET-*tseh-roh*
syllable	sillaba, f.	SEEL-*lah-bah*
sympathy	pietà, f.	*pyeh-*TAH
table (furniture)	tavola, f.	TAH-*voh-lah*

ENGLISH	ITALIAN	PRONUNCIATION
tablecloth	tovaglia, f.	*toh*-VAH-*lyah*
tailor	sarto, m.	SAHR-*toh*
take, to	prendere	PRENN-*deh-reh*
talk (conversation)	conversazione, f.	*kohn-vehr-sah-*TSYOH-*neh*
talk, to	parlare	*pahr*-LAH-*reh*
tall (of persons)	alto	AHL-*toh*
tall (of things)	alto	AHL-*toh*
tap (faucet)	rubinetto, m.	*roo-bee-*NETT-*toh*
tap (rap), to	battere legger-	BAHT-*teh-reh*
	mente	*ledd-jehr-*MENN-*teh*
tape recorder	registratore a	*reh-jee-strah-*TOH-*reh ah*
	nastro, m.	NAH-*stroh*
tariff (duty)	dazio, m.	DAH-*tsyoh*
taste (flavor)	gusto, m.	GOO-*stoh*
taste (sample), to	assaggiare	*ahss-sahd-*JAH-*reh*
tax (n.)	imposta, f.	*eem-*POH-*stah*
taxi	tassì, m.	*tahss-*SEE
tea	tè, m.	TEH
teach, to	insegnare	*een-seh-*NYAH-*reh*
teacher	maestro (di	*mah-*EH-*stroh (dee*
	scuola), m.	SKWOH-*lah)*
tear (rip), to	strappare	*strahp-*PAH-*reh*
tease, to	stuzzicare	*stoots-tsee-*KAH-*reh*
telegraph, to	telegrafare	*teh-leh-grah-*FAH-*reh*
telephone	telefono, m.	*teh-*LEH-*foh-noh*
telephone, to	telefonare	*teh-leh-foh-*NAH-*reh*
television	televisione, f.	*teh-leh-vee-*ZYOH-*neh*
tell (inform), to	informare	*een-fohr-*MAH-*reh*
temperature	temperatura, f.	*temm-peh-rah-*TOO-*rah*

ENGLISH	ITALIAN	PRONUNCIATION
temporary	provvisorio	*prohv-vee-*ZOH*-ryoh*
tenant	inquilino, m.	*een-kwee-*LEE*-noh*
tent	tenda, f.	TENN*-dah*
term (duration)	periodo, m.	*peh-*REE*-oh-doh*
term (expression)	termine, m.	TEHR*-mee-neh*
terms (conditions)	patti, m., pl.	PAHT*-tee*
terrible	terribile	*tehr-*REE*-bee-leh*
test (educ.)	esame, m.	*eh-*ZAH*-meh*
testify, to	attestare	*aht-teh-*STAH*-reh*
testimony	testimonianza, f.	*teh-stee-moh-*NYAHN*-tsah*
textile (n.)	tessuto, m.	*tess-*SOO*-toh*
than	che	KEH
thank, to	ringraziare	*reeng-grah-*TSYAH*-reh*
thankful	grato	GRAH*-toh*
thanks (gratitude)	ringraziamenti, m., pl.	*reeng-grah-tsyah-*MENN*-tee*
then (at that time)	allora	*ahl-*LOH*-rah*
then (in that case)	allora	*ahl-*LOH*-rah*
then (subsequently)	poi	POY
there (at that place)	là	LAH
therefore	perciò	*pehr-*CHOH
thick (not thin)	spesso	SPESS*-soh*
thief	ladro, m.	LAH*-droh*
thin (not fat)	magro	MAH*-groh*
thin (not thick)	sottile	*soht-*TEE*-leh*
thing (material object)	cosa, f.	KOH*-sah*
think (reason), to	pensare	*penn-*SAH*-reh*
thirst	sete, f.	SEH*-teh*
thirsty	assetato	*ahss-seh-*TAH*-toh*
thorough (complete)	completo	*kohm-*PLEH*-toh*
thought (idea)	idea, f.	*ee-*DEH*-ah*
thread (sewing thread)	filo, m.	FEE*-loh*

ENGLISH	ITALIAN	PRONUNCIATION
threaten, to	minacciare	*mee-naht-*CHAH-*reh*
throat	gola, f.	GOH-*lah*
through (by means of, prop.)	a mezzo di	*ah* MEDD-*dzoh dee*
through (from end to end of, prep.)	attraverso	*aht-trah-*VEHR-*soh*
throw, to	gettare	*jett-*TAH-*reh*
thumb	pollice, m.	POHL-*lee-cheh*
thunder	tuono, m.	TWOH-*noh*
ticket (entitling card)	biglietto, m.	*bee-*LYETT-*toh*
tide, high	marea alta, f.	*mah-*REH-*ah* AHL-*tah*
tide, low	marea bassa, f.	*mah-*REH-*ah* BAHSS-*sah*
tie (necktie)	cravatta, f.	*krah-*VAHT-*tah*
tie (fasten), to	legare	*leh-*GAH-*reh*
time (hour determined by clock)	ora, f.	OH-*rah*
time (interval)	tempo, m.	TEMM-*poh*
timetable	orario, m.	*oh-*RAH-*ryoh*
tiny	piccolino	*peek-koh-*LEE-*noh*
tip (gratuity)	mancia, f.	MAHN-*chah*
tire	pneumatico, m.	*pnoh-oo-*MAH-*tee-koh*
tired	stanco	STAHNG-*koh*
title (name)	titolo, m.	TEE-*toh-loh*
to (indicating destination, prep.)	a; in	AH; EEN
to (indicating direction, prep.)	a	AH
to (in order to, prep.)	per	PEHR
toast (bread)	pane tostato, m.	PAH-*neh toh-*STAH-*toh*
tobacco	tabacco, m.	*tah-*BAHK-*koh*
today	oggi	OHD-*jee*

ENGLISH	ITALIAN	PRONUNCIATION
toe	dito del piede, m.	DEE-*toh del* PYEH-*deh*
together	insieme	*een*-SYEH-*meh*
toilet (water closet)	gabinetto, m.	*gah-bee*-NETT-*toh*
tomorrow	domani	*doh*-MAH-*nee*
tongue	lingua, f.	LEENG-*gwah*
tonight	stasera	*stah*-SEH-*rah*
too (also)	anche	AHNG-*keh*
too (overly)	troppo	TROHP-*poh*
tooth	dente, m.	DENN-*teh*
toothache	mal di dente, m.	MAHL *dee* DENN-*teh*
toothbrush	spazzolino per i denti, m.	*spaht-tsoh*-LEE-*noh pehr ee* DENN-*tee*
tooth paste	pasta dentrificia, f.	PAH-*stah denn-tee*-FREE-*chah*
top (summit)	sommità, f.	*sohm-mee*-TAH
total (complete)	totale	*toh*-TAH-*leh*
total (sum)	totale, m.	*toh*-TAH-*leh*
touch, to	toccare	*tohk*-KAH-*reh*
tour	giro, m.	JEE-*roh*
toward	verso	VEHR-*soh*
towel, hand	asciugamani, m.	*ah-shoo-gah*-MAH-*nee*
town	città, f.	*cheet*-TAH
toy	giocattolo, m.	*joh*-KAHT-*toh-loh*
track (rails)	binario, m.	*bee*-NAH-*ryoh*
trade mark	marca di fabbrica, f.	MAHR-*kah dee* FAHB-*bree-kah*
traffic (flow of vehicles)	traffico, m.	TRAHF-*fee-koh*
train, railroad	treno, m.	TREH-*noh*
training (instruction)	istruzione, f.	*ee-stroo*-TSYOH-*neh*
transit (passage)	transito, m.	TRAHN-*see-toh*

ENGLISH	ITALIAN	PRONUNCIATION
transport, to	trasportare	*trah-spohr-*TAH-*reh*
travel, to	viaggiare	*vyahd-*JAH-*reh*
traveler	viaggiatore, m.	*vyahd-jah-*TOH-*reh*
tray	vassoio, m.	*vahss-*SOH-*yoh*
treat (behave toward), to	trattare	*traht-*TAH-*reh*
treatment (behavior toward)	trattamento, m.	*traht-tah-*MENN-*toh*
treatment (medical care)	cura, f.	KOO-*rah*
tree	albero, m.	AHL-*beh-roh*
trial (court proceeding)	processo, m.	*proh-*CHESS-*soh*
trick (ruse)	trucco, m.	TROOK-*koh*
trip (journey)	viaggio, m.	VYAHD-*joh*
trip (stumble), to	inciampare	*een-chahm-*PAH-*reh*
trolley (street car)	tranvia, f.	*trahn-*VEE-*ah*
trouble (distress)	guaio, m.	GWAH-*yoh*
trouble (exertion)	fatica, f.	*fah-*TEE-*kah*
trousers	pantaloni, m., pl.	*pahn-tah-*LOH-*nee*
truck (automobile)	autocarro, m	*ou-toh-*KAHR-*roh*
true	vero	VEH-*roh*
trunk (baggage)	baule, m.	*bah-*OO-*leh*
trust (confidence)	fiducia, f.	*fee-*DOO-*chah*
trust (rely on), to	fidarsi di	*fee-*DAHR-*see dee*
truth	verità, f.	*vehr-ree-*TAH
try (attempt), to	tentare	*tenn-*TAH-*reh*
tub (bathtub)	vasca, f.	VAH-*skah*
tuition (school fee)	tasse scolastiche, f., pl.	TAHSS-*seh skoh-*LAH-*stee-keh*
tumbler (glass)	bicchiere, m.	*beek-*KYEH-*reh*
tune (melody)	aria, f.	AH-*ryah*
turkey	tacchino, m.	*tahk-*KEE-*noh*

ENGLISH	ITALIAN	PRONUNCIATION
turn (face about), to	voltarsi	*vohl-*TAHR*-see*
turn (make rotate), to	far girare	FAHR *jee-*RAH*-reh*
tweed (cloth)	tweed, m.	TWEED
twice	due volte	*doo-eh* VOHL*-teh*
twilight	crepuscolo, m.	*kreh-*POO*-skoh-loh*
twin	gemello, m.	*jeh-*MELL*-loh*
twist (wind), to	torcere	TOHR*-cheh-reh*
type (kind)	tipo, m.	TEE*-poh*
type (typewrite), to	scrivere a macchina	SKREE*-veh-reh ah* MAHK*-kee-nah*
typewriter	macchina da scrivere, f.	MAHK*-kee-nah dah* SKREE*-veh-reh*
typhoid fever	tifoide, f.	*tee-*FOY*-deh*
ugly	brutto	BROOT*-toh*
ulcer	ulcera, f.	OOL*-cheh-rah*
umbrella	ombrello, m.	*ohm-*BRELL*-loh*
uncle	zio, m.	TSEE*-oh*
under (prep.)	sotto	SOHT*-toh*
underground (below-ground, adj.)	sotteraneo	*soht-teh-*RAH*-neh-oh*
underneath (prep.)	disotto	*dee-*SOHT*-toh*
understand (comprehend) to	capire	*kah-*PEE*-reh*
underwear	biancheria (intima), f.	*byahng-keh-*REE*-ah (*EEN*-tee-mah)*
uneasy (anxious)	inquieto	*een-*KWYEH*-toh*
unemployed	senza lavoro	SENN*-sah lah-*VOH*-roh*
unemployment	disoccupazione, f.	*dee-zohk-koo-pah-*TSYOH*-neh*
unequal	ineguale	*ee-neh-*GWAH*-leh*
unexpected (adj.)	imprevisto	*eem-preh-*VEE*-stoh*
unfortunate	sfortunato	*sfohr-too-*NAH*-toh*
unhappy (sorrowful)	infelice	*een-feh-*LEE*-cheh*

ENGLISH	ITALIAN	PRONUNCIATION
United Nations	Nazioni Unite, f. pl.	*nah-*TSYOH*-nee* *oo-*NEE*-teh*
university	università, f.	*oo-nee-vehr-see-*TAH
unjust (inequitable)	ingiusto	*een-*JOO*-stoh*
unknown	sconosciuto	*skoh-noh-*SHOO*-toh*
unless (conj.)	a meno che	*ah* MEH*-noh keh*
unlucky	sfortunato	*sfohr-too-*NAH*-toh*
unnecessary	inutile	*ee-*NOO*-tee-leh*
unpaid (due)	allo scoperto	AHL*-loh skoh-*PEHR*-toh*
unpleasant	sgradevole	*zgrah-*DEH*-voh-leh*
until (before, prep.)	prima di	PREE*-mah dee*
until (conj.)	fino a che	FEE*-noh uh keh*
until (up to the time of, prop.)	fino a	FEE*-noh ah*
up (adv.)	su	SOO
upon	sopra	SOH*-prah*
upstairs (at upper story, adv.)	al piano superiore	*ahl* PYAH*-noh soo-peh-*RYOH*-reh*
upstairs (to upper story, adv.)	al piano superiore	*ahl* PYAH*-noh soo-peh-*RYOH*-reh*
urgent	urgente	*oor-*JENN*-teh*
use (utilization)	uso, m.	OO*-zoh*
use (utilize), to	usare	*oo-*ZAH*-reh*
useful	utile	OO*-tee-leh*
useless	inutile	*ee-*NOO*-tee-leh*
usual	solito	SOH*-lee-toh*
utility (usefulness)	utilità, f.	*oo-tee-lee-*TAH
vacant (untenanted)	vacante	*vah-*KAHN*-teh*
vacation (work holidays)	vacanze, f., pl.	*vah-*KAHN*-tseh*
vaccination	vaccinazione, f.	*vaht-chee-nah-*TSYOH*-neh*
vain (futile)	vano	VAH*-noh*

ENGLISH	ITALIAN	PRONUNCIATION
valuable	di valore	*dee vah-*LOH-*reh*
value	valore, m.	*vah-*LOH-*reh*
value (prize), to	apprezzare	*ahp-prett-*TSAH-*reh*
variety (assortment)	assortimento, m.	*ahss-sohr-tee-*MENN-*toh*
various (different)	diverso	*dee-*VEHR-*soh*
veal	vitello, m.	*vee-*TELL-*loh*
veal chop	costoletta di vitello, f.	*koh-stoh-*LETT-*tah dee vee-*TELL-*loh*
vegetable	verdura, f.	*vehr-*DOO-*rah*
vehicle (conveyance)	veicolo, m.	*veh-*EE-*koh-loh*
venture (dare), to	arrischiarsi	*ahr-ree-*SKYAHR-*see*
vertical (adj.)	verticale	*vehr-tee-*KAH-*leh*
very (extremely)	molto	MOHL-*toh*
vessel (ship)	bastimento, m.	*bah-stee-*MENN-*toh*
vest	panciotto, m.	*pahn-*CHOHT-*toh*
vicinity	vicinanza, f.	*vee-chee-*NAHN-*tsah*
victorious	vittorioso	*veet-toh-*RYOH-*soh*
victory	vittoria, f.	*veet-*TOH-*ryah*
Viennese (adj.)	viennese	*vyenn-*NEH-*seh*
view (opinion)	opinione, f.	*oh-pee-*NYOH-*neh*
view (scene)	veduta, f.	*veh-*DOO-*tah*
village	villaggio, m.	*veel-*LAHD-*joh*
vine (grapevine)	vite, f.	VEE-*teh*
vinegar	aceto, m.	*ah-*CHEH-*toh*
visible	visibile	*vee-*ZEE-*bee-leh*
vision (eyesight)	vista, f.	VEE-*stah*
visit (social call)	visita, f.	VEE-*zee-tah*
visit (call on), to	visitare	*vee-zee-*TAH-*reh*
visitor	ospite, m., f.	OH-*spee-teh*
vital (essential)	essenziale	*ess-senn-*TSYAH-*leh*

ENGLISH	ITALIAN	PRONUNCIATION
voice	voce, f.	VOH-*cheh*
volume (book)	volume, m.	*voh-*LOO-*meh*
vomit, to	vomitare	*voh-mee-*TAH-*reh*
vote, to	votare	*voh-*TAH-*reh*
vow	voto, m.	VOH-*toh*
voyage	viaggio, m.	VYAHD-*joh*
vulgar (ill-bred)	volgare	*vohl-*GAH-*reh*
wages	salario, m.	*sah-*LAH-*ryoh*
waist	vita, f.	VEE-*tah*
waiter	cameriere, m.	*kah-meh-*RYEH-*reh*
wait for, to	aspettare	*ah-spett-*TAH-*reh*
wake (make awaken), to	svegliare	*zveh-*LYAH-*reh*
wake (rouse oneself), to	svegliarsi	*zveh-*LYAHR-*see*
walk (stroll)	passeggiata, f.	*pahss-sedd-*JAII-*tah*
walk, to	camminare	*kahm-mee-*NAH-*reh*
wall (inside)	parete, f.	*pah-*REH-*teh*
wall (outside)	muro, m.	MOO-*roh*
wander, to	vagare	*vah-*GAH-*reh*
want (desire), to	volere	*voh-*LEH-*reh*
war	guerra, f.	GWEHR-*rah*
wardrobe (apparel)	vestiario, m.	*veh-*STYAH-*ryoh*
warm	caldo	KAHL-*doh*
warm, to	riscaldare	*ree-skahl-*DAH-*reh*
warn, to	avvertire	*ahv-vehr-*TEE-*reh*
wash (cleanse), to	lavare	*lah-*VAH-*reh*
waste (squander), to	sciupare	*shoo-*PAH-*reh*
watch (timepiece)	orologio, m.	*oh-roh-*LOH-*joh*
watch (guard), to	vigilare	*vee-jee-*LAH-*reh*
watch (observe), to	stare a guardare	STAH-*reh ah gwahr-*DAH-*reh*
water	acqua, f.	AHK-*kwah*
waterproof	impermeabile	*eem-pehr-meh-*AH-*bee-leh*

ENGLISH	ITALIAN	PRONUNCIATION
way (route)	via, f.	VEE-*ah*
we	noi	NOY
weak	debole	DEH-*boh-leh*
wear (have on), to	portare	*pohr*-TAH-*reh*
weather	tempo, m.	TEMM-*poh*
week	settimana, f.	*sett-tee*-MAH-*nah*
weekend	fine di settimana, f.	FEE-*neh dee sett-tee*-MAH-*nah*
weekly (adj.)	settimanale	*sett-tee-mah*-NAH-*leh*
weep, to	piangere	PYAHN-*jeh-reh*
weigh, to	pesare	*peh*-SAH-*reh*
weight (scale weight)	peso, m.	PEH-*soh*
welcome (n.)	accoglienza, f.	*ahk-koh*-LYENN-*tsah*
welcome (receive hospitably), to	accogliere cordialmente	*ahk*-KOH-*lyeh-reh kohr-dyahl*-MENN-*teh*
well (commendably, adv.)	bene	BEH-*neh*
well (in health, adj.)	sano	SAH-*noh*
well (water pit, n.)	pozzo, m.	POHT-*tsoh*
west	ovest, n.	OH-*vest*
western	occidentale	*oht-chee-denn*-TAH-*leh*
wet	bagnato	*bah*-NYAH-*toh*
what (interrog. adj.)	che	KEH
what (interrog. pron.)	che cosa	*keh* KOH-*sah*
what (rel. pron.)	quel che	KWELL *keh*
wheel	ruota, f.	RWOH-*tah*
when (at the time that, conj.)	allorchè	*ahl-lohr*-KEH

ENGLISH	ITALIAN	PRONUNCIATION
when (at what time, adv.)	quando	KWAHN-*doh*
where (in, at the place that conj.)	dove	DOH-*veh*
where (in, at what place, adv.)	dove	DOH-*veh*
whether (either, conj.)	sia	SEE-*ah*
whether (if, conj.)	se	SEH
while (during the time that, conj.)	mentre	MENN-*treh*
whisper (utter softly), to	bisbigliare	*bee-zbee*-LYAH-*reh*
whistle, to	fischiare	*fee*-SKYAH-*reh*
white (adj.)	bianco	BYAHNG-*koh*
who (interrog. pron.)	chi	KEE
whole (entire, adj.)	intero	*een*-TEH-*roh*
whooping cough	tosse canina, f.	TOHSS-*seh kah-*NEE-*nah*
why	perchè	*pehr*-KEH
wide (not narrow)	largo	LAHR-*goh*
widow	vedova, f.	VEH-*doh-vah*
widower	vedovo, m.	VEH-*doh-voh*
width	larghezza, f.	*lahr*-GET-*tsah*
wife	moglie, f.	MOH-*lyeh*
will (power of choice)	volontà, f.	*voh-lohn*-TAH
win (be victor in), to	vincere	VEEN-*cheh reh*
wind	vento, m.	VENN-*toh*
window	finestra, f.	*fee*-NEH-*strah*
windshield	parabrezza, f.	*pah-rah*-BREDD-*dzah*
wine (beverage)	vino, m.	VEE-*noh*
winter	inverno, m.	*een*-VEHR-*noh*

ENGLISH	ITALIAN	PRONUNCIATION
wisdom	saggezza, f.	*sahd*-JETT-*tsah*
wise	saggio	SAHD-*joh*
wish	desiderio, m.	*deh-see-*DEH-*ryoh*
wish for, to	desiderare	*deh-see-deh-*RAH-*reh*
wit (humor)	spirito, m.	SPEE-*ree-toh*
with (prep.)	con	KOHN
without (lacking, prep.)	senza	SENN-*tsah*
woman	donna, f.	DOHN-*nah*
wonder (ask oneself), to	domandarsi	*doh-mahn-*DAHR-*see*
wood (lumber)	legno, m.	LEH-*nyoh*
wool (cloth)	tessuto di lana, m.	*tess-*SOO-*toh dee* LAH-*nah*
word	parola, f.	*pah-*ROH-*lah*
work (labor)	lavoro, m.	*lah-*VOH-*roh*
work (labor), to	lavorare	*lah-voh-*RAH-*reh*
worker	operaio, m.	*op-peh-*RYE-*oh*
world	mondo, m.	MOHN-*doh*
worry (feel anxious), to	stare in pensiero	STAH-*reh een penn-*SYEH-*roh*
worse (adj.)	peggiore	*pedd-*JOH-*reh*
worse (adv.)	peggio	PEDD-*joh*
worship, to (rel.)	adorare	*ah-doh-*RAH-*reh*
worst (adv.)	(il) peggio	*(eel)* PEDD-*joh*
worst (n.)	peggio, m.	PEDD-*joh*
worthless (valueless)	senza valore	SENN-*tsah vah-*LOH-*reh*
worthy (deserving)	meritevole	*meh-ree-*TEH-*voh-leh*
wound (injury)	ferita, f.	*feh-*REE-*tah*
wrist	polso, m.	POHL-*soh*
write, to	scrivere	SKREE-*veh-reh*
writer (author)	scrittore, m.	*skreet-*TOH-*reh*
wrong (amiss, adv.)	male	MAH-*leh*

ENGLISH	ITALIAN	PRONUNCIATION
wrong (erroneous, adj.)	sbagliato	*zbah*-LYAH-*toh*
wrong (injustice)	ingiustizia, f.	*een-joo*-STEE-*tsyah*
wrong (unjust, adj.)	ingiusto	*een*-JOO-*stoh*
X-ray (examine), to	radiografare	*rah-dyoh-grah-*FAH-*reh*
year	anno, m.	AHN-*noh*
yearly (adj.)	annuale	*ahn*-NWAH-*leh*
yellow (adj.)	giallo	JAHL-*loh*
yes	sì	SEE
yesterday	ieri	YEH-*ree*
yet	ancora	*ahng*-KOH-*rah*
young (adj.)	giovane	JOH-*vah-neh*
youth (period of life)	gioventù, f.	*joh-venn*-TOO
youthful	giovane	JOH-*vah-neh*
zero (n.)	zero, m.	DZEH-*roh*

CARDINAL NUMBERS

one	uno	OO-*noh*
two	due	DOO-*eh*
three	tre	TREH
four	quattro	KWAHT-*troh*
five	cinque	CHEEN-*kweh*
six	sei	SAY
seven	sette	SET-*teh*
eight	otto	OHT-*toh*
nine	nove	NOH-*veh*
ten	dieci	DYEH-*chee*
eleven	undici	OON-*dee-chee*
twelve	dodici	DOH-*dee-chee*
thirteen	tredici	TREH-*dee-chee*
fourteen	quattordici	*kwaht*-TOHR-*dee-chee*

ENGLISH	ITALIAN	PRONUNCIATION
fifteen	quindici	KWEEN-*dee-chee*
sixteen	sedici	SEH-*dee-chee*
seventeen	diciassette	*dee-chahss*-SET-*teh*
eighteen	diciotto	*dee*-CHOHT-*toh*
nineteen	diciannove	*dee-chahn*-NOH-*veh*
twenty	venti	VENN-*tee*
twenty-one	ventuno	*venn*-TOO-*noh*
twenty-two	ventidue	*venn-tee*-DOO-*eh*
thirty	trenta	TRENN-*tah*
forty	quaranta	*kwah*-RAHN-*tah*
fifty	cinquanta	*cheen*-KWAHN-*tah*
sixty	sessanta	*sess*-SAHN-*tah*
seventy	settanta	*set*-TAHN-*tah*
eighty	ottanta	*oht*-TAHN-*tah*
ninety	novanta	*noh*-VAHN-*tah*
one hundred	cento	CHENN-*toh*
one hundred one	cento uno	CHENN-*toh* OO-*noh*
two hundred	duecento	*doo-eh*-CHENN-*toh*
two hundred one	duecento uno	*doo-eh*-CHENN-*toh* OO-*noh*
one thousand	mille	MEEL-*leh*
one thousand one	mille uno	MEEL-*leh* OO-*noh*
two thousand	due mila	DOO-*eh* MEE-*lah*
two thousand one	due mila uno	DOO-*eh* MEE-*lah* OO-*noh*
one million	un millione	*oon mee*-LYOH-*neh*
one billion	un miliardo	*oon mee*-LYAHR-*doh*

ORDINAL NUMBERS

first	primo	PREE-*moh*
second	secondo	*seh*-KOHN-*doh*
third	terzo	TEHR-*tsoh*
fourth	quarto	KWAHR-*toh*
fifth	quinto	KWEEN-*toh*
sixth	sesto	SEH-*stoh*

ENGLISH	ITALIAN	PRONUNCIATION
seventh	settimo	SETT-*tee-moh*
eighth	ottavo	*oht*-TAH-*voh*
ninth	nono	NOH-*noh*
tenth	decimo	DEH-*chee-moh*
eleventh	undicesimo	*oon-dee*-CHEH-*zee-moh*
twelfth	dodicesimo	*doh-dee*-CHEH-*zee-moh*

DAYS OF THE WEEK

Sunday	domenica, f.	*doh*-MEH-*nee-kah*
Monday	lunedì, m.	*loo-neh*-DEE
Tuesday	martedì, m.	*mahr-teh*-DEE
Wednesday	mercoledì, m.	*mehr-koh-leh*-DEE
Thursday	giovedì, m.	*joh-veh*-DEE
Friday	venerdì, m.	*veh-nehr*-DEE
Saturday	sabato, m.	SAH-*bah-toh*

MONTHS OF THE YEAR

January	gennaio, m.	*jenn*-NAH-*yoh*
February	febbraio, m.	*fehb*-BRAH-*yoh*
March	marzo, m.	MAHR-*tsoh*
April	aprile, m.	*ah*-PREE-*leh*
May	maggio, m.	MAHD-*joh*
June	giugno, m.	JOO-*nyoh*
July	luglio, m.	LOO-*lyoh*
August	agosto, m.	*ah*-GOH-*stoh*
September	settembre, m.	*set*-TEMM-*breh*
October	ottobre, m.	*oh*-TOH-*breh*
November	novembre, m.	*noh*-VEMM-*breh*
December	dicembre, m.	*dee*-CHEMM-*breh*